UNVANQUISHED PURITAN

A
Portrait
of
Lyman Beecher

UNVANQUISHED PURITAN

A Portrait of Lyman Beecher

by

STUART C. HENRY

WILLIAM B. EERDMANS PUBLISHING COMPANY
Grand Rapids, Michigan

Copyright © 1973 by William B. Eerdmans Publishing Company
All rights reserved
Printed in the United States of America

Library of Congress Cataloging in Publication Data

Henry, Stuart Clark.
Unvanquished Puritan.

Includes bibliographical references.
1. Beecher, Lyman, 1775-1863. I. Title.
BX7260.B33H4   285'.9'0924 [B]   72-94608
ISBN 0-8028-3426-4

*To
the memory
of
my sister
Mabel Aubrey Henry*

Contents

	Preface	9
	The Family of Lyman Beecher	12
I	God's Business: A Decision for the Frontier—1832	13
II	Yale Conversion: Collegiate Deism in Flight—1775-1799	29
III	Early Testing: Battling Apathy in East Hampton—1800-1810	47
IV	Mixed Blessings: Ministering Without State Support—1810-1826	67
V	Workaday Theology: Faith in the Common Life—1810-1826	85
VI	In Extremis: Confidence in the Face of Despair—1810-1826	99
VII	Threatened Orthodoxy: The Rise of Unitarianism—1826-1832	115
VIII	Boston Prophet: Traditional Answers to New Questions—1826-1832	131
IX	An Exclusive Gospel: Old Prejudices in a Young Republic—Interlude	147
X	Lane Seminary: A Western School of the Prophets—1832-1833	167
XI	Rebels and Martyrs: A Conflict Over Abolition—1834-1835	187
XII	Heresy Trial: An Attempt to Liberalize Calvin—1835	207

XIII   Divided Company: Schism of Old and New School
Presbyterians—1835-1846   225

XIV   Quo Warranto: A Search for Meaning—
1838-1863   247

XV   Soul Marching On: Heirs of Beecher's Spirit—
Before and After 1863   265

    Epilogue   287

    Appendix   289

    Index   295

Preface

Lyman Beecher, 1775-1863, celebrated clergyman and educator, spanned an age of national metamorphosis. His famous children pieced together a fascinating patchwork of letters and transcribed reminiscences of their father, which they published shortly after his death as an *Autobiography of Lyman Beecher*. Reissued and edited with excellent introduction and notes by Barbara Cross (Cambridge, Massachusetts, 1961), the so-called autobiography provides a rich account of the man's career, but only an oblique indication that he was substantially related as both author and actor to a drama being played out in American religion. During his lifetime, and partly through his effort, the acknowledged authority of the established New England theocracy was being displaced in the national culture by the right of the individual to choose for himself, and the confidence that he could bring off the option. When not dismissed simply as the father of his children, Lyman Beecher has usually appeared in literature as a charming eccentric, or as the activist preacher who popularized the theology of Nathaniel Taylor.

The present work is neither a conventional biography nor a systematic treatment of Lyman Beecher's theology. His numerous endeavors were continuously varied, overlapping, abandoned, reactivated through many years; but the measure of the man does not turn upon a complete chronicle of the externals of his life. Readers interested in conventional presentation of Beecher's thought are advised that a volume directed to that task has been in parallel composition with the work at hand. The aim of the study here offered is to depict Beecher the man, who believed what he wanted to believe, but who did what the exigencies of the moment required. He was a living illustration of an evolving optimistic anthropology in American religion. Not always aware of the

9

theological assumptions on which he acted, he was, nevertheless, effective in cultivating in his generation a new sense of
freedom in relation to God. Beecher's theology is, therefore,
considered in the life of the man—what he did, as well as
what he said. The impact of his confession is indicated in the
lives of his children.

Friends who have read the work in manuscript have
strongly suggested that what follows is best understood as a
whole, as a picture is considered in its entirety, and not in
individual chapters or scenes. The perspective is appropriate
for a composition that essays to achieve portraiture. In this
case, as with any portrait, the effort has been to capture
essence and convey likeness through suggestion and significant detail; but the parts are best understood when viewed
together. The feeling of the subject is nowhere more
authentically indicated than in the words of the time, and the
persistent echo of the King James English that informed
Beecher's speech as spontaneously as breathing. Extensive
quotation permits the use of original language that without
identification of source would appear artificial, and in contemporary paraphrase would be weak. Both detail and
vocabulary have been selected with a view to recapturing the
attitudes and climate of another day.

Primary materials for the study of Lyman Beecher and his
family are numerous. The Beechers were writers, copiers, and
keepers. In addition there are extant many original documents of significance for the study of the early days of Lane
Seminary, as well as letters and other papers of Beecher's
contemporaries. The materials are scattered over many loca-
tions. The principal collections, in terms of volume and
variety, are to be found in the libraries of Oberlin College,
McCormick Theological Seminary, Radcliffe College, the
Stowe-Day Foundation of Hartford, Connecticut, and Yale
University, and in the Historical Societies of Cincinnati,
Ohio, and Litchfield, Connecticut. Other libraries and many
individuals have smaller, sometimes single, holdings of importance. Use of these materials is indicated as they appear in
the text. I am deeply grateful for permission to reproduce
them.

Chapter 1
God's Business:
A Decision for the Frontier – 1832

Divining the theological implication of Western expansion was a natural function for American ministers after the War of 1812. The new form of Christianity that became visible early in the nineteenth century fused religion with patriotism, and created unique problems for the church. By 1814 most people acknowledged the frontier opportunity, and many believed that the nation's future lay beyond the Alleghenies. Clergymen committed to bringing in the kingdom, therefore, could not ignore responsibility for the West. Although patriots then were by no means uniformly religious, most religious folk in the United States were likely to equate or confuse Christianity with patriotism in the emotional way typified by Samuel Smith in his poem of 1832, "My Country, 'Tis of Thee." For a minister to go West in that year was an act of theological significance.

Lyman Beecher, 1838 (Stowe-Day Foundation)

When the Reverend Doctor Lyman Beecher, the most celebrated clergyman in the United States in the year 1832,[1] alerted Boston of his intention to remove to the West, he was like some new Moses, daring the bold to come with him and possess a promised land. At that time Beecher shared more with Moses than a sense of being God's man. He was middle-aged, and beyond, well past the period when crusade is appropriate in a man's life. Also, having relentlessly hunted sinners and fought Satan for over thirty years, he had become a legend in his own day. If the distinction was uncomfortable, it relieved him of any need to seek further celebrity. Long since established in the affections of a city that had at first given him a frosty reception,[2] he was, against Boston's objection, and without undue visible pressure, departing for the frontier. To "a very attentive and crowded auditory,"[3] he announced that he would leave his distinguished pulpit in New England and identify himself with a school in Ohio that existed in little more substantial form than a name.

Though a preacher of renown, Beecher was, as a speaker, neither impressive in appearance nor graceful in gesture. Rather, he was given to nervous "pump-handle strokes of his right hand,"[4] and annoying habits of provincial speech.[5] But there was an arresting, spirit-driven look from the man's steady, wide-set, burning eyes[6] by which all knew when he rose to speak that he did so from no ordinary necessity, and that they were likely to hear no commonplace word. Neither did they at this time: Beecher spoke of the West like a prophet.

Cincinnati, his destination, was no wilderness in 1832; indeed, the river town reflected and rivaled Eastern centers, where, if at times grudgingly, she was already acknowledged a queenly city.[7] Beecher, however, spoke of himself as bound for a frontier, the appointed place of national destiny, and the resort of raw, undisciplined life, "rushing up to a giant manhood."[8]

Base men had looked greedily at the West since the Revolution. Thoughtful folk had marked the complex implication for national policy of the lusty civilization that flourished beyond the Appalachians. Protestants, watching on the walls of Zion, early saw that the opening West was at once opportunity and obligation to extend the borders of the kingdom: unless some prophet of God galvanized her conglomerate population to the gospel life, the West would degenerate into savagery or—far worse—lose her wealth and liberty to a predatory Catholic hierarchy, whose strength daily augmented through the continuing stream of European immigrants.[9] Thus, pressed by conscience and spurred by circumstance, aggressive evangelicals concluded to establish at Cincinnati (which "in twenty years," they said, would be "at the heart of twelve millions") a "great central theological institution of the first character."[10] Ministers educated in the West and for the West could save America. The dreamers, honoring an early sponsor, named the school "Lane,"[11] and they doubted not that Dr. Beecher of Boston, "if he could be obtained," would "immediately" bestow "elevation and success" to the seminary.[12] His relentless valor as a champion of Calvinistic orthodoxy was such that "no minister in New England" was "so uniformly dreaded and hated by Unitarians as Dr. B."[13] Bostonians, surely, would understand that while "the enemy" was "coming in like a flood," one of "their best generals should occupy the very seat of Western warfare."[14]

Invited to become president of the infant school, Beecher felt himself tapped for destiny. When the heady thought first "flashed" in his "mind like lightning," it threw him into such a state that—rare indeed for a Beecher—temporarily he could not speak.[15] For a much longer time, almost two years, he could not finally decide to turn to the West and face the "vacant stear [sic] of ignorance" and the "sly leer eyed look of infidelity."[16] Catherine, however, his firstborn, who of all his children was most like him in taste and temperament, had sensed all along what the outcome would be. Ten months before Lyman's conscience allowed him publicly to confess what he privately determined, to go to Cincinnati, Catherine began quietly setting her Hartford house in order, and putting affairs of her school there "on such a footing" that she could in contented mind "immigrate with father to the West."[17]

Meanwhile Lyman wrestled with himself as passionately as ever he had in his fifty-six years. The effort affected his "nerves and health, and was a very, very severe thing,"[18] for to immigrate to Ohio meant to retreat from the battle that was joined in New England between the faithful and the Unitarians.

Boston evangelicals—a decreasing tribe in 1826—had brought Beecher in that year from Litchfield, Connecticut, to their city for the express purpose of stanching the tide of Unitariansim that threatened to engulf them.[19] All agreed that he was the logical one *who could, who would,* and *who ought to* come to Boston as pastor of the newly organized Hanover Church.[20] Not only was he known abroad as the "great gun" of Calvinism, but at the time Lyman Beecher was confident that in "several years" Unitarianism in Boston could be destroyed "roots and all."[21] The misguided ministers of the liberal movement he judged but "feeble men," and their parishioners "no more Unitarians than any uninformed people."[22] Alas, when he reached Boston he had found "the literary men of Massachusetts . . . all the trustees and professors of Harvard College" and the "elite of wealth and fashion crowded" into Unitarian churches.[23] Hanover Church boasted a splendid new structure with walls of roughhewn granite, and a thriving fellowship of vigilant saints who were unyielding in their rigorous campaign against Satan. The floor of the "main audience room" sloped toward the pulpit so that those furthest away could not only hear but see[24] as Beecher "took off his spectacles, twirled them with his fingers" and looked over his shoulder in ironic ridicule of some fashionable heresy. Or they could tremble at the appearance and the sound of him when toward the climax of his sermon he was likely to stop "as suddenly as did the white horse and his rider in the apocalyptic vision" and, leaning over the pulpit, transport his listeners as he fixed them "with a fiery penetration of eye, and a marvellous inflection of voice."[25] Well might the flock expect such a shepherd to secure the fold from the Unitarian "wolf"[26] and, moreover, to bring safely to pasture those lost lambs and stray sheep, born or enticed to the dangerous paths of heresy.

Almost the longed-for happened. Revival began at once in the Hanover Church and was hardly interrupted by the fire that reduced the still new building to an ash heap. The Bowdoin Street Church rose phoenixlike from the ruin, and revival continued.[27] So, too, did the Unitarians. They were not dead, nor even moribund. Though the quarrel by 1832 was not so quick, nor the combat so severe as at the time of Beecher's arrival, the contest with the Unitarians had remained critical. If Lyman Beecher left Boston, it might be said with a measure of accuracy that he was deserting the field of battle before the enemy was vanquished. Nathaniel Taylor, aristocratic and authoritarian minister of Centre Church of New Haven, was the dearest idol of Beecher's heart, and a sympathetic professional friend. He said bluntly that Beecher ought not to go to the West, that "truth and the interests of religion" required him to remain in New England.[28] Impatient Cincinnatians insisted that "the good of the Church . . . loudly demanded" that he come to Lane, and quickly. So Beecher took the matter to the Lord, explaining his situation point by point, and carefully preserved his brief, so that it is known exactly how he argued.

After reviewing the history of his "burning desire . . . for the West," which had been with him long before God's voice said to him, "Go and fulfill thy desires," he acknowledged himself willing to "stay and finish" the grim business at hand or equally agreeable "to leave all and serve . . . at the West." Then he confessed his faith that the Omnipotent would not suffer the eternal "cause to be injured" merely by a Beecher's departure from the East, commended his Boston parish to God's care and his family to heaven, and arose from his knees ready to travel.[29] Already he perceived the dimension of the danger that America's "intelligence and virtue" might in the West "falter and fall back into a . . . reckless mass of infuriated animalism . . . set on fire of hell."[30] Plainly he believed that God called him to the West. By the time he preached his farewell sermon in Boston, Beecher could trace with utmost clarity the "leadings of Providence" that had brought him to the decision.[31] He presented his case with such force and with such cogent "solemnities" that some said he could never again return to New England.[32]

The decision for Cincinnati was a testament of faith, the westward journey a pilgrimage. Increasingly Beecher had granted that the saintly Jonathan Edwards had accurately predicted that the "millennium would commence in America."[33] The place, of course, would be, as Lyman expressed it, "at the West." For there in the wilderness men might through God's strength revive in their lives the lost puritan ideal, and release it for the healing of the nations. "Indeed, if it had been the design of heaven . . . to show the world by experiment, of what man is capable; and to . . . awake the slumbering eye, and rouse the torpid mind, and nerve the palsied arm of millions," would not America, Beecher asked, have been the proper setting for so grand a drama? Did not the course of the nation's history "indicate the purpose of God to render" America's children "almoners of his mercy" to all the world?[34] The time had come, he felt, when "the experiment" had to be tried whether the world would be "emancipated and rendered happy" or whether "the whole creation" should "groan and travail together in pain until the final consummation."[35] The "world's hopes" turned "on the character of the West," and if the West were lost, all was lost.[36] Earlier than most, Beecher had realized that the faith of the Puritans had struck a spark that was still bright and was yet destined to be the light of the world, because it could no more be extinguished than "the fires of Aetna." Only yesterday, as it were, he had spoken passionately of his confidence that the darkness could not swallow up the light of it—had voiced his faith that the flame would continue to blaze in glowing warmth for the hearts of God's children, and in fearful destruction of the places of wickedness: "Still it burns, and still the mountain heaves and murmurs; and soon it will explode with voices, and thunderings, and earthquakes. Then will the trumpet of Jubilee sound, and earth's debased millions will leap from the dust, and shake off their chains, and cry, 'Hosanna to the Son of David.' "[37] The fateful hour was at hand. Beecher could hardly have spoken of it less certainly or less dramatically if the intelligence had been given him by an angelic messenger descending through a rift in the skies.

Lyman Beecher was not disobedient to his heavenly vision. Instinctively he moved to action; for he saw a garden, ordered in design and free of thorns, precisely because men who uprooted devil's tares from their souls could successfully establish a conforming morality in the landscape. Beecher was clear-eyed in his estimate of "naked, ferocious human nature" more prone to depravity than loosened rocks to "thunder down the precipice."[38] For this sinfulness no expedient had "been discovered to avert entirely its deadly influence," so sadly confirmed in the "history of individuals, of families, societies and nations."[39] The prophet put his case, however, with disarming naiveté: "But because nations have never yet resisted the influence of sin, is it certainly to be inferred that they never will?"[40] A full generation earlier Beecher had remarked New England's departing glory and mourned her "institutions, civil and religious," which had "outlived that domestic discipline" and "vigilance in magistrates which rendered obedience easy and habitual." Necks unaccustomed to the yoke were stretched in defiance even then. It was nothing strange to see "drunkards reel through the streets," or find profane swearing accepted by "magistrates as though they heard it not." And as for "travelling on the Sabbath," efforts to stop such were everywhere "feeble, and in many places wholly" abandoned.[41] Yet there was still hope for the West. With uncommon insight regarding the indistinguishable identity of faith and action in his own life, of which the removal to the West was in every way typical, Beecher observed: "The Lord drove me, but I was ready." [42] In this situation—as usual—what he chose for himself he chose as well for his family. After expressing a willingness to go to the West for himself he added, "and I will send my children."[43]

Lyman Beecher thought it no injustice (to say nothing of

impropriety) to plan his children's lives. Rather it was a duty. Directing their affairs, early and late, he managed when he could, maneuvered when he had to, always in the interest of moral government. He outflanked the adolescent Henry Ward (ready to run away to sea) by agreeing enthusiastically with his son's intention, while, in the very act of packing him off to an academy to learn the necessary mathematics of navigation, commenting as the lad walked happily into the trap: "I shall have that boy in the ministry yet."[44] After William was grown and established as a minister in the church (shakily, some feared) his father still prescribed for him a daily schedule to be followed "rigidly," setting forth, for example, exactly the hours at which he should study. Beecher also warned son William not to say anything "openly" about the Masons.[45] In watchful care over his children, the father was impartially zealous about large, profound concerns, such as Edward's opportunity and desire to join the Dartmouth faculty ("By no means accept or consent. . . . I believe this is all I need to say"[46]) and about picayunish, personal matters, such as whether Catherine were wearing flannels in the "new and raw climate" of Hartford ("Purchase and make you some"[47]).

The children of Lyman Beecher did not necessarily resent this autocratic trait in their father and, indeed, though they did not always accede to it, were sometimes quite pleased by the developments it occasioned. "I fairly *danced* the first half hour after I read your letter," wrote Henry Ward, upon hearing from his sister Harriet of the Lane decision. "I sang, whistled, flew around like a mad man. Father's removal to the West is my 'heart's desire,' tho I cannot say that it had been my prayer."[48] Operating characteristically on the assumption that his children could do anything that he set his mind to, and assuming, with some measure of justification, that his choice for them would be right and acceptable, Doctor Beecher resolved quite simply the matter of what his family should do about his going to the West: they should come with him. There was never a question about the matter. Three months before the idea of his becoming president of Lane first came to his ears[49] Beecher had written Catherine of how "greatly excited" was his "interest in the majestic West" and of how he "thought seriously of going over to Cincinnati, the London of the West, to spend the remnant" of his days. "But if I go," he continued, "it will be part of my plan that *you* go, and another that Edward, and probably all my sons and all my daughters who are willing to, go."[50] He assumed that they would do so. They did, every last one, save Mary, married and already settled in Connecticut, and the clairvoyant Edward, who, by this time, had preceded his father to the frontier.

If there was some question whether the Beecher children should accompany their father to the West, there was none about Aunt Esther. Daughter of David Beecher's fifth wife by former marriage, Esther, considering herself (as did others) a Beecher, accepted responsibility for Lyman's household after his first wife died, leaving eight motherless children, the youngest not yet a year old.[51] Esther Beecher, neat and energetic as the house wren she rather resembled, made war upon dirt and disorder with the same indignant zeal that Lyman turned on the unconverted, and, at least in her own bailiwick, with a considerably greater measure of success. Her attempt, however, to impose system upon the irrepressible family she was called "to take charge of" achieved only indifferent victory. The Beechers "admired and commended" her inflexible rules; but they violated them shamelessly, offering, by way of lame apology, their "contrite confession or droll excuse."[52] Still, they liked nothing better than to retreat to Aunt Esther's "spotlessly neat" room, marveling at the reflections in the brass andirons, or watching as she fetched some delight from her "deep, shady, mysterious closet" which housed grand, beautiful things. More than the appointments of her room, though, the furniture of this remarkable woman's mind charmed her wards. She was "forever reading," and could answer their questions about chemistry, philosophy, and natural history, or entertain them with an inexhaustible succession of anecdotes. Once she told *"nineteen rat stories* all in a string." Aunt Esther it was who introduced Lyman's daughter, the young Puritan, Harriet, to Byron's poetry, and then dismissed her niece's question about an unpuritanical line with a cryptic, "Oh, child, it's one of Byron's strong expressions."[53] The Beechers could not have parted with so endearing a person, even had she been inclined or able to go elsewhere.

Esther, of course, found the spasmodic progress and haphazard accommodation of the trip to Cincinnati distressing to her disciplined nature. Though greatly inconvenienced, she was not visibly disturbed. Her philosophy of tribulation was to "howl all day if it would do any good," but otherwise to keep silent.[54] The member of the crusade who was truly in dismay was poor, long-suffering Harriet Porter, Beecher's second wife, who understood him, perhaps, even less than he understood her, which was not at all.

Miss Porter was gently born and gently reared, and was called "quiet and lady-like" in a generation when the distinction was not lightly granted.[55] She had met Lyman Beecher in 1817 while she was visiting in Boston, where he had come to preach an ordination sermon. The Connecticut celebrity swept her into engagement within a week and rushed her into a marriage her parents thought hasty rather than ill-considered.[56] To the "rough, red-cheeked . . . country children" of the Litchfield manse she seemed "a strange princess" with beautiful hands "made of pearl."[57] Presently it was plain that she was, indeed, a stranger to them, and to their father as well, because their habits and attitudes in many "respects were directly contrary to her own."[58] On surface it was the difference between her naturally dainty and disciplined way of life—as orderly as Aunt Esther's—and the spontaneous harum-scarum of the rowdy Beechers. The dimension of that difference appears in Lyman's baffled inability to understand her despair on discovering that in the interest of a nutting expedition for the children he, like an "omnipotent marauder," had commandeered her stocking, patch, linen, yarn, and thread baskets, and pitched their contents together "into a promiscuous heap."[59] Less obviously, but more darkly, it was an alienation born of the older Beecher children's fierce and worshipful loyalty to their mother's ghost. Calling her father's second marriage a "sudden and unforeseen mercy," Catherine asked pointedly,

"Who can fill a *mother's* place?" In candor Harriet replied, "I am not to take the place of that mother. Oh no," and then, wistfully, inquired, "but have you not room for me also?"[60] The request was nonetheless sufficiently threatening to brand Harriet Porter as a reproach to the sainted Roxana. Subsequent years separated the children of Harriet and the children of Roxana by an unbridgeable stream of misunderstanding, which, when finally made public, was wide and deep. Meanwhile the agony was more exquisite because the persons most immediately concerned steadfastly refused to recognize or admit its nature and origin.[61]

Living thus under attrition, the naturally pious Harriet found compensation at Boston, in the lively revival at Hanover Church, and especially in the "secret history" of the city's intellectual life. By her own confession she had begun "to be really comfortable," and was undone by the shattering decision to leave that place which had been "pressed by the feet of the Pilgrims."[62] The measure of her despair and the mettle of her character, occasioned and elicited by the departure for Lane, are transparent in her obituary published subsequently in the *Cincinnati Journal:* "When called of Providence, by a removal to the West, to forsake all her earthly friends and near relatives, though she felt it to be a great trial and privation, yet she felt it to be a duty, and gave her consent without a murmur of complaint."[63] No less quick of conscience than the Beechers (and often a bit more tender), Harriet was mindful of the moral obligation involved. But whereas the Beechers, acknowledging the risks, leaped joyfully into the breach, confident of the ministering assistance of legions of angels, she stood like a martyr, mute in the face of a certain death.

The company traveling toward Ohio appeared normal enough statistically: of Lyman's older sons and daughters there were Catherine, already growing self-important and opinionated; George, happily in a period of euphoria; and Harriet Beecher, belying turbulence of heart with tranquillity of expression. There were also the young children of Lyman's second marriage: Thomas, Isabella, and James (only four). And, of course, there were Aunt Esther, always poised, and Harriet Porter, withdrawn and resigned. Their movement, though, may well have arrested even those accustomed to odd and motley immigrants; for the Beechers were gospel gypsies, singing hymns, scattering tracts and, between private prayer meetings, engaging strangers in conversations about the soul.[64] They marched to Lyman's music, surer than any piper's tune. Lyman, though, was no piper: he was a warrior-prophet, "bold as thunder,"[65] and with "bones of brass."[66] He had sent from his trumpet no uncertain sound. The recruits gathered about him, and now they advanced to the West, as the Beechers were fond of describing any righteous progress, "terrible as an army with banners."

At their head Lyman was "in high spirits" and "confident for the future."[67] Only Providence could have brought him through the days of his years to this good hour. With commendable foresight Providence had begun the preparation with Lyman's ancestry.

Notes to Chapter I

1. E. D. Mansfield, *Personal Memories, Social, Political, and Literary with Sketches of Many Notable People, 1803-1843* (Cincinnati, 1879), pp. 139, 279; Gilbert H. Barnes and Dwight Dumond (eds.), *Letters of Theodore Dwight Weld, Angelina Grimké Weld, and Sarah Grimké, 1822-1844*, 2 vols. (New York and London, 1934), I, 12n.

2. *Cincinnati Journal*, October 12, 1832, quoting *Boston Courier*.

3. Newspaper clipping of March, 1830, unidentified otherwise, in the Yale collection of Beecher papers.

4. David Bartlett, *Modern Agitators: or, Pen Portraits of Living American Reformers* (New York, 1856), p. 200.

5. ALS, "Nancy," Walnut Hills, Cincinnati, February 25, 1848, to her mother, from the collection of the Connecticut Historical Society. The writer was associated with Catherine Beecher in educational work.

6. David Bartlett, *Modern Agitators*, p. 200.

7. Alvin F. Harlow, *The Serene Cincinnatians* (New York, 1950), p. 33.

8. Lyman Beecher, *A Plea for the West*, 2nd ed. (Cincinnati and New York, 1835), p. 12.

9. *Ibid.*, pp. 54-60. Beecher admitted the "excellence and intelli-

gence and value of a portion" of the immigrants, but denied that there were enough such to "avert the danger," p. 52n.

10. Charles Beecher, ed., *Autobiography, Correspondence, Etc., of Lyman Beecher, D.D.*, 2 vols. (New York, 1865), II, 241. Hereinafter cited as *Autobiography.*

11. *Cincinnati Journal*, September 8, 1829.

12. *Autobiography*, II, 242.

13. *Trial and Acquittal of Lyman Beecher, D.D., Before the Presbytery of Cincinnati, on Charges Preferred by Joshua L. Wilson, D.D., Reported for the New York Observer, by Mr. Stansbury, of Washington, D.C.* (Cincinnati, 1835), p. 33.

14. *Autobiography*, II, 242.

15. *Ibid.*, p. 246.

16. *Weld-Grimké Letters*, I, 87. The description of the West, particularly that part of it in which Lane Seminary is set, is from a letter of A. A. Stone to Theodore Weld, written in November of 1832.

17. ALS, Catherine Beecher, Hartford, Connecticut, September 4, 1831, to Mary Dutton, Manuscript Collection of the Beinecke Library. Catherine Beecher had opened the Hartford Female Seminary on May 20, 1823, over a harness store on Main Street. Modest in origin, the school twice outgrew its quarters within three years, was incorporated in 1827, and in November of that year moved into new buildings where six other women and a man joined Catherine as faculty members. Catherine announced her resignation in the 1831 *Catalogue*, but the school lasted until 1888.

18. *Autobiography*, II, 248.

19. Winthrop S. Hudson, *Religion in America* (New York, 1965), pp. 160-161, gives a succinct and perceptive statement regarding the concentration of Unitarianism in the Boston area.

20. Minutes of the August 24, 1825, meeting of the committee to consider adaptability of Old South, Park, and Union Church rules to the Hanover Church, from the collection of the Congregational Library, Boston, Massachusetts.

21. Carlos Martyn, *Wendell Phillips: The Agitator* (New York, 1890), p. 41.

22. *Autobiography*, I, 542.

23. *Ibid.*, II, 110.

24. *Congregational Quarterly*, VII (1865), 30.

25. James C. White, *Personal Reminiscences of Lyman Beecher* (New York, 1882), p. 14.

26. *Autobiography*, I, 448.

27. The society of the Bowdoin Street Church did not survive after 1865. The building that housed the organization is now occupied by the Church of St. John the Evangelist, Cowley Fathers, S.S.J.E.

28. *Autobiography*, II, 248.

29. *Ibid.*, pp. 270-272.

30. Lyman Beecher, *A Plea for the West*, p. 39.

31. *Autobiography*, II, 273.

32. ALS, A. W. Weston, Groton, September 17, 1836, to Debora Weston, in the Weston Papers, Boston Public Library.

33. Lyman Beecher, *A Plea for the West*, p. 10.

34. Lyman Beecher, *The Memory of our Fathers, A Sermon delivered at Plymouth, on the twenty-second of December, 1827* (Boston, 1828), p. 17.

35. *Ibid.*, p. 33.

36. *Autobiography*, II, 224.

37. Lyman Beecher, *The Memory of our Fathers*, p. 21.

38. Lyman Beecher, *Lectures on Skepticism, Delivered in Park Street Church, Boston, and in the Second Presbyterian Church, Cincinnati* (Cincinnati, 1835), p. 79.

39. Lyman Beecher, *The Practicability of Suppressing Vice, by Means of Societies Instituted for that Purpose. A Sermon Delivered before the Moral Society in East Hampton, September 21, 1803* (New London, 1804), p. 4.

40. *Ibid.*

41. *Autobiography*, I, 261-262.

42. *Ibid.*, p. 70.

43. *Ibid.*, II, 247.

44. Harriet Beecher Stowe, "Henry Ward Beecher," in *Men of Our Times, or Leading Patriots of the Day* (Hartford, 1868), pp. 518-519.

45. *Autobiography*, II, 226.

46. ALS, Lyman Beecher, Boston, August 4, 1826, to Edward at Yale, Beecher Collection, Yale University.

47. ALS, Lyman Beecher, Litchfield, May 26, 1819, to Catherine, Beecher-Stowe Collection, Schlesinger Library, Radcliffe College.

48. ALS, Henry Ward Beecher, Amherst College, March 8, 1832, to Harriet, Beecher Collection, Yale University.

49. *Autobiography*, II, 239.

50. *Ibid.*, p. 224.

51. *Ibid.*, I, 292-300. Catherine Cebra Webb's "Diary," quoted in Emily Noyes Vanderpoel, *Chronicles of a Pioneer School from 1792 to 1833*, Elizabeth C. Barney Buel, ed. (Cambridge, 1903), pp. 148-149, also indicates the suddenness of Mrs. Beecher's decline.

52. *Autobiography*, I, 320-323.

53. *Ibid.*, pp. 527-528. The line, "One I never loved enough to hate," is from Byron's *Corsair*, III, 133.

54. ALS, E[sther] B[eecher], October 24, 1848, to Eunice [Mrs. Henry Ward Beecher], Beecher Collection, Yale University.

55. Catherine E. Beecher, *Educational Reminiscences and Suggestions* (New York, 1874), p. 23.

56. ALS, Harriet Porter, Portland, Maine, October 13, 1817, to Lyman Beecher, Beecher Collection, Stowe-Day Foundation.

57. *Autobiography*, I, 363.

58. Catherine E. Beecher, *Educational Reminiscences*, p. 24.

59. *Autobiography*, I, 523.

60. *Ibid.*, pp. 358-360.

61. Lyman Beecher's family suffered serious rift on the occasion of the Beecher-Tilton affair, in which Henry Ward was variously charged and tried concerning his relationship with Mrs. Theodore Tilton. *Theodore Tilton vs. Henry Ward Beecher, Action for Crim. Con.* . . . *Verbatim Report by the Official Stenographer*, 3 vols. (New York, 1875), and Austin Abbott, *Official Report of the Trial of Henry Ward Beecher*, 2 vols. (New York, 1875), record the matter. Robert Shaplen, *Free Love and Heavenly Sinners: The Story of the Great Henry Ward Beecher Scandal* (New York, 1954), is a popular, essentially correct, account of the case. Beecher was acquitted.

62. *Autobiography*, II, 62-63.

63. *Cincinnati Journal*, July 24, 1835.

64. *Autobiography*, II, 278-281.

65. *Cincinnati Journal*, July 31, 1835.

66. H. P. Hedges, "Anecdotes, Recollections, Impressions and Traditions of Lyman Beecher," *Sag Harbor Express*, January 31, 1901.

67. *Autobiography*, II, 278.

Chapter II
Yale Conversion:
Collegiate Deism in Flight – 1775-1799

American revivalism is rooted in the religious fervor that has periodically crested in the nation's life. The so-called Great Awakening of the colonial era was succeeded by a second, 1797-1805, in which the Western manifestation was markedly unsophisticated. The Eastern phenomenon began in colleges. Timothy Dwight, President of Yale, won undergraduates back to orthodoxy through reason and the new democratic emphasis on man's worth. He initiated a season of several generations of student revivalists and of religious activity spreading beyond the campus. Rigid forms now associated with revivals were less characteristic then than the zeal of converts, but conventions were crystallizing. From that time until the 1920's revivalism was increasingly adopted as a method of evangelization by most Protestant bodies and, in moderation, by quasi-liturgical and minority groups.

Yale College as It Was Then

Lyman Beecher's father, David, was a strong man who could lift a full barrel of cider. So could his grandfather, Nathaniel, and his great-grandfather, Joseph; and Joseph, moreover, could hold the barrel above his head and drink from the bunghole.[1] Lyman inherited the sturdiness of these titans, all of whom were blacksmiths. On the morning of his eighty-first birthday he was hurrying to a lecture, running "across lots," for fear of being late, when he found his way blocked by a "five-barred fence." Placing his hand on the top rail, he "cleared [it] at a bound," and, nimble as a cricket, arrived at his appointment on time.[2]

Oddly, his beginning had been precarious. Just "by a hair's-breadth," he mused, did he get a "foothold in this world." At his birth the attending midwife considered him such a "puny thing" that she "actually wrapped [him] up and laid [him] aside," thinking, and hoping, that he would surely die.[3] Characteristically, he refused to do so, and was, accordingly, after the death of his mother two days later, put into a basket and taken by horseback to the home of his mother's sister, Catherine Benton, and her husband, Lot.[4] There, near Guilford, Connecticut, the seven months' child held on to life with a tenacity often seen afterward in his children.

The Beechers—at least those born to Lyman—were hardy.[5] Roxana Foote, his first wife, died early. Harriet Porter, his second, declined quickly. But whatever the weakness of body or will that laid them untimely in their graves, it succumbed to that Beecher vitality with which it was fused in Lyman's children. Their stubborn health, however, was a blessing they exhibited rather than affirmed. Regarding their own state of well-being they were very apt to be pessimistic, always reporting their illnesses (real or imagined) in minute and clinical detail, and often predicting imminent death. A visitor at the Walnut Hills home in 1833, writing that the Beechers happily were in a "tolerable state of health for the first time

31

since their" arrival in Ohio, casually included in her report the following catalogue of infirmities: "Catherine has had a bilious fever and a sprained ankle. George has the dyspepsia all the time dreadfully. Mrs. Beecher is always sick—and Aunt Esther is suffering with a sore mouth." As a marginal gloss the correspondent added, "and they all have *nerves.*"[6] The curious union in the Beecher children of a deep anxiety about health with the unusual hardihood (which for the most part they enjoyed) was even more decidedly marked in their father. As early as his twenty-fifth year Lyman, indisposed, doubted if he "should ever go out again."[7] At the height of his celebrity, he lay on the floor and wailed so convincingly that it was "done over" with him that his son William (who had often seen Lyman in the depths), "almost feared it was so."[8] It was not, of course. Lyman lived another thirty-eight years, though not without many periods of despondency. In the end his body so outlasted his senile mind that friends had sadly to concede that the "hull" had "proved better than the engine."[9] That it did so was a testimony to the vein of iron bequeathed to him from the blacksmith Beechers.

Lyman's foster parents gave him "the nurture and training of a Connecticut farmer's boy" generally understood in that day to mean "catechising in the house," and "plenty of hard work" out-of-doors.[10] The Bentons were distinguished by native goodness rather than by surface sophistication. Aunt Benton's ultimate expression of affection for the lad was to tell him that he did not "look *well*" and urge him to "go into the milk-room and get a piece of cake."[11] This indicated more than the simple woman could articulate, but Lyman, who was sensible of her worth, had the wit to appreciate her then, and the grace to remember her later. The news of her death "completely overwhelmed" him,[12] and he subsequently called his first child "Catherine" in her memory.[13] Uncle Lot was a tall and upright man who, even in old age, never "learned to stoop,"[14] and, "under a don't-care look," was quite warm and appealing.[15] If the lad forgot to "blow out the candle when he went to bed" (which was frequently the case), his uncle would always say on the following night,

"Lyman, you shan't have no candle," and then with unfailing indulgence allow him the privilege of taking a fresh one.[16]

As much as he loved the Bentons, though, the youth abominated the tedium and monotony of life on a farm. He grew "deadly sick of ploughing a hilly, swampy, fifteen acre corn-field with a yoke of slow-moving oxen."[17] To his life's end Lyman thrived in the out-of-doors; but he could not bear the laggard existence of North Guilford. The fact is that Lyman inherited more from his father than a strong back. David Beecher was a man of native intellect, which he cultivated intensely, if not systematically. Grimy and soot-streaked he undoubtedly was, but to see him only thus, "forging . . . 'hoes as blunt as a beetle,' "[18] is neither accurate nor kind, though, if it comes to that, he made "the best hoes in New England."[19] In David Beecher's mind ideas struck fire that burned brighter and longer than the sparks from his anvil. He rented rooms to Yale students, partly for the convenience of borrowing their books in the evenings, and he boarded legislators, because he was fond of discussing politics. Squire Roger Sherman, who had signed the Declaration of Independence, "always calculated to see Mr. Beecher as soon as he got home from Congress, to talk over the particulars."[20] The intellectual smith fathered in his son a passion for ideas, and a facility for relating them to Connecticut life. The seed was slow to sprout, but it lived. Lyman enrolled in college to escape the farm. Once there, he discovered that he was where he belonged.

In the same year in which Lyman Beecher entered Yale, caterpillars overran the city of New Haven. They "almost covered the trees," and they blanketed "houses to the tops of chimneys." More seriously, "scarlatina anginosa" prevailed generally in the area. Also "for many months preceding the invasion of the fever, the oysters" along the coast "were in a very sickly state."[21]

Doubtless there were residents of New Haven who read these circumstances as signs of warning. Certainly Puritans of another generation would have detected the judgment of God in such "derangement of the elements." And what was more

likely considering the breed of infidel arisen among them? If
the faithful noted the stranger in the camp, how could
heaven ignore the enemy at the very gates of Zion? New
England—so long a fortress of orthodoxy and rectitude—was
now in the eyes of the faithful invaded by a horde of foes
more repulsive than caterpillars, and beset by a plague dead-
lier than any fever. God-defying atheists in their midst
brazenly abandoned, even attacked, the church; and their
private lives were scandalous and lewd. Hoping to build a new
Jerusalem, the founding fathers had fled the heresy and
wickedness of Europe; but the sin they thought to evade had
stubbornly pursued them and overtaken their children. Currents of foreign thought, blowing steadily into New England
for some years past, had become winds of chilling fury. It
was not possible in the last decade of the eighteenth century
to say whether Calvinism would be swept away from Connecticut, whether the old order could withstand the gale.

At Yale the youthful Lyman first witnessed the ordeal of
the tradition as a contest that was both reflection and result
of the grander struggle that had engaged all New England.
The quarrel now was between the godless and the elect. Men
of righteousness were set against a motley swarm of deists,
atheists, and infidels. In the eyes of the orthodox these were
varmints of hell, and all of a kind; for however idiomatic
their individual blasphemies might be, alike they spurned the
faith of the past. The issue was less the distinctive variety of
belief than their common apostasy and the threat it posed to
the puritan way of life. From the beginning Lyman found the
fray exciting, and in the end it shaped his life. The struggle
was inseparably bound to the young nation's successful
breaking of the British yoke.

During the French and Indian wars militia from the colonies had shared barracks with British regulars. In association
with these Englishmen the simple and uneducated among the
New Englanders had first learned—or at least observed—
freedom from the binding influence of religion. They were
fascinated. Strict protocol obtained while soldiers were on
duty; but the gross indulgences and shocking notions of the
militia at their leisure quickly established the army's final

commitment only to "Infidelity and Gratification of the appetites." Fighting men, therefore, returning to colonial villages and towns, brought with them the "polite Mysteries and vitiated morals of Deism."[22] When the War for Independence exposed colonists in greater number and from wider background to the infidelity of their French comrades at arms, religion in New England suffered an even heavier blow than she had sustained earlier from the English. "Far more dissolute of character" than the British, the French also held "that loose and undefined Atheism which neither believes, nor disbelieves."[23] English deists, though obviously not inhibited by religion, still had manners enough to exhibit "in appearance at least, some degree of reverence for the Creator." Continental infidels not only "despised" God; they were disdainful of provincials in the bargain. "The Frenchman," said a contemporary, stares at you with "surprise and contempt." Considering you an "ignorant rustic," he pities your weakness and patronizes your stupidity.[24] Citizens of young America, eager to be accepted by theological dandies from the Continent, were gladly seduced.

The apostasy plain folk met in the attitudes and actions of the soldiers, men of letters read in a growing volume of foreign literature that washed over America like a tidal wave. Along with useful merchandise, Europe in those days annually shipped west an "assortment of toys and mischief" so that there were means of corruption in "plentiful supply." The very "dregs of Infidelity were vomited" upon America. An enormous French edition of the *Age of Reason* was sent with specific instruction "to be sold for a few pence a copy, and where it could not be sold, to be given away." "Impudent beyond example," the scullions who wrote such tracts were also skillful in propaganda, and resourceful in distribution.[25]

In every area of New England, mourned the orthodox, men came under the influence of these varlets of Satan, and never more willingly or more boastfully than at Yale. When Lyman arrived at college, he discovered that undergraduates, assuming the names of their idols, affectedly called each other "Voltaire," "Rousseau," or "D'Alembert." Not unexpectedly, their profligate lives reflected what their foolish hearts espoused. They were, indeed, a godless lot: "intemperance, profanity, gambling, and licentiousness were common." Even before he came to college, Lyman had read Tom Paine, hiding in the barn, lest he shock his uncle or wound his aunt. But whereas the lad at North Guilford had instinctively rejected the infidel and, in his own words, had "fought him all the way," his future and fellow classmates had "believed."[26] Though unconverted at the time, Lyman watched with growing sympathy as evangelists at Yale, seeking to pluck brands from the burning, clashed with the powers of darkness.

It was this grand battle for the faith, and the revival of religion attending it at Yale, that finally involved young Lyman Beecher and determined his career. The contest between truth and error, more demanding than any match of brawn, was combat for which he was able. That he did not immediately join ranks with the angels was doubtless because there was when he first came to Yale no general exciting enough to capture his imagination, or daring enough to command his loyalty. Certainly Ezra Stiles did not do so.

Although he was only five feet, four inches tall, Stiles, Yale president of Beecher's first college days, was impressive, even majestic.[27] Formal and austere in performance of official duties, the "dry old man," wearing a black robe and all but "extinguished" under a great white wig,[28] awed students, whether lecturing on divinity or levying fines.[29] Fantastically erudite, and almost indiscriminately curious, he stunned undergraduates with his exact knowledge of sea water and silkworms, of syntax and Shaftesbury; and he delighted them when, in the grip of his obsession, compulsive as a magpie's, he was busy collecting or exhibiting the vast hoard of his treasure, diverse enough to embrace a penguin from Cape Horn[30] and a leaf from Virgil's tomb.[31] But though he impressed and amused the students, Stiles did not convert them. They were more likely to remember an unusual outburst of rage than his faithfulness in prayer.

Beecher considered Stiles the "most urbane gentleman" he ever knew.[32] The judgment may well be exact, for that ordained clergyman was equally at his ease in the company of a fellow minister or as host to the visiting Thomas Jefferson.[33] Deflected neither by immediate turbulence nor distant threat, Stiles pursued the goal of a more excellent Yale, taking scant notice, for example, of New Haven's "great Combustion about the Dancing School,"[34] nor suffering his industry to slacken for the sake of the prospect of the "pity and neglect" with which "pious posterity" would probably view the accomplishments of his generation.[35]

Stiles was no deist. He looked upon the divinity of Jesus as one of the "pillar truths."[36] Indeed, he was a more committed evangelical for having, in his salad days, associated with the skeptics.[37] The proper place and the certain fate of this particular heresy and its advocates no longer puzzled Ezra Stiles by the time he reached maturity. Once in a sermon, with more dramatic flair than was his wont in the pulpit, he summoned the "father of deism" and the whole group of "self-opinionated deniers of the Lord" together with their "cloud of deluded followers" to "step forth" and be reckoned at the bar of judgment. According to Stiles' fancy, the Sovereign of heaven would dismiss them with a single word: *evanish.* Their destiny along with their "bloated wisdom" was eternal residence in the "blackness of darkness."[38] All this, though, was for the future, and meanwhile, in civilized tolerance, Stiles acted upon his announced assumption: that "many considerable errors, if let alone, will correct themselves in time."[39] Ezra Stiles, though a wise and sensitive Christian, was no man to start a revival.

Timothy Dwight, who succeeded Stiles, was of a different order. He entertained no doubt regarding the ultimate destruction of the kingdom of evil, but he did not propose meanwhile to suffer the devil and his advocates even interim victory, if he, by God's grace, could be the agent of their defeat. Nor was it his idea to win a war by waiting. Dwight never made the mistake of viewing the conflict exclusively in the theoretical terms of demonic powers: he found the issues as well in the narrow and specific area of undergraduate behavior, even at Yale. When freshmen, much put upon, had come to Stiles praying relief from degrading servitude at the hands of arrogant upperclassmen, the aristocratic old doctor had sent them packing.[40] But Dwight, a no-nonsense man, who sought in true puritan fashion to order all things under God, abolished the traditional practice of fagging,[41] and along with it the ridiculous law forbidding students to approach their betters closer than ten rods without doffing their hats, "rain or no rain."[42]

The new president's close application of Christian truth to cases of common life impressed Beecher. But it was Dwight's passion in the quest for souls that Lyman could not escape. On arrival at New Haven to assume the presidency of Yale, Dwight, most recently come from the idyllic parish of Greenfield Hill, had discovered in the college an unspeakable situation. Having left a community in which the Bible-reading, peaceable inhabitants made orthodoxy pleasant and the pastorate an honor, he was confronted, not by mistaken ideas born of ignorance and default, but by shameless and aggressive apostasy. Students openly scoffed at the church and, with more zeal if less grace than their mentors, took example from the French in putting "arguments to flight with a sneer" and stifling "conscience with a smile."[43] The college church, fallen on evil days, was reduced to but two members; and soon after Dwight's arrival "it dwindled to a single person."[44]

Dwight's challenge came early: Yale students at the turn of the century (and for some generations thereafter), forced to furnish, rather than borrow, their entertainment, often disported themselves in various forms of debate, all of which were enormously popular. As the first day of "forensic disputations" during Dwight's tenure drew near, the possible subjects for contention were, according to custom, submitted to the president for endorsement and recommendation. Whether by the hand of low comedian or honest seeker is of no matter, but the list included the question: "Are the Scriptures of the Old and New Testaments the Word of God?" Dwight amazed the students by selecting this very topic, and he assured them that all who chose to declare openly for infidelity (as most of them did) would enjoy perfect freedom to do so and suffer no discrimination because of their candor. Students who had grumbled that the faculty were afraid to grapple firmly with thorny matters were delighted. Had they been half so keen as they were cavalier, they would not have rushed as brashly as they did into the snare. Dwight, who had served as Chaplain to General Parson's brigade during the Revolution, had seen spies flushed and traitors hanged. He knew the value of swift movement and surprise attack in combating defection, ecclesiastical or otherwise. On the appointed day, the president, always genteel, ever poised, waited with patience while the undergraduates affirmed and denied. Then he blasted their arguments with such an ammunition of cogency and data that even the most wayward admitted defeat. Those who battled with sophistry he laid low with logic; and those who foolhardily attempted to redeem ignorance with enthusiasm he demolished with hard fact. "The effect upon the students was electrical." From that moment, "Infidelity was not only without stronghold" but was in want even of a "lurking place." Students whose lips were yet warm with the words of Voltaire now confessed the Christ.[45] Beecher was charmed.

Steadily, and quietly, the president reclaimed at Yale the lost "respectability and influence" of the Pilgrim religion. Skepticism, shortly out of fashion, was soon disreputable.[46] Dwight's weapons were sound reasoning and overwhelming eloquence. Although he never employed ridicule or reproach, he did on occasion allow himself a gentle irony: how fantastic, he speculated, to imagine the splendid marvel of the human body a product of chance. If such were the case, the eyes, for example, so sensibly placed by the present arrangement, might just as easily have been fixed "on the top of the head or on the soles of the feet."[47] Such drollery—to say nothing of such wisdom—appealed to Beecher.

The measure of his admiration is apparent years after Dwight's death when Lyman, like a man in the "cave of the Vulcans," stood "in the dim light and sooty atmosphere of a Cincinnati iron foundry"[48] preaching to the workers. He spoke, among many other things, of the utter absurdity of thinking that in the "fortuitous concourse of atoms" the "sinews and muscles" simply came and "took their place" in the miracle that is man.[49] There was nothing insidious about the situation; nevertheless it was true, and in many another instance, that the voice was the voice of Lyman, but the thoughts were the thoughts of Dwight.

There was also a downright quality in Dwight's preaching which made it difficult to misunderstand his intention or to deny his logic. His genius for putting theological problems in metaphors as plain as mustard seed is clear in a word of his about human responsibility. Many churchmen of Dwight's day who agreed on the urgency of the soul's salvation were often at decided odds regarding man's competence to mend the matter. Some were sadly convinced that man could do nothing, that any attempt to help oneself was at best futile (because only God could save) and at worst disastrous. (They shook their heads and said that it presumed to the office of the Holy Spirit.) Even with those not lost in the "sloughs of high Calvinism,"[50] there was perplexity about just how far a man should press his own case. What would happen, Dwight asked of these disputants, if a farmer, waiting and hoping for a crop, should refuse to "plough, and sow, and reap" because, since only God could effect the miracle of a harvest, to try oneself was to doubt God's providence and defy divinity? Dwight never forgot that the earth was the Lord's; neither did he forget to plant the seed and prune the limb. Those who had ears to hear caught the echo of the Word in this parable.[51] Here was theology of a character and presentation that Lyman approved. Keenly aware of the sovereignty of God and of man's dependence upon him, Dwight's creed was, nevertheless, distinguished by an eminent common sense that took due account of man's ability and, consequently, held mortals responsible for doing what they could, which was a great deal.

The busy life his theology endorsed was the life Dwight lived. Faced with the responsibility of building a university from a ruined college—no mean task—he found it possible and necessary to teach daily, travel widely, preach often, study constantly, and still guard time for regular physical exercise. He rode horseback in all winds and weather, and "when no other mode of exercise was convenient," chopped

firewood, almost as an act of faith.[52] Neighbors who
bothered to look could see the celebrated doctor any spring
morning, shortly after daybreak, happily working the rows of
cucumbers and radishes in the garden that was his forgivable
pride.[53] Dwight's activity was the more remarkable, because
ill health (largely induced, it is true, through self-imposed
asceticism) had plagued him from his youth. Also since early
manhood the threat of blindness had continually shadowed
his days, and, because he had read by candlelight too long
and too late, use of his eyes was virtually denied him. No
matter. When he could not read he listened, and remembered.
None of this was lost on Beecher, who believed in controlling
circumstance, rather than being controlled by it. Nor was
Dwight's intent foreign to Beecher's instinct. Already Lyman
had the habit of undertaking tasks that overtaxed his strength
and schedule; and his bond with nature was strong enough
that it would attend and color his activities to his life's
end—whether he was planning a preaching tour to Portland,
while planting cabbages at Litchfield,[54] or solving "knotty
problems in divinity at the same time" he was rooting stumps
out of his Cincinnati garden.[55]

Quite as much as Lyman's religion was stamped with
opposition to infidelity and commitment to man's ability, it
was oriented to a desire to escape from the wrath to come.
His was a grim and unshakable confidence that the future
wrath had sulphur to spare and was most acutely fervid. Hell
was dreadfully important to Lyman Beecher.

A playmate of childhood had frightened Lyman half out
of his wits with an alarming description of a burning, unend-
ing hell. It "took hold" of him, said the mature Lyman,
because he knew "what fire was," and he understood "forever." The notion became a "mainspring" and never left him
from that time.[56] Not long before Lyman died, his son
Charles said that his father's "whole career" would have been
changed if the idea of hell had been struck "out of his
mind."[57] Young Lyman, the future scourge of the "no-
hellite" universalism[58] and other forms of wickedness, arrived at Yale with "a sort of purpose to be a preacher,"[59]
but his decision was without spark, and his effort without

fire. His lips were not yet touched with a coal from the altar. Heaven caught him unaware. During his junior year at college he was on a visit to his home when his innocent and honest stepmother, marking through the window the town drunkard's uncertain progress along the street, expressed the charitable hope that the poor man would not spend eternity in hell. Lyman was so unnerved by her comment that he completely lost control of himself, and returned to Yale under what was then described as "conviction."[60] Soon thereafter Dwight's sermon on the text "The harvest is past, the summer is ended, and we are not saved"[61] left him utterly defenseless. It was as if "a whole avalanche rolled down" upon him, and he went home, "weeping every step." His despair was the occasion for the kindly Dwight to lead him away from that "state of permanent hypochondria" into which Lyman had recently settled after reading in the works of Jonathan Edwards, and to bring him to the door beyond which he felt "reconciled and resigned."[62] It was perfectly natural that Lyman Beecher's conversion should have been accomplished through the agency of Timothy Dwight, astonishing only that it should have been so long in arrival, even though the Beecher mind was constitutionally disposed to suspect the right of any lamb to enter the fold without first having been "chased all over the lot by the shepherd."[63]

Enemies of Yale's president called him "Old Pope Dwight." Lyman joined the throng of those New Englanders who regarded him "as second only to St. Paul."[64] "I loved him as my own soul," Lyman recalled, "Oh, how I loved him"; and he added, with more piety than proof, "and he loved me as a son."[65]

In the long years beyond and between Lyman's conversion and the sad twilight interim of his last days in Brooklyn, he never deserted the path upon which this Father in Israel had set his feet. The vague purpose of his youth became a verified portion. In revelation's impartial light Lyman saw men of his feckless generation empty of hope, ignorant of promise. It was his destiny to spur them to self-knowledge and tax them with the duty to achieve that conquest of fallen creation which their fathers essayed. Early ordained to the ministry, he made the life of the church the breath of his nostrils. Diligently, doggedly, he labored for revival, never doubting that divine initiative and human industry could save the world. Always in his theology he maintained (or thought he maintained) that fine balance in which man's utter dependence upon God is tempered with the unique mortal ability to be and to do. Thus had Dwight sensibly corrected the forbidding orthodoxy of his own day, and thus did Beecher, using at his best Dwight's combination of practical zeal and reasonable evangelism, of lofty thought and common touch, declare his debt to his old teacher.

More frequently than he knew, Lyman appeared in the mantle of Timothy Dwight. He wore it with pride always, and often with grace and honor.

Notes to Chapter II

1. *Autobiography*, I, 18.
2. Calvin E. Stowe, "Sketches and Recollections of Dr. Lyman Beecher," *Congregational Quarterly*, VI (1864), 234.
3. *Autobiography*, I, 21-22.
4. Leonard Bacon, *Sermon at the Funeral of Rev. Lyman Beecher, D.D., in Plymouth Church, Brooklyn, Jan. 14, 1863* (New York, 1863), pp. 5-6.
5. It is true that two of Beecher's thirteen children died in infancy. Of the remaining eleven, however, three lived well past seventy, four past eighty, and two past ninety; the lives of George and James were cut short by accidental or unnatural death.
6. ALS, Mary Foote Shotwell, Cincinnati, February 10-18, 1833, to Mrs. George A. Foote, Beecher Collection, Yale University.
7. *Autobiography*, I, 127.
8. *Ibid.*, II, 57.
9. D. Howe Allen, *The Life and Services of Rev. Lyman Beecher, D.D., as President and Professor of Theology in Lane Seminary* (Cincinnati, 1863), p. 28.
10. Leonard Bacon, *Sermon at the Funeral*, p. 6.
11. *Autobiography*, I, 27.
12. *Ibid.*, p. 113.
13. *Ibid.*, p. 125.
14. Leonard Bacon, *Sermon at the Funeral*, p. 6.
15. *Autobiography*, I, 24.
16. Calvin E. Stowe, "Sketches and Recollections," p. 223.

17. *Ibid.*

18. Theodore Parker, *The World of Matter and the Spirit of Man,* George Willis Cooke, ed. (Boston, n.d.), p. 147. This is Volume VI in the American Unitarian Association's Centenary Edition of Parker's *Works.*

19. *Autobiography,* I, 19.

20. *Ibid.*

21. Frederick H. Hoadley, "A Review of the History of the Epidemic of Yellow Fever in New Haven, Conn. in the Year 1794," in *Papers of the New Haven Colony Historical Society,* Vol. VI (New Haven, 1900), 237.

22. Richard J. Purcell, *Connecticut in Transition, 1775-1818* (Washington and London, 1918), p. 7.

23. Timothy Dwight, *Travels in New England and New York,* 4 vols. (New Haven, 1821-1822), IV, 366.

24. *Ibid.,* p. 367.

25. *Ibid.,* p. 380.

26. *Autobiography,* I, 43.

27. William Buell Sprague, *Annals of the American Pulpit, or, Commemorative Notices of Distinguished American Clergymen of Various Denominations, from the Early Settlement of the Country to the Close of the Year Eighteen Hundred and Fifty-Five,* 9 vols. (New York, 1857-1869), I, 476.

28. Calvin E. Stowe, "Sketches and Recollections," p. 223.

29. *Autobiography,* I, 40.

30. Franklin Bowditch Dexter, ed., *The Literary Diary of Ezra Stiles, D.D., LL.D.* (New York, 1901), III, 497.

31. Franklin Bowditch Dexter, "Student Life at Yale College under the First President Dwight (1795-1817)," in *A Selection from the Miscellaneous Historical Papers of Fifty Years* (New Haven, 1918), p. 384.

32. *Autobiography,* I, 40.

33. Franklin Bowditch Dexter, *Diary of Ezra Stiles,* III, 126.

34. *Ibid.,* p. 11.

35. Ezra Stiles, *The United States elevated to Glory and Honor. A Sermon preached before his excellency Jonathan Trumbull, Esq., LL.D., Governor and Commander in Chief, and the Honorable the General Assembly of the State of Connecticut, Convened at Hartford, at the Anniversary Election, May 8, 1783* (New Haven, 1783), p. 96.

36. *Ibid.,* p. 75.

37. Stiles, who was of scrupulous intellectual honesty, did not achieve firm belief until after long and extensive study of the Bible. He was not ordained as minister of the Second Congregational Church of Newport, R.I., until two years after he had been admitted to the bar. Even then he insisted that deism could not be fought by suppressing sympathetic literature and risking suppression of the truth.

38. Ezra Stiles, *The United States elevated*, p. 86.

39. Ezra Stiles, *A Discourse on the Christian Union. The substance of which was delivered before the Reverend Convention of the Congregational Clergy in the Colony of Rhode-Island, Assembled at Bristol, April 23, 1760* (Boston, 1861), p. 94.

40. *Autobiography*, I, 40.

41. Timothy Dwight, *Theology, Explained and Defended in a Series of Sermons by Timothy Dwight, S.T.D., LL.D., Late President of Yale College with a Memoir of the Life of the Author in four volumes*, 2nd ed. (New Haven, 1823), I, 23.

42. Edmund S. Morgan, *The Gentle Puritan: A Life of Ezra Stiles, 1727-1795* (New Haven and London, 1962), p. 368.

43. Timothy Dwight, *Travels*, IV, 368.

44. Timothy Dwight, *Theology*, I, 51.

45. *Ibid.*, p. 22.

46. William Buell Sprague, *Annals*, II, 164-165.

47. Timothy Dwight, *Theology*, I, 95. Dwight not only possessed wisdom, but he recognized it in others. He assembled a distinguished faculty, with whom he willingly shared governance of the college, and advocated the broadening of the curriculum to include courses in science, medicine, theology, and law.

48. James C. White, *Personal Reminiscences*, p. 44.

49. Lyman Beecher, *Lectures on Skepticism*, p. 70. The particular quotation represents a characteristic note which Beecher sounded in his case for God's existence on the basis of evidences in the creation.

50. *Autobiography*, I, 47.

51. Timothy Dwight, *Theology*, I, 261.

52. *Ibid.*, p. 28.

53. *Ibid.*, p. 27.

54. *Post Script*, by LB to ALS, Harriet Porter Beecher, Litchfield, July 4, 1819, to Catherine Beecher, Beecher-Stowe Collection, Schlesinger Library, Radcliffe College. Beecher in ALS, Litchfield, December 3, 1823, to Catherine Beecher, Beecher-Stowe Collection, *ibid.*, wrote: "I cannot peddle potatoes but I can make Pork & eat it comfortably at home & enrich my land to make corn and potatoes grow to raise more—and thus furnish to myself health & pleasure & profit & mental vigor."

55. *Autobiography*, II, 306.

56. *Ibid.*, I, 34.

57. ALS, Charles Beecher, Andover, April 12, 1857, to Henry Ward Beecher, Beecher Collection, Yale University. Emotionally unconvinced of the centrality of such doctrine, Charles inquired in the same letter: "What *danger* if he believed in no future endless ruin? Yet Isabella & Mary I fear reflect father's belief on that point, & Hatty's mind is I fear shaken—do *you* believe in it? Do you really believe the wicked will exist forever, & continue forever in sin?"

58. Charles Grandison Finney, "Traditions of the Elders," in *Sermons on Important Subjects* (New York, 1836), p. 65, first designated the Universalists as divisible into two categories, the no hell-ites (the worst of the lot) and the limitarians or restorationists.

59. *Autobiography*, I, 45.

60. *Ibid.*

61. Timothy Dwight, *Theology*, I, 51.

62. *Autobiography*, I, 46-47.

63. Charles Edward Stowe, *Life of Harriet Beecher Stowe compiled from Her Letters and Journals* (Boston and New York, 1889), p. 35.

64. Samuel Griswold Goodrich, *Recollections of a Lifetime, or Men and Things I Have Seen: Historical, Biographical, Anecdotical, and Descriptive* (New York and Auburn, 1856), I, 348-349.

65. *Autobiography*, I, 44.

Chapter III
Early Testing:
Battling Apathy in East Hampton — 1800-1810

The type of deism that was introduced to America in the late nineteenth century reflected recent scientific advances in Europe and offered a cosmology and a view of man that quickly found expression in the national literature. Prominent figures such as Thomas Jefferson and Thomas Paine were commonly identified as deists, and many lesser celebrities were so known, or suspected of leaning strongly in that direction. Clergymen frequently attributed to the imported philosophy the low state of public morals that obtained after the Revolution. In seeking to promote revival they did not always distinguish between criminal offense against society and religious indifference. Orthodox ministers of the Federalist period especially deplored rejection of Biblical authority and the neglect of public worship, faults they considered exceedingly grave, even in law-abiding citizens.

East Hampton Church

East Hampton was plain, but substantial, a quiet town of puritan ancestry and respectable age, situated toward the southeastern tip of Long Island. Henry Hudson's men (landing there eleven years before the Pilgrims set foot on Plymouth) found the natives friendly, and marked the rugged beauty of dark woods and tangled vines.[1] Not long thereafter the admiring Indians sold the site to white men for hatchets, and less, valued at thirty pounds; and the wild grandeur of the island of shells began to retreat before the industry of the settlers.[2] By the early nineteenth century beach plum and scrub bush covered the hills where the forests had stood,[3] and, until suddenly and unaccountably killed by blight, neat hedges of prim fenced the homestead boundaries.[4] The single street of the village, a grassy stretch of perfectly level ground where geese wandered at their will, divided the town's two straight rows of sturdy, unpainted houses,[5] each with a pile of firewood before the door. The only trees were a scant line of poplars between the chief residences, and one elm of "enormous height" that served as a "conspicuous waymark for miles around." Windmills, like sentinels, kept watch at the ends of the roadway.[6] Strong damp winds from the sea blew steadily across the strip of blazing white sand that lay drifted in dunes between the town and the shore.[7] Travelers on first coming to the hamlet were "forcibly struck with a sense of stillness" and absorbed into the quietude that seemed to envelop the island.[8] Visitors who remained met endurance as well as repose, and discovered that East Hampton lived less tranquilly than she appeared. There was a certain propriety in the meeting of East Hampton, looking so little like her essence, and Lyman Beecher, whose five feet, seven-and-one-half-inch stature in no way indicated his strength when he battled for the Lord, and even less betrayed the formidable character of the resistance he could offer to the minions of hell.[9]

After his graduation from Yale, Beecher had spent a year studying divinity with Dwight,[10] and then, in October, had been licensed to preach by the New Haven West Association of ministers.[11] About that time, his eye happened to fall—as he said—"on the obituary notice" of Samuel Buell,[12] who for half a century had ministered to East Hampton.

The vacant charge was no mean appointment. The congregation boasted a tradition of Puritanism that until quite recently had reigned "without even 'a dog to move his tongue' against it," and was still strong after a century and a half.[13] Whaling, not yet affected by the embargo, afforded the town industry and income, for men regularly responded to the "weft" that signaled the appearance of a whale spout. Clinton Academy, first in the state of New York of those schools that rejected the musty emphasis on Latin and Greek and offered courses in practical and modern subjects, flourished in the very shadow of the church.[14]

Fascinated by the prospect but not at all sanguine of obtaining the settlement for himself, Lyman concluded that the folk there would certainly not have him. Scarcely three weeks later, though, he was engaged to preach as a candidate on probation. The opportunity had come about through his friend, Tudor Davis, who had learned that the orthodox element of the community was seeking a man who could "stand his ground in argument, and break the heads of" the infidels.[15] Under such necessity, it was a trustworthy instinct, indeed, that led the Long Islanders to accept Davis' recommendation and invite Lyman Beecher to their pulpit. The wind stood fair for Sag Harbor when at ten o'clock in the morning, on Thanksgiving Day, 1798, he set sail from New London.[16] Save for his horse and harness, all he owned had been easily packed into the small hair trunk he carried on the pommel of his saddle.[17] Also, he traveled with a consuming passion to revive the church. That passion never thereafter left him completely free, and sometimes it drove him close to madness and despair.

Religious zeal and fidelity were no novelties for the natives of East Hampton. Dr. Buell had been so enraptured with the Word that he routinely preached for at least an hour, and often for much, much longer. He once outmaneuvered a languishing auditory by announcing, after he had already passed the two-hour mark, that having finished admonition to sinners (who were now free to go) he would proceed to address the elect.[18] During seasons of revival that flowered under Buell's ministry, worshipers saw him frequently interrupt divine service to dash from the pulpit and mount the gallery stairs in search for souls newly awakened to the gospel.[19] Thomas James, a somewhat earlier minister, and an acknowledged eccentric, had given explicit "orders that his remains should be deposited in the grave contrary to those of his people" so that he might "arise up" to face them on the "solemn morning of the resurrection,"[20] and his affectionate flock had indulged his quaint conceit.[21] East Hamptoners rather enjoyed their colorful clergy. Even so, they were hardly prepared for the vitality and fire of the quixotic Beecher, which he employed equally in pursuing sinners and chasing whales.

Before the first winter was past, Lyman's parishioners nicknamed him the "snow-bird" because neither storm nor season dampened his spirit nor stopped his movement.[22] He roamed, or, more correctly, rushed, all over the island: Amaghansett, Three-mile Harbor, The Springs, Wainscott, and the Negro settlement, Freetown.[23] Between times he took to the sea with all the zest of the local residents, who hardly breathed "land air" at all.[24] Twice he came near death by drowning, once while attempting to land a shark without losing his line, which, foolishly, he had tied to his waist,[25] and once when, swimming in the surf, he ventured too far out and fell into that meeting of the waves which the islanders called a "sea-poose."[26] But most significantly, and most ardently, he preached, with such carefully planned campaign, and such shrewdly cast sermons, as only his account of them can tell:

> I did not attack infidelity directly. Not at all. That would have been cracking a whip behind a runaway team—made them run the faster. I always preached right to the conscience. Every sermon with my eye on the gun to hit somebody. Went through the doctrines; showed what they didn't mean; what they did; then

> the argument; knocked away objections, and drove home on the conscience. . . . At first there was winking and blinking from below to gallery, forty or fifty exchanging glances, smiling, and watching. But when that was over, infidelity was ended.[27]

Infidelity on the island, though, was not quite dead. Members of the Infidel Club[28] simply settled down to wait for an opportunity to tilt with this knight on a fair field. At the same time, older members of the parish with no little uneasiness kept an eye on the zealot, because, as it happened, Beecher had not been unanimous, or even first, choice to fill the shoes of Samuel Buell. The saintly doctor had recommended a Mr. K. as his successor, and the mature element of the church, regarding the advice on a level but little lower than revelation, sought unsuccessfully to establish the former parson's choice. The youth of the town objected so strenuously that, after a series of flinty encounters, opposing factions agreed in an armed truce on Beecher, not so much as a candidate of their common choice, as upon one not unacceptable to the old and not forced upon the young. Until it should be perfectly clear, therefore, whose colors this gallant horseman wore, the gossips, though it surely taxed them to follow so sprightly a figure, kept strict account of his activity: Mr. B. had dined with a deist on Christmas. Mr. B. had taken tea at Captain Isaac's. Mr. B. had asked Miss Esther Hand to sing for him all the songs she knew. Mr. B. had himself spent an evening singing with Mr. H. Mr. B. had gone hunting with a doctor of unsound faith, a questionable pastime that, by the town crier's estimate, "lowered his character twenty-five percent."[29] Little wonder that Beecher felt himself watched "as narrowly as a mouse is watched by a cat,"[30] and no marvel at all that he long remembered the bright intervals when he could "saddle his horse, ride post haste" and visit with Aaron Woolworth, minister at Bridgehampton,[31] or join the human, if heterodox, Dr. Abel Huntington to fish the streams of Montauk Point. Fifty years later, when Beecher returned to East Hampton, the old physician pleaded with his dear friend to stay yet another day that they might once more go casting along the Alewife Brook.[32]

From the moment he arrived at his charge, Beecher was impatient for revival. Believing then, as he admitted afterward, that God intended East Hampton "as a theatre on which to make memorable displays" and had accordingly planted it with "the choicest vine,"[33] Beecher worked for a miracle, which refused to happen. With the sense of frantic immediacy that only the God-possessed may know, Lyman, at a single stroke, wrote an oblique testimony of fear and faith: "Immortal souls are sleeping on the brink of hell. Time is on the wing. A few days will fix their eternal state. Shall I hide the truth?" "O my God!" he cried, "lift up my voice like a trumpet."[34] East Hampton stopped her ears. "My preaching seems not to move," he wept. "I speak against a rock."[35] Sadly, it was true.

Lyman's despondency over his parish explains in part his curious exchanges at this period with Roxana Foote. During their courtship he wrote passionate letters, declaring less his love for her than inquiring of her love for God, and pressing so hard to be certain it was genuine that her distressed family justifiably feared lest he should push her over the brink of sanity. Lyman's behavior was but added evidence that his sense of divine commission waited upon nothing—not even upon the equanimity of his betrothed. Nor would it ever. Yet Lyman delighted in Roxana, and he loved her after his fashion. He never gave as much of himself to another. Shortly before he died, the senile old man came upon one of her letters, carefully preserved after fifty-six years. Across the faded paper he wrote, "Roxana, beloved still," and signed his name and the date as boldly as his shaking hand would allow.[36]

Roxana Foote grew up in the Connecticut home of her grandfather, General Andrew Ward, who served under Washington in the Revolution. The old patriot had taken his widowed daughter and her ten children to live at "Nutplains" when Eli Foote, his son-in-law, died of yellow fever in North Carolina.[37] Life at the Ward farm was comfortably religious, wholesomely intellectual. The general's mother, an inflexible patrician of granite orthodoxy, who outwitted death till her hundredth year, was a daily reminder of a Puritan past. She

did not suffer fools gladly. Eli Foote's gentle widow was a
devout churchwoman who could speak of "our Lord" without seeming proprietary. And Andrew Ward, himself, was a
bottomless reservoir of strange fact and serious question. The
kindly soldier, maddeningly casual about household matters,
had systematically read through every book in the public
library. In such a setting Roxana was early sensible of the life
of the spirit and of the limits of the mind.[38] Of his three
eldest granddaughters, the general said, laughingly, that when
he first heard their voices in the morning, Harriet would be
saying, "Here! take the broom," Betsy Chittenden asking
"what ribbon it's best to wear," and Roxana inquiring,
"Which do you think was the greater general, Hannibal or
Alexander?"[39]

Roxana tied books to her distaff that she might read
French while she spun flax. In her leisure she painted minia-
tures on ivory. To the end of a tragically short life her
brilliance did not tarnish, nor her interests flag. Her letters,
written in the pitiful scraps of time left after caring for a
family against the odds of inadequate budget and an absent-
minded husband, speak excitedly of the "discovery that the
fixed alkalies are metallic oxyds";[40] or again, offer "new
poems" as a lure to a desirable house guest,[41] and give
reliable instructions for planting fruit trees identified with
such enchanting names as "Gargonelle," "St. Michael," and
"Swan's Eggs."[42] Vastly knowledgeable, Roxana was painfully modest: in presence of strangers she could not speak
without blushing, and she was "absolutely unable" to "lead
the devotions in . . . female prayer-meeting."[43]

No sooner had Lyman seen her than he rightly judged
Roxana of "uncommon ability."[44] Presently he exclaimed
that she shone "pre-eminent."[45] Roxana had said that she
would never marry until she found a Sir Charles Grandison.
Lyman put a stop to that. Less polished, but more persistent,
than the model Englishman, he was irrepressible. Roxana and
Lyman were betrothed soon after they met, although a
wedding was out of the question for at least two years.

In the fall of 1799 Beecher had received ordination over

the parish of East Hampton, an event that he felt would "stand prominent" during his lifetime, and just possibly through "eternity."[46] Following a period of probation the town had called him to remain permanently. East Hampton had promised her first minister forty-five pounds per annum and a quarter of all the whales stranded on the beach.[47] The parish agreed to pay Lyman three hundred dollars a year and firewood. Still mourning the lack of revival, but by no means conceding defeat, Beecher had accepted, which meant, also, that he agreed to spend the remainder of his days on Long Island.[48] Save for open break with the parish or serious fraction of the moral code, there was as yet in New England no defensible circumstance short of death or act of God to remove a man from the charge to which he had been ordained.

As soon as the settlement was effected Lyman had returned to Connecticut to marry Roxana. Parson Bray performed the ceremony on a morning, late in September, 1799. The occasion was festive, in spite of a drenching rain. Roxana's friends were there, and Lyman's family from New Haven. Afterward Uncle Lot Benton, still gruff and still generous, hired a sloop to take the bride and groom to the island. They faced the future with the outrageous faith of the young. "Nobody," said Lyman, "ever married more heart and hand than we."[49]

Lyman was potentially compatible with the community. His background was that of Connecticut Congregationalism. So for that matter was that of his charge, the East Hampton Presbyterian Church. Only in the time of Samuel Buell had the body left Congregationalism, and then not enthusiastically so. Also, every minister who had served the parish had come from the Standing Order of New England.[50] Moreover, in those years there was operative a Plan of Union for Congregationalists and Presbyterians by which individual churches could call men of either persuasion without sacrificing denominational affiliation or complicating ecclesiastical administration. Ministers moved between the two without difficulty or embarrassment.[51]

Lyman was not overly tender about sect—especially where
Calvinism was affirmed or alleged. Naturally, he regarded
Episcopalians as scarred by the mark of the papal beast, but
he did not attack them; and he snorted, but without rancor,
at the upstart Methodists. His chief concern in East Hampton
was to bring the town first to salvation, and then to church;
and in reaching for this mark he was tireless. In a letter to her
sister, Roxana called him "every body's man." "Last week,
for example, he preached twice in town and two lectures,
besides a funeral sermon on Gardiner's Island, and five sermons to the Indians," and, between time, she wrote, there
were "meetings afternoons, and evenings, and sometimes in
the forenoon." Roxana added wistfully that he had not had
"much leisure."[52]

Neither had he had much response. There was a stirring in
the winter, and for several weeks "the work was powerful
and glorious,"[53] but the awakened fell asleep again, and the
glory departed. It was more than Beecher could understand
or absorb. Perplexed in mind, and troubled of heart, he fell
into deep despair. His health failed, and for almost a year he
did not preach. Insensitive visitors, no wiser than the friends
of Job, demanded that he "cheer up" and urged upon him
the necessity of going outside. Lyman moaned that he could
not. For a time neighbors agreed that he might not indeed
recover.[54]

A lesser man would have died—at least in spirit. Beecher
held relentlessly to life. Venturing from the shelter of his
house, he risked at first no more than long hours in the sun
and deep breaths of salt sea air. In time he put his hand to
building turf fences and cutting hay fields. Before he returned to the pulpit he could pile a cart high with seaweed
and haul it home from Three-mile Harbor. Slowly he reclaimed his strength and former ebullience. When Mr.
Fithian, hateful and stingy, threatened to stop paying because Beecher had stopped preaching, Lyman was ready for
him. "What is the reason," the wretched old man had asked,
"you ministers are so hungry for money?" "I don't know,"
replied the fiery young parson, "unless it is that we see our

people growing covetous and going to hell, and want to get it away from them."[55]

A miniature of Lyman, painted by a traveling artist at about this time, struck Mrs. Woolworth as the likeness of one just ready to preach. It was. During his remaining years in East Hampton, he blasted the parish with prophecy that made their ears tingle and echoed far beyond Sag Harbor.

On July 11, 1804, Alexander Hamilton and Aaron Burr, entangled in a web of political intrigue and personal animosity, met at Weehawken, New Jersey, in an overt duel that was fatal to both: Hamilton lost his life, and Burr became a political outcast. Shocked over the death of Hamilton, the nation was offended by the behavior of Burr, who, under indictment for "willful murder," appeared to take "his seat as president of the senate of the United States."[56] Moreover, rumor charged him with making sport of the matter at the very moment Hamilton lay dying.[57] A stunned populace began to consider *affaires d'honneur* in a new light. There was an English dissertation on duelling at the August Commencement of Harvard. Timothy Dwight, preaching in the Yale Chapel in September following, condemned duelling; and although he disclaimed any concern with personalities, no one misunderstood the context of the discourse.[58] On Long Island, Beecher read about the death of General Hamilton and was inflamed. "I kept thinking and thinking," he said, "and my indignation did not go to sleep."[59] The outcome of his brooding was a sermon[60] that waked up his flock at hand, and warned the morally insensitive afar. "More than anything else, it made the name of brave old Andrew Jackson distasteful to the moral and religious feeling of the people. It hung like a millstone on the neck of Henry Clay."[61]

Beecher excoriated duelling as the "great national sin," which defiled a whole land. Its terror cut wives down to widowhood and slashed fathers away from their children, while those whose guilty hands had let the flow of blood stood brazen and secure. Had Beecher but deplored the sin and damned the wickedness, men could have endured (and

forgotten) his rage. As it happened, they could not put his
wrath aside, for he had had the temerity to suggest a practical
approach to the enemies of God.

> There is no way to deal with these men . . . but to take the
> punishment of their crimes into our own hands. Our conscience
> must be the judge, and we must ourselves convict, and fine, and
> disgrace them at the polls. Here . . . will our voice be heard, and
> our will become law.[62]

Underlying this challenge and appeal is the confidence that
man—regardless of whether he can lay hold of heaven without assistance from God—can most assuredly by his own
effort shape earth to the likeness of Eden and that to attempt
to do less is to ignore the power that is his. Early and late this
was Lyman Beecher's message, that man is obligated and able
to turn himself to God, and able also to establish and maintain society as testimony of his submission to heaven and joy
in the gospel, refining the old and initiating the new in strict
conformity to that law of God which is plainly declared in
the Bible. The sermon on duelling was but one of many
variations of the constant theme.

Softly at first, to his own people, "to see how it would
sound," and then to the villagers on the north side of the
island, Beecher spoke the remedy for duelling. With authority
he preached it to presbytery and received a firm mandate:
"Publish."[63] Gathering momentum, Lyman introduced on
the floor of the synod a resolution for forming anti-duelling
societies. Opposition "came up like a squall, sudden and
furious," but the prophet with thunder and lightning in his
face "rose and knocked away their arguments," and in swift
and shattering attack was able to "switch 'em, and scorch
'em, and stamp on 'em." He carried every vote in the
house.[64] Thus was there lifted up for reform a voice that
silence did not overtake for half a century. Men listened; they
had no choice. They could, however, resist, and they did.

Not so serious for the Beechers as sin, but dreadfully
vexing, was the problem of finance. Lyman was deeper in
debt by the year. His salary was more than when he came to
the island,[65] but so was his expense. Six children arrived

almost as rapidly as nature would allow. One of them had died.[66] Lyman was quite sentimental about his family: "Kiss the babies," he wrote Roxana when he was even briefly absent. "I cannot think of them or you without tears."[67] He could also be almost cavalier about such mundane matters as food or dress, and once in the midst of the snow season, rode away on a preaching tour without providing adequate firewood for the family in his absence.[68] Expansive and unfeeling by turns, he might fetch lobster and oysters for the same meal,[69] or send a child on a long journey without any money.[70] Devoid of all greed, Lyman misunderstood and therefore misused money with the touching naiveté of an open-handed child; but no measure of watchful care could have accommodated his modest stipend to the growing demands upon it. Something had to be done. Teaching (although Lyman thought it "perfect torture," just "like driving Uncle Lot's old plow, only worse"[71]) was respectable, ancillary occupation for clergymen, so the Beechers opened a school for select young ladies, teaching, and even in some cases boarding, them in the crowded quarters of the manse. Roxana made the classes a success, but the paltry income was, almost literally, eaten up as soon as it was in hand. Eventually Lyman had to ask for a raise.

As the whole community, and not the church alone, had called Lyman to East Hampton,[72] any increase of salary had to be granted in the town meeting. Such an arrangement made multiplication of Lyman's grief ever potential, and, in this instance, unfortunately actual. Men of the town (especially members of the Infidel Club) complained that Beecher was orthodox; the church objected to him because he was not. The secular mind-set is unmistakable in an incident involving Clinton Academy, of which Beecher was for a while both trustee and principal.

During his days at Yale, Beecher had written a satire on skepticism that turned back upon the enemies of religion their own "shafts of ridicule."[73] A presentation of this *Dialogue* was planned for the 1807 exhibition day at the Academy. Though wonderfully amusing in the character of the drunken Toperus, the piece was no real threat to infidelity nor any boon to faith. Pedestrian for the most part, it is often tedious; but there is clear and unflattering allusion to Jefferson's philosophy. Free-thinkers, therefore, alarmed and angered, "wire-worked among the Democrats"[74] and succeeded in forbidding the presentation,[75] even though the offending instructor and the chairman of the board proved expendable in the conflict.[76]

Church disapproval was subtler in expression—stronger in effect. Members of the congregation nursed the suspicion that the Beechers just might have planted their feet in this world more firmly than they had fixed their eyes upon the next. They feared the family was "growing too splendid" and making idols of their "fine things."[77] When Lyman (typically without plan) bought a bale of cotton because it was cheap, Roxana spun it and made a canvas carpet of it herself, painted it with bright flowers, and laid it grandly on the parlor floor. It was the wonder of the island—the only rug in the village. Deacon Tallmadge refused to enter the room where it was, because he couldn't " 'thout steppin' on'it," but he stayed to inquire if Roxana thought to have "all this *and heaven too.*"[78]

Harassed thus from without, badgered from within, and ground down by the weight of problems of finance, Lyman moved toward inevitable departure, knowing before he openly said it that he must go from East Hampton. Until that time, however, he did not slack his effort for revival, confident of coming showers, although as yet "there was no cloud nor sign of rain."[79] Such was his zeal that members of the parish could not finally resist. They began to show sparks of life, making Lyman "think of hens in the night, when you carry a candle into the hen-roost, how they open first one eye and then the other, half asleep."[80] Striving "to preach cut and thrust, hip and thigh, and not to ease off," Lyman finally waked them. Sharpened warnings stabbed them into consciousness, even as grace described intoxicated them with thoughts of salvation. Lyman preached election; but it was plain from his sermons that there would be far fewer in hell than gloomy Puritan fathers had thought, and many, many more in heaven. "God will not illumine heaven with His glory," Lyman assured East Hampton, "by sacrificing help-less, unoffending creatures to eternal torment." This time his hearers believed, and took heed. "Oh! what a time that was," said Lyman. There were a hundred converts.[81]

The delayed revival that flowered in the last months of Beecher's Long Island residence only underscored the irony of his resignation. For years he had struggled for this hour. Now that it had come, he was compelled to turn his face away because he could not support his family on air—even the fine sea air of. East Hampton. He advised his sister, Esther, that he would surely be dismissed by spring, that "not more than half" were willing to increase his salary. It fell out as he had feared. Even Roxana's customary calm dissolved in the tension, and she came closer to bitterness than the record ever shows again: "The very low estimation which people appear to have of the blessing of the Gospel ministry is strikingly exemplified when we compare what they are willing to pay for it with what they are willing to pay for their own gratification."[82]

Beecher took the step in the spring of 1810. Having preached on trial and having been well received at Litchfield, Connecticut, he began to set in motion the slow-turning wheels of ecclesiastical machinery that would accomplish his release. In shocked disbelief, East Hampton, seeing a blessing taking flight, endeavored in vain to keep him. Roxana wrote to him how it went: some called him "runaway" to her face. Others vilified him with words that mercifully she did not hear. At the eleventh hour there were offers of money, ill-timed as compliment and unrealistic as enticement.

In his farewell sermon Lyman spoke baldly, almost brutal-ly, to his parish, the severity of his judgment relieved only by his poignant regret that the revival had not come earlier and spread wider. "I had hoped before the close of my ministry," he said, "to be able to present you as dear children to God. But I shall not. My ministry is ended, and you are not saved." He should love them, though, he said, until the "lamp of life" expired.[83]

Restless for the new parish, Beecher looked for a better life at Litchfield. Folk he had met there were gracious and

62   UNVANQUISHED PURITAN

concerned, and he felt already that "had the people in New York been thus predisposed," he would "not have failed" in East Hampton.[84]

Beecher was yet to learn that the drama that involved him in Long Island would continue in Connecticut—with fresh scenery, with new lines, but with identical agon. Actor and action remained the same; they only removed to another part of the forest.

Notes to Chapter III

1. *Autobiography*, I, 94-95.
2. Lyman Beecher, *A Sermon, Containing a General History of the Town of East-Hampton, (L.I.), from its first settlement to the present time. Delivered at East-Hampton, January 1, 1806* (Sag Harbor, 1806), p. 3. The articles of payment were 20 coats, 24 looking-glasses, 24 hoes, 24 hatchets, 24 knives, and 100 mugs. Regarding the name of the island, a footnote in the *Autobiography*, I, 64, volunteers: "So named by the natives from the abundance of white shell used in the manufacture of wampus, for the production of which this island was celebrated, as is still attested by vast heaps of broken shells."
3. *Autobiography*, I, 96.
4. Lyman Beecher, *East-Hampton*, p. 29.
5. Timothy Dwight, *Travels*, III, 311.
6. *Autobiography*, I, 97.
7. Timothy Dwight, *Travels*, III, 316.
8. *Ibid.*, p. 315.
9. Lyman Beecher Stowe, *Saints, Sinners, and Beechers* (Indianapolis, 1934), p. 17.
10. *Autobiography*, I, 68. Yale Divinity School was not established until 1822. Roland H. Bainton, *Yale and the Ministry* (New York, 1957), pp. 79-95, gives a sprightly account of the early history of the institution.
11. Franklin Bowditch Dexter, *Biographical Sketches of the Graduates of Yale College with Annals of the College History. Vol. V, June, 1792-September, 1805* (New York, 1911), p. 247.
12. *Autobiography*, I, 89.
13. Nathaniel S. Prime, *A History of Long Island, from its First Settlement by Europeans, to the Year 1845, with Special References to its Ecclesiastical Concerns* (New York, 1845), p. 185.
14. Benjamin F. Thompson, *History of Long Island, from its Discovery and Settlement to the Present Time*, 3rd ed., 3 vols. (Port Washington, L.I., 1962), II, 136-138.

15. *Autobiography*, I, 89.
16. *Ibid.*, p. 92.
17. *Ibid.*
18. William Buell Sprague, *Annals*, III, 105.
19. *Autobiography*, I, 89.
20. Lyman Beecher, *East-Hampton*, pp. 19-20.
21. Nathaniel S. Prime, *History of Long Island*, p. 175.
22. *Autobiography*, I, 101.
23. *Ibid.*, pp. 96-97.
24. Timothy Dwight, *Travels*, III, 316.
25. H. P. Hedges, "Anecdotes."
26. *Autobiography*, I, 113.
27. *Ibid.*, II, 100-101.
28. Luther A. Weigle, *American Idealism*, vol. 10, *The Pageant of America* (New Haven, 1928), p. 139, notes that "Jacobin clubs and societies of 'Illuminism' were founded in various sections of the country, devoted to the destruction of Christianity and the general revolutionizing of government and society."
29. *Autobiography*, I, 102.
30. *Ibid.*, p. 103.
31. H. P. Hedges, "Anecdotes."
32. *Ibid.* Dr. Huntington is reported to have added, " . . . and if you will stay a month I don't know but I will go to Heaven with you."
33. Lyman Beecher, *East-Hampton*, p. 32.
34. *Autobiography*, I, 104.
35. *Ibid.*, p. 103.
36. *Ibid.*, p. 86. The document thus endorsed by Lyman contains Roxana's declaration of faith in God as love. Much of it is incorporated in a letter, often a verbatim quotation of the original, occurring in Harriet Beecher Stowe, *The Minister's Wooing* (New York, 1859), pp. 291-294, in which the character Mary Scudder affirms the same position. Lyman's enduring devotion and the circumstance of Mrs. Stowe's quotation support the near worshipful attitude of the Beechers toward Roxana. A manuscript in the Beecher Correspondence, Yale University, unidentified except by date, though obviously (to this author) in the handwriting of Henry Ward Beecher, expresses a similar sentiment: "I found the correspondence of my father & our mother . . . O my mother! I could not help kissing the letter—I looked & . . . tho't that her hand had rested upon it. . . . I found out more of her *mind* than I ever knew before—more of her *feelings*, her *piety* . . . and I could not help observing that her letters were superior—more refined & conclusive than the corresponding ones of father's."
37. *Autobiography*, I, 54.
38. "It was his custom to read aloud to his family, with remarks and discussions to excite thought and interest." *Ibid.*
39. *Ibid.*, p. 56.

40. *Ibid.*, p. 232.

41. *Ibid.*, p. 285.

42. ALS, Roxana Beecher, East Hampton, October 7, 1809, to George Foote, Beecher Collection, Yale University.

43. William C. Beecher and Samuel Scoville, assisted by Mrs. Henry Ward Beecher, *A Biography of Rev. Henry Ward Beecher* (New York, 1888), p. 23.

44. *Autobiography*, I, 62.

45. *Ibid.*, p. 65.

46. *Ibid.*, p. 115.

47. *Ibid.*, p. 99. Ralph Henry Gabriel, *Toilers of Land and Sea*, vol. 3, *The Pageant of America* (New Haven, 1926), p. 314, describes the community enterprise of Long Islanders in disposition of whales washed ashore during the eighteenth and nineteenth centuries.

48. *Autobiography*, I, 105.

49. *Ibid.*, p. 119.

50. Leonard Bacon, *Sermon at the Funeral*, p. 9.

51. E. H. Gillett, *History of the Presbyterian Church in the United States of America*, rev. ed., 2 vols. (Philadelphia, 1864), I, 396-398.

52. *Autobiography*, I, 121-122.

53. Nathaniel S. Prime, *History of Long Island*, p. 183.

54. *Autobiography*, I, 132.

55. *Ibid.*, p. 135. Lyman's ready retorts are almost invariably mentioned in any reminiscence of him. Henry Howe, *Historical Collections of Ohio*, 2 vols. (Norwalk, Ohio, 1896), I, 825, records a classic instance. Crowded from a road that was hardly more than a shelf on a muddy hillside, Beecher rolled perhaps thirty feet down a precipice and was so badly injured that he was incapacitated for three weeks. Answering his cries for help, the careless teamsters responsible for his plight asked how they could get down to where he was. "Easy enough," he answered, "come down as I did."

56. William Oliver Stevens, *Pistols at Ten Paces: The Story of the Code of Honor in America* (Boston, 1940), p. 162. Stevens is quoting from a November 11, 1804, entry of John Quincy Adams' diary.

57. *Autobiography*, I, 150.

58. William Oliver Stevens, *Pistols at Ten Paces*, p. 162.

59. *Autobiography*, I, 150.

60. Lyman Beecher, *The Remedy for Duelling: A Sermon Delivered before the Presbytery of Long-Island, at the Opening of their Session, at Aquebogue, April 16, 1806* (New York, 1809).

61. Leonard Bacon, *Sermon at the Funeral*, p. 11. Beecher said that Democrats distributed 40,000 copies of the sermon during Clay's campaign for the presidency.

62. *Ibid.*, p. 22.

63. The manuscript of the sermon was lost when it fell from the

jacket of the friend taking it to a literary critic, and was washed ashore on Gardiner's Island a month later.

64. *Autobiography*, I, 153.

65. *Ibid.*, p. 139.

66. E. E. Eells, *A Sermon on the Pastorate of the Rev. Lyman Beecher, D.D. in the Old Town Church, East Hampton, N.Y. Preached November 17, 1835* (n.p., n.d.), pp. 23-24, relates that after the Beechers' departure, the coffin of the infant was disinterred and moved to his own plot by one of the town's leading skeptics, who insisted that he had done so because the grave was lonely, and added that there was "buried in it one of the reasons why Lyman Beecher grew unhappy in his pastorate" at East Hampton. The child's name was subsequently given to another Beecher, who in due course became Mrs. Stowe.

67. *Autobiography*, I, 131.

68. *Ibid.*, p. 232.

69. Henry Ward Beecher, "Diary," February 24, 1836, Beecher Collection, Yale University, records that "no one provided better dinners, soups, codfish, and mutton chops even. Upon great days he has been known to have a turkey."

70. ALS, Lyman Beecher, Litchfield, April, 1821, to Catherine, Beecher-Stowe Collection, Schlesinger Library, Radcliffe College.

71. *Autobiography*, I, 126.

72. E. E. Eells, *Sermon on Beecher*, p. 9.

73. Lyman Beecher, *A Dialogue, Exhibiting Some of the Principles and Practical Consequences of Modern Infidelity* (Sag Harbor, 1806).

74. *Autobiography*, I, 180. The offending passage relates to the character Theoret, who is represented as thinking for himself, rising above vulgar prejudice, and eschewing priestcraft, bigotry, and fanaticism. In the second scene he says: "You must possess some knowledge of geography, and natural history, or how could you decipher from strata of lava, and beds of oyster-shells the era of creation, to prove that Moses was a liar. You must know also that some men are black, and some white, or how would you ridicule the scriptures for pretending that all men descended from one pair. And if you knew nothing of the Andes, and their height, how could you prove that the Almighty could not get water enough to cover them, at the time of the flood?" The ease of relating such sentiment to Jefferson's *Notes on Virginia*, together with the reprehensible character, and miserable end (justly, according to the author) ascribed to spokesmen of the same, accounted for the free thinkers' opposition to Beecher's offering.

75. Nathaniel S. Prime, *History of Long Island*, p. 186.

76. ALS, Lyman Beecher, East Hampton, April 6, 1806, to Rev. Richard S. Storrs, Beecher Correspondence, Yale Divinity School.

77. *Autobiography*, I, 125.

78. *Ibid.* Roxana even ground and mixed the pigment.

79. *Ibid.*, p. 161.
80. *Ibid.*, pp. 161-162.
81. *Ibid.*, pp. 165, 167.
82. *Ibid.*, p. 182.
83. *Ibid.*, pp. 202-203.
84. *Ibid.*, p. 186.

Chapter IV
Mixed Blessings:
Ministering Without State Support – 1810-1826

Where the Anglican church in colonial America had been regarded primarily as extension of the crown (which was the case in Georgia, Maryland, the Carolinas, and New York City together with three adjoining counties), disestablishment of Tory religion was almost routine in the course of organizing state governments subsequent to the Declaration of Independence. Even in Virginia, where the church was firmly, as well as legally, established, state support was cut off in 1779, and Jefferson's bill of religious freedom passed in 1785. But in New England, where Congregationalism—the religion of the patriots—was established, separation of church and state came more slowly and with much greater difficulty. Liberals (seeking freedom) and dissenters (seeking toleration) made common cause and over strong opposition achieved disestablishment in Connecticut in 1818, in New Hampshire in 1819, and in Massachusetts in 1833. It was soon apparent that separation of church and state did not necessarily indicate lack of sympathy between them.

Eng.d by W.G.Jackman

Lyman Beecher, Age 28

On the twenty-first day of August, 1770, an elegant equestrian statue of George III, imported from London and richly gilded, was erected in the Bowling Green at the lower end of Broadway, in the city of New York.[1] The likeness was wrought in lead (a parable according to Henry Guy Gould),[2] and was unveiled "amidst the discharge of cannon and music by the band."[3] Six years later a mob toppled it to the ground. The statue was taken, by what transportation it is impossible to say, to Litchfield, Connecticut. There, in a shed constructed in his apple orchard for the very purpose, Oliver Wolcott "chopped it up with the wood axe," and the women of his family "had a frolic" melting the pieces and making bullets (over forty-two thousand) to be used against the British.[4]

The episode demonstrates the character of Litchfield residents. Calvinism had nurtured in them a courage and a fortitude that did not easily disintegrate in the face of earthly mischance. Men who had contemplated eternal ruin without flinching did not shrink before the comparatively minor threats of temporal conflict. "Accustomed to combats with the Devil," they found it "rather a recreation to fight only [the] British,"[5] but they did not forget nor doubt that in so doing they upheld the divine purpose. America was God's garden, and they were his angels.

When during the War for Independence news reached Litchfield that General Cornwallis was landing on the coast with a large fleet, the Reverend Judah Champion, able and eloquent pastor of the parish, addressed the God of battles in words Litchfield considered sufficiently appropriate and choice to preserve for the edification of succeeding generations:

> O Lord, we view with terror the approach of the enemies of Thy Holy religion. Wilt Thou send storm and tempest to toss them upon the sea, and to overwhelm them upon the mighty deep, or to scatter them to the uttermost parts of the earth. But peradven-

ture any should escape Thy vengeance, collect them together
again as in the hollow of Thy hand, and let Thy lightnings play
upon them.[6]

The seat of such sentiment would seem to have been a fine
place of settlement for one who, like Lyman Beecher, was
convinced that it was "Christianity which, in this country,
rocked the cradle of our liberties, defended our youth, and
brought us up to manhood";[7] but by the time Beecher
arrived in Litchfield love of country in America wore a
different complexion from that which some had found or
fancied in earlier days. After the Revolution patriotism was
likely to express the attempt to invent value rather than any
effort to discover it. Men were more concerned to idolize
their own achievement than to bend their energies to the will
of God. Rationally, Lyman acknowledged the human condition, though he tended to reject it emotionally. "We are
becoming another people," he said in 1812.[8] Fifteen years
later he was still referring to the "vandal spirit of innovation
and overthrow." He insisted that the puritan fathers, looking
"down upon their descendants with approbation or reproof,"
according as they might "follow or depart from the good
way," exercised a "censorship inferior only to the eye of
God."[9] Lyman lived in the present, but his heart was often in
bondage to the past. Unwisely he sought to perpetuate the
value of a tarnished tradition by holding to the outward
forms of the Pilgrims instead of capturing their inner spirit.
Lyman was moved by the puritan fusion of true virtue with
true patriotism, and he refused to believe his generation
incapable of or unsympathetic to such union.

At least, though, Lyman's continuing frustration was set in
pleasant places. Litchfield was completely different from his
first parish. Roxana's star-crossed sister, Mary Hubbard, had
found East Hampton as "dull" and "inactive" as a "frog
pond," the residents able neither to "laugh nor cry," and
totally unaware of any life, even "wars, murders, and violence," beyond the island;[10] but Litchfield society, utterly
charming and infectiously lively, she said she would prefer,
though she might have opportunity to "go the world over"

and choose what she would.[11] This was a sensibility that natives, with neither pride nor wonder, generally shared, acknowledging the superior quality of the local gentry as objectively as they accepted the order of the seasons or the structure of the universe. When a British ambassador, intending to compliment the grace and beauty of Mrs. Chauncey Goodrich, observed to Uriah Tracy that she would be an ornament at the court of St. James's, the senator, bowing in agreement, immediately replied, "She is distinguished even on Litchfield Hill."[12]

Litchfield was on the highroad to everywhere, and the stages speeding between New York and Boston, or between Hartford and Albany, stopped briefly at its taverns, and rushed on again.[13] Huge "red, four-horse coaches with whips cracking and horns blowing came and went at a great pace all day long through the town."[14] Such excitement was suitable in a place as industrious as an ant hill. In 1810 there were in Litchfield

> 4 forges, 1 slitting mill, and one nail factory . . . 1 cotton mill, 1 oil mill, 1 paper mill, 2 carding machines, 6 fulling mills, 5 grain mills, 18 saw mills, 5 large tanneries . . . 2 comb factories, 2 hatters shops, 2 carriage makers, 1 cabinet furniture maker, 5 saddlers, and a number of house carpenters, joiners, and smiths, and other mechanics.[15]

There was also much liveliness of a less serious nature. Young blades went for winter sleigh rides to nearby Goshen, where there were turkey or oyster suppers, with "Black Caesar to play jigs on a cracked fiddle."[16] In summer they took steamboat rides on Bantam Lake, or anticipated delights of the promised "Aerial Phaeton," by which eight persons could sit in carriages attached to a wheel and "in regular succession be raised to the distance of Fifty Feet in the air," at a "velocity equal to ten miles a minute" for recreation and amusement "highly recommended by the most eminent Physicians in the United States."[17] And, of course, when some justly celebrated visitor such as General Lafayette arrived, there was an elaborate reception at Phelps' Tavern, where the whole top floor was given over for a ballroom.[18]

Litchfield was also beautiful. The streets, laid out around a village green, were shady and wide, and the chiefest of them "had a row of dignified white houses," which bespoke the solid substance and impeccable taste of their cultivated residents. There were "deep dooryards and large side gardens," and in front of each and "along the grassy streets on either side were over-shadowing, long-branching trees."[19]

Prominent on the green was the Congregational meeting house, the second such occupied by the local Society. The splendid building had been finished in twenty weeks, after the Society voted a committee the "good right to furnish Rum, Grindstone, and Ropes sufficient for framing the meeting house according to their best discretion," and appointed an overseer to direct the issue of liquor at the raising, allowing "two drams per day to the spectators."[20] With a high "belfry, projecting out at the east end," and a "double row of windows" in the side walls, the structure was imposing from without, and altogether grand from within, where the pulpit, flanked by panels of carved tulips painted "flaming red," dominated the square, boxed pews of the faithful.[21]

As the meeting house was conspicuous on the hill, so was her minister eminent among men. Litchfield soon learned to recognize the peculiar rattle of Beecher's sulky, bound for the lake, or "spinning up North Street" about eleven o'clock on Sunday nights, when he would return from preaching at Bantam, where, as he said, the community "having hunted and fished all day, were tired enough to sit down and hear him talk in the evening."[22] Litchfieldians enjoyed Beecher's wit and respected his wisdom; but his celebrity among them was that of a man who takes his turn in a company of brilliant folk where each may shine because all are bright. Beecher there was part of a galaxy, not a comet unattended. Dan Huntington, Beecher's immediate predecessor, who called Litchfield a "delightful village on a fruitful hill," had pointed out how richly it was "endowed with schools" and how distinguished with statesmen in a population that was generally "enlightened and respectable."[23] It was true.

Among those honored and honorable in Litchfield, Sarah Pierce was set apart. Her teaching career, which began modestly in her own dining room with a single pupil, lasted for forty years.[24] During that period she taught almost two thousand students and earned the deep gratitude of her town, which twice by subscription erected a building better than the one in use to accommodate the expanding program of the Litchfield Female Academy.[25] In an era when "map-drawing, painting, embroidery and the piano" were the subjects principally sought by young ladies, Sarah Pierce pioneered in educating women in the "higher branches," as well as in the disciplines of the drawing room.[26] Her academy attracted students not alone from distant Michigan and Florida, but from Canada and the Indies as well.[27] They came quite as much in search of social grace as in quest of sharpened intellect. Often they were vastly successful in acquiring both, and betrothal to a promising young lawyer in addition.

Consistently practical and deeply religious, Miss Sally, while she stretched the minds of her wards, was also careful for the health of their bodies and the state of their souls. Periodically she pressed them for answers to questions that tabulated fraction of the moral code and revealed the proximity of hygiene and godliness—at least in the view of Miss Pierce: "Have you rose early enough. . . ? Have you prayed . . . ? Have you spoken any indecent word. . . ? Have you been neat in your person. . . ? Have you combed your hair with a fine tooth comb. . . ? Have you eaten any green fruit during the week?"[28] Afternoons the young ladies, even in the face of the roughest March wind, took a prescribed constitutional, sedately walking, two by two, down North Street, and "moving to the music of a flute and flageolet." [29] Daily they met for prayers and exhortation. Though instructing them herself in divinity, Miss Pierce frequently presented to her girls the ministers of the community, among whom none was more welcome than Lyman Beecher. In return for his counsel and assistance she bartered free education for his children. Beecher sons as well as daughters attended her school and, resplendent in paper helmets and borrowed ostrich plumes, participated in the end of term exhibitions when "Jephthah's Daughter," or some other such didactic drama of Miss Pierce's personal authorship, was presented to the amazement and delight of large audiences.[30] On these occasions students from Judge Reeve's Law School were always in attendance.

Tapping Reeve was genuinely pious, impressively portly, and an inflexible Federalist. He had once been indicted for libeling President Jefferson, although happily the charge was not pressed.[31] Openhandedly generous, he lived and died a poor man, but he was ever gallant in behavior and gracious in speech. Contemporaries said of him that he "never saw a little girl but that he wished to kiss her, for if she was not good," he was certain that "she would be."[32] Sinners also remembered his diligence in attending their spiritual rebirth, and his incessant and sensitive prayers for their salvation. He was established in Litchfield as a practicing attorney before Lyman Beecher was born.[33]

In other days aspiring lawyers had attached themselves to a member of the profession whose character and ability they admired and had read law under the direction of that mentor until sufficiently self-confident to hang out their own shingles. Reeve attracted students in such number that it soon seemed wise and necessary for him to offer formal lectures on the interpretation of the law.[34] Somewhat later, to spare his invalid wife the inevitable noise and confusion of fledgling attorneys arguing cases in a moot court, Reeve, in 1784, erected in his dooryard a separate building to the south of his residence.[35] There he housed his library, taught his classes, and counseled his students. Thus did the law school in America become a reality, and for some years Reeve conducted it alone. After his appointment to the bench in 1798, he associated the urbane James Gould in the enterprise.[36] Between them they educated more than a thousand lawyers, numbering among the future civil servants who passed through their doors six cabinet members, twenty-eight senators, and fourteen governors of states.[37] As late as 1850, a congressman newly come to the Capitol was welcomed by "over thirty members of the House" who had studied law at Litchfield, or had married one of Miss Sally Pierce's graduates.[38]

The Law School was at its zenith when Lyman, protégé

and ally of the Messrs. Reeve and Gould, arrived in Litchfield to join his voice with theirs in the defense of the Standing Order. Indeed, it was through their effort that he came to Connecticut at all.

James Gould, whose treatise on "Pleading" was considered the ablest law book of the generation,[39] knew a cogent argument when he met one and could thereby measure the mind that created it. Gould had been Lyman's tutor at Yale, and when he came upon his former pupil's published sermon "The Government of God Desirable,"[40] he doubtless began it with interest. In any case he finished it with enthusiasm and at once brought it to Reeve, whose spontaneous reaction was, "Who is that man?" "Why can't we get him?"[41] As it happened, they could and did get Beecher. The invitation for him to become pastor was unanimous, the vote to pay him eight hundred dollars annually (a handsome salary) *almost* unanimous.[42] It was abundantly clear that Judge Reeve was the new minister's constituent.

When Lyman Beecher came to Connecticut, the Congregational Church still enjoyed state support; but her days of privilege were numbered. After the Revolution, as state governments were formed, established churches for the most part disappeared rather as a matter of course. The transition, as a rule, was accomplished easily, partly because the popular mind identified Anglican and Tory, and thought the business a political affair. Even Virginia denied tax support to the Church of England, though somewhat tardily. In New England, though, the Congregational Church, established by law, was the church of the patriots, and the struggle was hotly fought, harder won. There was never, however, serious possibility that men who had thrown off the British yoke would tolerate church-state union indefinitely. A new and liberal generation of voters favored separation. Episcopalians (uncomfortable as pensioners on "uncovenanted mercies") requested the severance; and a growing company of dissenters demanded it.

In Litchfield, as in neighboring towns, older men and former leaders were mostly Federalists. They identified society's well-being with that of its prosperous citizens and were angered and alarmed by the clamorous upstarts of the age. The younger element were Democrats. So it came about that clergy and Federalists in Connecticut were banded together in a struggle to maintain the old ways, which included state support of the church. From the first the combat was unequal, the outcome assured. Beecher, as able as any, and far more resourceful than most, was a champion of the Standing Order. As such he was personally and politically welcome to Tapping Reeve, who was convinced that—without Government support—the gospel would never survive.

When Roxana and the children arrived in Litchfield, they went directly to their patron's home. Mrs. Reeve (the judge's second wife) was a warm, good-natured woman, so enormously fat that she could hardly walk, but so droll about her bulk that she relieved friends and visitors of any embarrassment of being in her presence.[43] She was also intelligent, and as deadly serious about the faith as her husband. After the Beechers moved into their own quarters, Mrs. Reeve's chaise was to be seen almost daily outside their home. There with Roxana she read aloud the poems of Miss Hannah More (a religious star of the period), and with Lyman she discussed the plight of the Hindus and their possible conversion. Inordinately fond of the Beechers, Mrs. Reeve remained realistic in assessing them. When the parish commissioned a portrait of Lyman, some of the ladies suggested that the canvas be sent to the parsonage as soon as it was finished. Mrs. Reeve, absolutely immovable, refused: "By no means," she said, "not until everything is ready for its hanging—even the spike driven in the wall. If it is not hung at once those Beecher children will have the eyes punched out."[44] But her devotion and sterling character appear in her acceptance of Lyman's second wife, warmer by far than that which the hapless woman received from her stepchildren. Mrs. Reeve ministered to the Beecher family after Harriet Porter became mistress of the manse as faithfully and as willingly as she had served Roxana.[45] As for the judge, he demonstrated his loyalty many times, and never more tangibly than when, in an effort to relieve his "beloved and highly respected Minister" entirely from embarrassment, he collected some two thousand dollars for Lyman, who in the space of six years had managed to fall into debt in excess of twenty-eight hundred dollars.[46]

Having known Tapping Reeve and his wife, Beecher ever thereafter referred to homes in which he felt himself especially cherished as his "Judge Reeve places."[47] Lyman did not, however, experience such cordial treatment indiscriminately in Litchfield. For that matter, no ordained Congregationalist would have. The fact is that the Standing Order was threatened.

By the Standing Order not only was the Congregational Church supported at public expense, but her clergymen were accorded many privileges normally enjoyed only by nobility. There was a time, much to the dismay of dissenters and deists, when Congregational ministers made a "festival" of election day. It was their custom to "walk in procession, smoke pipes, and drink . . . they would talk over who should be governor, and who lieutenant governor, and who in the Upper House, and their counsels would prevail."[48] To be sure, by the time of Beecher's generation, this vested interest, already shorn of much of its influence, was openly opposed. The Reverend Nathanael Emmons, still visiting in his parish, clad like a colonial divine in small clothes and a "three cornered hat," was a curiosity whom street boys flocked after as a freak. Less related to his times than his costume was that tyranny over society which ministers exercised before the war.[49] But there was still in New England a tax support of the church, and it was fought by both saints and sinners. Episcopalians, who had for years grumbled quietly, joined for the nonce with the multiplying Baptists and Methodists, and shouted their dissatisfaction. Especially they voiced acrid complaint over the "imposition of a tax for religious purposes."[50] It was at this point that the dissenters made common cause with the deists and Democrats, who, as a part of their effort to unseat the old guard, were striving to throw off all religious restrictions of state. If they were successful, a man would be free to support any church (a circumstance that insured status for the religiously disgruntled) or none (a solution preferred by political radicals). So doubtful an alliance was, understandably, of short duration; but it was a caution for a season. As Beecher put it, the rising democracy "included nearly all the minor sects, besides the Sabbath-breakers, rum-selling tippling folk, infidels and ruff-scuff generally, and made a dead set at . . . the standing order."[51]

The challenge to preserve an established church excited Beecher, but the task was beyond him, as he seemed instinctively to have known. For while on the one hand he made "Herculean efforts to uphold the system of Church and State," on the other he lavished "almost superhuman energies in laying the foundations of the voluntary system."[52] His technique was a combination of revival and reform.

Revivalists were a breed suspect in the Bantam hills. During the days of the Great Awakening, Litchfield, haughtily aloof from the goings on of the distracted followers of George Whitefield and Jonathan Edwards, went so far as "in regular Church meeting, called expressly for the purpose" to let these disturbers of the peace know "by a unanimous vote, that they did not wish to see them."[53] The scruple was primarily aesthetic. Civilized folk frowned upon the irregular itinerancy of the awakeners, and deplored the enthusiastic vulgarity of their converts. But renewal under the direction of a resident minister, especially one who equated their own interests with the will of heaven, they would approve and abet. Initially Beecher fanned their Laodicean faith back into flame, and even brought them to that point of regarding with jaundiced eye such innocent (and formerly indulged) diversions as the "Curious and Ingenious Art of Dancing on the Slack-Wire"; they abandoned gaming and balls as unseemly in those who "aimed for the better life."[54] Week after week, the large and "ancient meeting-house" was "filled to overflowing." Lyman lighted some fires that burned for years. One early stirring "continued as a revival, first in the center of town, next in the west, then in the east, and on the extreme outskirts," and eventually flamed as border warfare in remote localities "where Satan had long held control." [55]

For Beecher, reform, like revival with which it was inseparably bound, was, in large part, the decisive action that man's memory demanded and God's grace informed: reformation meant not "to reshape," but, as a dictionary tells, "to restore to a former good state." In revival, therefore, Lyman called upon churchmen to remember old promises and to rekindle forgotten fires; and he urged unconfessed sinners to look back even beyond the distance the fall of man had placed between him and God. Preaching reform, Beecher pressed men to return to puritan ways—to that life in which men acknowledged what was good and acted accordingly. Lyman understood that a culture is what it is because people determine its shape on the basis of their common faith regarding true value. Stable worlds arise only from stable faiths; and true faith makes the wilderness an Eden. Thus Beecher was tireless in the fervent sermon of revival, and the feverish activity of reform societies, shoring up the dikes of law that stood against the surging sea of human willfulness. How could he—or any man of reason—risk or invite the inevitable chaos that would result when mother church was disestablished and a "brood of infidels, heretics, and profligates" allowed to "undermine the deep laid foundations of . . . civil and religious order"?[56]

Yet while Beecher strove for the Standing Order, he "foresaw the result as it afterward came to pass."[57] He was well advised, for in the end, all his piety and wit could not stay the tide. Just after five o'clock on the afternoon of September 15, 1818, members of the convention at Hartford, Connecticut, adopted by a vote of one hundred thirty-four to sixty-one a state constitution that disestablished religion. Popular ratification followed in October.[58] Religion became purely voluntary, and the state no longer forced any man to pay his tithe.

Although he had already accepted the revolt as accomplished, Lyman was nevertheless stung by the defeat. "They slung us out like a stone from a sling," he said.[59] Long afterward daughter Catherine remembered seeing the warrior the day after the election, "sitting on one of the old-fashioned, rush bottomed kitchen chairs, his head dropping on his breast, and his arms hanging down." When she asked her father the subject of his thought, the battered prophet groaned solemnly, "THE CHURCH OF GOD."[60]

Beecher was absolutely inconsolable—but only for "several

days." Resilient at core, he shortly announced that disestablishment was the "best thing that ever happened to the State
of Connecticut." Now churches would be thrown "wholly on
their own resources and on God," and it would soon appear
that they could accomplish by "voluntary efforts, societies,
missions, and revivals" far more than ever they could have
gained "by queues ... and cocked hats and gold-headed
canes."[61]

After the downfall of the Standing Order, timid clergymen
in Connecticut were careful to guard their tongues until
bitterness and danger were past. Not so Lyman. Deliberately
(and with some difficulty) he secured an invitation to speak
in New Haven, a stronghold of toleration, and thick with
Beecher-haters. It would be a "stimulus" for him, he said, to
show himself and preach "in the midst of all attacks, before
the community" where he was still slandered and where there
was "tremendous and deliberate effort" to crush him.[62] Also
it would serve his enemies notice that though he accepted,
even now approved, disestablishment, he still opposed the devil
and all his cohorts. Denied the shield of state, he sought the
same ultimate goals he had always sought, and possibly with
greater chance of success. When he had finished his address in
New Haven the audience had understood. Their "sneering
and hissing" had dissolved first into attentive quiet, and then
into approval. "I preached as I used to preach," said Lyman.
"It answered the end for which it was intended."[63]

The whole maneuver had been a natural ploy in one who
thrived on contest. As a youth, he had felt his "nerves braced
up" at the signs of an approaching storm and, "as it grew
darker," had realized that his "excitement increased, till,
finally when the thunder burst, it was like the effect of a
strong glass of wine."[64] If Lyman did not yet stand at
Armageddon, he felt himself already battling for the Lord.

Notes to Chapter IV

1. George M. Woodruff, "Address at the 200th Anniversary of the Congregational Church, August 1, 1920," in Esther Harriet Thompson, "Life in Old Litchfield: History and Gossip of People and Events Through Two Centuries," in "First Ecclesiastical Society Scrap Book, I" (n.p., n.d.), in the Litchfield Historical Society Library. See also Morris W. Seymour, "Historic Litchfield" (privately printed, 1920), p. 8, in the collection of the Litchfield Historical Society.

2. Emily Noyes Vanderpoel, *Chronicles*, p. 27.

3. George M. Woodruff, "Address."

4. George C. Woodruff, *History of the Town of Litchfield, Connecticut* (Litchfield, 1845), p. 47.

5. Harriet Beecher Stowe, *Oldtown Folks* (Boston, 1882), p. 374. Many of Mrs. Stowe's writings illuminate the religious and social situation of her father's time. The clergyman, Mr. Avery, of *Oldtown Folks* is a portrait of Lyman Beecher.

6. *Autobiography*, I, 208.

7. Lyman Beecher, *Lectures on Skepticism*, p. 104.

8. Lyman Beecher, *A Reformation of Morals Practicable and Indispensable: A Sermon Delivered at New Haven on the Evening of October 27, 1812*, 2nd ed. (Andover, 1814), p. 22. In the sermon Beecher is specific: "Drunkards reel through the streets, day after day, and year after year with entire impunity. Profane swearing is heard, and even by magistrates, as though they heard it not. Efforts to stop travelling on the Sabbath have, in all places, become feeble, and in many places, even in this State, they have wholly ceased."

9. Lyman Beecher, *The Memory of Our Fathers*, pp. 22-23.

10. *Autobiography*, I, 140. Mary Hubbard, Roxana's sister, married a West Indies plantation owner, and, completely shattered to discover that he was father of children by slave mistresses, returned to make her home with the Beechers. She died in 1813.

11. *Ibid.*, p. 235.

12. E. D. Mansfield, *Personal Memories*, p. 125.

13. Elizabeth C. Barney Buel, *Old Time Industries of Litchfield Town* (Litchfield, 1952), p. 2.

14. Emily Noyes Vanderpoel, *Chronicles*, p. 21.

15. Elizabeth C. Barney Buel, *Old Time Industries*, p. 1.

16. E. D. Mansfield, *Personal Memories*, p. 136.

17. Emily Noyes Vanderpoel, *Chronicles*, p. 34.

18. Alain C. White, *The History of the Town of Litchfield, Connecticut, 1720-1920* (Litchfield, 1920), p. 96.

19. Harriet Beecher Stowe, *Poganuc People* (Toronto, 1878), p. 184.

20. George C. Woodruff, *History of Litchfield*, p. 55.

21. *Autobiography*, I, 210-211. One of the tulip panels is preserved in the Litchfield Historical Society's collection.

22. ALS, Jonathan Beace, Milford, Connecticut, September 28, 1857, to Henry Ward Beecher, Beecher Collection, Yale University.

23. *Autobiography*, I, 213.

24. Emily Noyes Vanderpoel, *More Chronicles of a Pioneer School, from 1792 to 1833* (New York, 1927), p. 1.

25. In 1798 grateful citizens subscribed three hundred eighty-five dollars to erect a building just south of the Congregational Church for housing the Female Academy, *ibid.*, p. 4.

26. *Autobiography*, I, 226.

27. Emily Noyes Vanderpoel, *More Chronicles*, p. 7.

28. Emily Noyes Vanderpoel, *Chronicles*, p. 147.

29. E. D. Mansfield, *Personal Memories*, p. 122.

30. *Autobiography*, I, 228. It was Miss Pierce's custom to write the dramas herself. A single quotation from *Ruth*, Emily Noyes Vanderpoel, *Chronicles*, pp. 84 ff., is indicative of the tone of the productions: "The fatal day, which blasted all my joys / Which banish'd hope, the wretches latest compact / And black despair erect her empire here. / My loved daughters, well may ye remember / This fatal morn, black with impending woe / Which hid forever, the last ray of comfort. / Your hopes like mine fled like morning dew / Before the scorching blast of dire disease. / Then join with me once more, to weep this day / Fatal to love, a too maternal fondness."

31. Morris W. Seymour, "Address," in *Presentation of the Reeve Law School Building to the Litchfield Historical Society at Litchfield, Conn., August 22d, 1911* (Litchfield, 1911), p. 20.

32. *Autobiography*, I, 223-224.

33. Lyman Beecher, *A Sermon Preached at the Funeral of the Hon. Tapping Reeve, Late Chief Justice of the State of Connecticut; Who Died December Thirteen, Eighteen Hundred and Twenty-Three, in the Eightieth Year of his Age* (Litchfield, 1827), p. 5.

34. *Ibid.*, p. 10.

35. Dwight C. Kilbourn, "Presentation Address," in *Presentation of Reeve Building*, p. 11.

36. *The Litchfield Law School, Litchfield, Connecticut: A Brief Historical Sketch* (n.p., n.d.), in the collection of the Litchfield Historical Society, p. [1].

37. *Ibid.*, p. [2]; Litchfield County, *Litchfield County Centennial Celebration* (Hartford, 1851), p. 51.

38. Morris W. Seymour, "Historic Litchfield" (n.p., 1920), p. 4.

39. E. D. Mansfield, *Personal Memories*, p. 123.

40. Sermon I in Lyman Beecher, *Sermons Delivered on Various Occasions* (Boston, 1828).

41. *Autobiography*, I, 181.

42. *Ibid.*, p. 192.

43. *Ibid.*, p. 224.

44. Esther Harriet Thompson, "Life in Old Litchfield."

45. *Autobiography*, I, 367.
46. "Ecclesiastical Scrap Book" preserves the instrument relative to the subscription of the money, together with the list of donors.
47. *Autobiography*, I, 210.
48. *Ibid.*, p. 259.
49. Jacob Ide, ed., *The Works of Nathanael Emmons, D.D.* (Boston, 1846), I, 130-131.
50. E. D. Mansfield, *Personal Memories*, p. 134.
51. *Autobiography*, I, 342.
52. *Ibid.*, p. 345. The comment is that of Charles Beecher, who admired his father's zeal, even when he was puzzled by his motivation.
53. *Ibid.*, p. 213.
54. Emily Noyes Vanderpoel, *Chronicles*, p. 322.
55. *Autobiography*, I, 217-218.
56. Lyman Beecher, *A Sermon, Delivered at Woolcott (Conn.) Sept. 21, 1814, at the Installation of the Rev. John Keyes, to the Pastoral Care of the Church in that Place* (Andover, 1815), pp. 9-12. Beecher referred to this sermon subsequently as "my sermon on the 'Building of Waste Places,'" an admirable example of a title that summarizes and underscores the thrust of the whole work.
57. *Autobiography*, I, 260. It was in an effort partially to anticipate the inevitable that Beecher had preached his *Reformation of Morals* sermon.
58. Disestablishment was delayed longer in New England than in Virginia (1785), because the Congregational Church (which was established in New England) did not suffer the accusation of implied Tory sympathy that was often directed against the Anglican establishment in Virginia. Legal separation of church and state was accomplished in Connecticut in 1818, in New Hampshire in 1819, but not until 1833 in Massachusetts.
59. *Autobiography*, I, 343.
60. *Ibid.*, p. 344.
61. *Ibid.*
62. *Ibid.*, pp. 344-346. Forrest Wilson, *Crusader in Crinoline; the Life of Harriet Beecher Stowe* (Philadelphia, London, and New York, 1941), pp. 44-45, makes this episode and its sequence, Beecher's preaching the ordination sermon of Sereno Edwards Dwight (*The Bible a Code of Laws* [Andover, 1827]), a key to understanding the man's character.
63. *Autobiography*, I, 346.
64. *Ibid.*, p. 29.

Chapter V
Workaday Theology:
Faith in the Common Life – 1810-1826

*As the strength of Calvinism was never more evident
than in the lives of common folk who gladly faced exile
and danger for their faith's sake, so the security of the
system was never more precarious than when descendants of the early advocates found it no longer possible
to express the creed in everyday life. In post-Revolution
America, political events and expanding opportunity
seemed to invite activity and require a faith the Calvinistic system neither permitted nor required. Where holi-
ness was a mysterious, unverifiable state and justification a gift, the common man was frustrated. If both sin
and righteousness were imputed, activity was worthless
and without meaning, a judgment the young nation
could not accept. While clergymen endeavored to bridge
the gap between colonial Calvinism and the philosophy
of the new republic, common folk, often assuming already man's adequacy and freedom, externalized religion by demonstrating at a practical level that outward
expression was an appropriate and trustworthy index to
true faith.*

Beecher Home at Litchfield

Years after Lyman Beecher had moved from Connecticut, the great, square house[1] where the Beechers dwelt in Litchfield was called a "Puritan penitentiary." Lyman was designated "one of the wardens" of a "prison with very narrow and closely-grated windows," which lay always under the heavy "shadow of God's eternal frown" and sheltered the "rayless, hopeless and measureless dungeons of the damned." Life within those walls, said the critic, was an absurd and cruel "inquisition," where conformity was enforced and cowed children were "tortured for the good of their souls."[2]

Not one of the boisterous company congregated in the parsonage would have recognized or accepted the description. To be sure, Lyman extolled Calvinism to his children. To have done less would have been to deny his own faith. Without repeal of the laws of nature, however, no child of his could ever have stood mute in the presence of a sentiment or situation he disapproved, and had the rebel dared to do so, the "doctor would have disowned" him.[3] In the often Spartan economy of the Beecher household, speech was one of the few commodities (outside of God's good grace) that was both plentiful and free. "Opinions were canvassed without ceremony," and Lyman habitually prodded his family into the forum. "He expected originality; he encouraged independence"; and "he inspired boldness."[4] His children, being neither geese nor mice, responded with spirit. Quite apart from their Beecher heritage, they came naturally by a tendency to speak to their father's face and to quarrel with his theology. Before her marriage, Roxana, Lyman's first wife, had rather the better of her husband in astringent exchange over the love of God.[5] The usually diffident Harriet Porter would have none of it when Lyman attempted to read to her from Jonathan Edwards' "Sinners in the Hands of an Angry God." "Dr. Beecher," she declared, "I shall not listen to another word of that slander against my Heavenly Father." Then she swept elegantly from the room.[6] Connecticut orthodoxy was austere as Sinai's rocks; but acceptance of such doctrine was neither commanded nor achieved at the Beechers'. Moreover, members of Lyman's household were exposed to richer variety in belief than that normally allowed within the lean and narrow range of Congregationalism.

In the days before the embargo throttled the merchant marine, New England traded briskly in ports of the Caribbean and the Orient. Litchfield did not often meet seamen of the sort who swarmed wharf town streets, wearing varnished hats and carrying monkeys or parrots, or exhibiting other evidence of their romantic travels. But Roxana's brother, Samuel Foote, who captained his own square-rigged clipper, used now and again to visit the Beechers, bringing with him a great sea chest filled with curios from far places. His gifts of "Moorish slippers" and "strange implements from the tombs of the Incas" dazzled the children only slightly less than the tales that he told. Also he spoke of Roman Catholic bishops he had known "as learned and as truly pious" as any Christian; and he startled them with the intelligence that he had found "Turks were more honest" than Connecticut Congregationalists. While Lyman engaged his brother-in-law in "good-natured skirmishes" over these outré notions, the young Beechers listened, fascinated.[7]

No more subdued in mien than in mind, the Beecher brood were such a lusty, uninhibited lot that Aunt Esther sometimes felt that the only cure for the mutinous crew was to "condemn and hang half a score of them."[8] There were hardly so many, though, when they lived in Litchfield. By 1815 they numbered but eight. Of the nine children Roxana had borne Lyman, only one—the first Harriet—had died. (Her name, though not her place, had been given to another.[9]) Beecher got on well with all children, even when he tangled with their elders.[10] His own adored him. The youngest was always taxed with the responsibility of bringing Lyman to breakfast, which meant first taking him "by the nose" in order to wake him, and then assuring him that no beast lay hidden "under the bed" waiting to pounce upon him if he exposed so much as a great toe.[11] The older children Lyman complimented more subtly, affording them the privileged status of participating as equals in his clever, though commendable, schemes for the family welfare. "I'll tell you what we'll do," he said once to weary children who had been impressed in the preparation of the annual barrel of apple sauce, George and "I'll take turns, and see who'll tell the most out of Scott's novels." And so they did, scene by scene, as the wide-eyed children worked without flagging, intoxicated by the exploits of Ivanhoe, or the picture of Jeannie Deans walking barefoot from the Scottish Highlands to London to save her sister's life.[12] On winter evenings, when Litchfield snow was piled in drifts against windows and doors, and Bantam Lake was locked in ice, Pa—as the children called him—would take his violin and play rollicking tunes for them, always including their favorite, "Go to the Devil and Shake Yourself," and sometimes, even, take off his shoes and, to their uncontrolled delight, exhibit the wonders of the double shuffle, which he had danced on the barn floor when he was a young man and went to corn huskings.[13]

Nor did the Beecher children enjoy the freedom and celebration of the Litchfield parsonage in isolation. There were also gathered under the same roof Betsy Burr, an orphaned relative;[14] several young ladies from Miss Pierce's academy, boarders, who thrived on the excitement but smarted under the lack of privacy;[15] and Rachel and Zillah, two bound Negro girls brought from East Hampton to manage the kitchen. Next door lived Aunt Esther and Grandma Beecher, David's fifth and last wife, who had outlived him. Mother and stepdaughter had moved nearby before necessity brought them within; but it was much the same, since they were only "half a minute's walk" away.[16] And always, always there were visitors from the roving band of Connecticut clergy, forever bound for meetings, or on their way to exchange pulpits, and never passing up opportunity for conference and debate with Dr. Beecher.

Curiously, children and ministers alike were radically discomfited by Calvinism, and, as a result, expressed, one perhaps as unwittingly as the other, the kindling American spirit that was completely foreign to the older orthodoxy. The young Beechers, clamoring for attention, were only seeking recognition through achievement; but this was scandalous endeavor in the eyes of strict Congregationalists, because it assumed intrinsic worth and native ability in man. Their spontaneous heresy persisted throughout childhood and, in due course, informed the words of their mature years. Optimism and self-confidence, even in children, were not easily adaptable to the canons of Calvinism.

The clergymen, on the other hand, discovered themselves strangers to the faith, not because they turned away from the tradition, but because when they looked at it closely they found its essence unacceptable. The case for human inability was difficult to explain to a generation who had conquered the wilderness, subdued the savages, and humbled a world power; and the cogency of election to eternal life on the basis of God's secret will was lost to an age that extolled reason. The clergymen essayed unsuccessfully to make logical a system that at its heart turned upon decrees of a sovereign God, inscrutable always, and often arbitrary. In their reaction to the theology of their ancestors, the ministers, as the Beecher children, displayed that disposition to self-determining individualism which, as the world moved into the nineteenth century, seemed characteristic not alone of America, but of men and movements on both sides of the Atlantic.

The year 1815 marked the end of America's second war with Britain, a conflict Litchfield assessed less by ideology than by income. Had it not been for the alarmingly increased cost of living (every article "double or treble the former price, and some things even more"), Litchfieldians, preponderantly sound Federalists, would have thought no more of the conflict than of a contest between "Turks and Crim Tartars."[17] Lyman seems not to have understood the War of 1812—when it happened, or afterward.[18] Yet the war and its outcome affected Lyman and all Litchfield with him. In spite of their halting support of the war and their truculent unwillingness to furnish militia for the Canadian campaign, Beecher's fellow townsmen absorbed much of the national vanity and the spirit of self-sufficiency that were born of the struggle, and akin to a world sentiment more vigorous and more widespread than old regimes knew.

In the year in which the war terminated, two emperors, four kings, a few grand dukes, and many plain ones, gathered in ridiculously solemn assembly at the Vienna Congress to try to piece together the sundered world Napoleon's armies had hewn apart. Too dull to understand or too frightened to admit that the emperor was defeated by an upsurgence of patriotism—the same force that had catapulted him to victory—the diplomats in Vienna acted in total disregard of the principle of national self-determination, and in so doing built destruction for themselves. Overweening pride of country was abroad in the world, like a creature that had been released from Pandora's box and could not be contained again. Simon Bolivar, exiled in Haiti at the very season, was fiercely pledged to the principle of national independence. Stephen Decatur, blindly worshipful of fatherland, was wildly admired.

Such attitudes and events sprang from the soil that they enriched: there was growing optimism regarding what mortals could accomplish and with it a strong conviction about the rights man is due. As much a child of his times as were his peers, Lyman also evinced the humanistic bias that stamped them. For him, however, the insistence on man's rights and his confidence in man's ability were both related to the drama of redemption. Above all else Lyman was a sojourner toward eternity and never relaxed the struggle to redeem man's conceit by directing human efforts into worthy channels, and replacing pride of accomplishment with the wonder of being party to God's great scheme of salvation. Beecher was at once more and less optimistic than the worldlings. Confident that the generation had not yet understood that of which man is capable,[19] he also believed that the millennium of Christ's universal reign was just at hand.[20] The times augured a splendid, coming society in which redemption, no longer confined to "favored spots," would be "co-extensive with the ruin" infesting life.[21] Not all could grasp the bright destiny and the grave responsibility he preached. The issue was not whether victory would be realized, but whether America would have a part in it. Such orientation made critical for the patriot any decision regarding loyalties and definition of man's freedom. To answer the questions honestly meant, for Lyman, to understand the Christian's obligation to fuse America's future with the purpose of God. America could not be great without being good.

Within such a framework of reference Lyman preached reform. It made action mandatory, but it also maintained a proper perspective, holding that the world was good only in its place, and that "its place" was "the footstool, not the throne."[22] A tender area upon which Lyman focused his attention and to which he applied his theory was the respected and entrenched New England habit of dramming.

At the beginning of the nineteenth century, hard liquor was a staple in the American economy, "an established article of diet almost as much as bread" and with many "in much more frequent use."[23] Rich or poor, families offered it to every male visitor as "an essential point of hospitality, or even good manners."[24] Its uses above courtesy and pleasure were numerous and varied. "Females or valetudinarians courted an appetite with medicated rum, disguised underneath the chaste name of 'Hexam's Tinctures' or 'Southon's Elixir,' " and nurses soothed children with rum-laced remedies. Employers who denied workers a daily ration of spirits were "held niggardly." Generally "thought necessary," alcohol was not "considered indecorous" even at "the most formal or sacred" gathering.[25] By Lyman's day persistent abuse had made at least token reaction inevitable. Ministers who did not object to "taking a little bitters before breakfast, and after breakfast" now condemned the constant "dramming, dramming, dramming at all hours of the day."[26] In *The Drunkard's Looking Glass,* Parson Weems insisted that his picture of the derelict "Snug under the Table with the Dogs," and able to "stick to the floor without holding on"[27] was a faithful reflection of a familiar figure. Moreover, clergymen, however shocked, could not speak in the security of professional innocence. Censure scored their own fraternity.

When Beecher was installed at Litchfield, Grove Catlin, the innkeeper who entertained the participating clergy, discovered that whereas they consumed but one "bole of lemonade" he was due payment for seventeen bottles of wine, four bottles of "Branday," five bottles of spirits, one bottle of bitters, and a bowl of punch.[28] Such hospitality was not unusual and focused Beecher's concern upon a vice that hitherto he had largely ignored. Indeed, it was the immoderate clergy who first provoked Lyman to action. A larcenous grog-seller of East Hampton who cheated Indians out of their corn, Lyman had despised more for his mendacity than his merchandise.[29] Not until he came to Litchfield, though, did the enormity of intemperance overwhelm him.

Shortly after his arrival Beecher attended an ordination at Plymouth where, for the "creature comforts" of the clergy, there were set out "all the various kinds of liquors then in vogue." The visiting ministers on that occasion took something to drink on arriving, and before the service, and after the service. They crowded the sideboard so eagerly that they had to form a line, "obliged to stand and wait as people do when they go to a mill." With all the "spillings of water, and sugar, and liquor," Lyman thought the setting "looked and smelled" like a "grog-shop." No one was drunk, he insisted, but at times there was "a considerable amount of exhilaration."[30] When the sordid business was presently repeated at an ordination in Goshen, Lyman vowed never to attend another such, nor to remain silent longer.[31]

Seething over clerical intemperance, Beecher appeared at the 1812 General Association of Connecticut ministers and, pleased to discover a committee considering the very problem, was stunned when that body confessed that they did not "perceive that anything could be done" about the alarming increase of drunkenness.[32] Lyman Beecher "rose instanter," demanded and secured another committee, as chairman of which he produced a report that was, in his opinion, the "most important paper" he ever wrote. His recommendations were disarming in their practical simplicity: let clergy and lay folk abstain from the use of alcohol, and let both organize to fight it. "If our streets swarmed with venomous reptiles and beasts of prey," he asked, would there be no effort to "expell these deadly intruders"?[33] Timothy Dwight, himself a fervent man, feared lest Lyman's ardor "transcend the sanction of public sentiment."[34] Undaunted, Lyman persisted, and the movement went "marching" through Connecticut, and New England, and far beyond.[35]

Early in his Litchfield pastorate Beecher had "blocked out" a series of jeremiads against liquor and "laid them on the shelf" until Providence should bid him to preach them.[36] Unsettled by the knowledge that his parishioners were often involved in carousals and brawls (such as one "battle wherein salted codfish figured as weapons"[37]), Beecher was moved to take down the sermons and sound the tocsin when a particular favorite of his fell victim to alcoholism. The sermons, lurid in their details of degeneration and death, and terrifying in their simplicity, came always to the same solemn admonition: "Touch not, taste not, handle not." Long since opposed not only to ardent spirits, but even to wine and small beer, Lyman sided with that division of the movement styled "teetotalers," because in signing the pledge, they wrote the word "total," or—more frequently—a large "T," after their names to indicate that they renounced the use of alcohol in every form or in any degree.[38]

Inflexible in commitment, Lyman was, for the most part, objective in analyzing the complexities of the problem. But although he was perceptive at the point of acknowledging that civil coercion could never banish social evil,[39] Beecher naively assumed that men would turn to truth if it were pointed out to them. Litchfield was electrified with the graphic sermons. So, for that matter, was half the world beside. As *Six Sermons on the Nature, Occasions, Signs, Evils, and Remedy of Intemperance*,[40] they were translated into many languages, including Hottentot and Greek. Lyman's victory, however, was less than complete, even with his own children. Catherine, the authoress of temperance hymns for Christian youth ("Ne'er shall the guilty bowl, O'er us its poison roll"[41]), endorsed spirits as pudding flavoring, or for medicinal use;[42] and Harriet Stowe, working feverishly to complete a manuscript before an approaching deadline should overtake her, wrote to her publisher requesting him to send her "half a dozen bottles of Catawba to support the hot weather and the long pull."[43] With reform, as with revivalism, zeal burned brighter in Beecher than in his converts. The cause lay deeper than fickleness of human nature.

A generation after Lyman had departed Connecticut, members of the first Congregational Society of Litchfield concluded to replace the meeting house in which Dr. Beecher had preached with a "neat and tasteful edifice" that would be "in more modern style."[44] The raising lasted for a whole week, and on the last day the timbers of the great spire were reared in testimony against the sky. The company of townspeople who thronged the green thanked God for yet another witness to the faith. The end of the matter, as it happened, had proved happier than the beginning. From time remembered such feats had been accomplished in New England by volunteers who always had expected and received free whiskey for their pains. Sensible of the mockery of paying men thus when the work of their hands should stand, at least in part, as memorial to Lyman's labor among them, the Society determined to break with time-honored custom. In place of ardent spirits there was supplied a hogshead of small beer that had been brewed in the cellar of Galpin and Goodwind's, a store convenient to the location. The few men who bothered to come to the green looked upon this insipid innovation with apathy. There were not enough of them to lift the ground beams into place. When it was apparent that the grumblers would not work for beer, Dr. William Buel sent some of the boys who stood by to fetch a "certain box" from his office. The lads found it quite heavy. When the doctor opened the case, the men saw that it was filled with square bottles of rum and whiskey. After that there were hands aplenty for the work. The day they raised the spire three Shaker tubs of rum punch were set out at the edge of East Park, along with a supply of tin cups so that men and boys could drink freely.[45]

The whole affair was a parable of Beecher and his times, but the truth of it was not yet writ large enough upon history's walls for a running man to read.

Notes to Chapter V

1. *Autobiography*, I, 281.

2. Joseph Lewis, *Ingersoll the Magnificent, to which has been Added a Special Arrangement of Some Gems from Ingersoll for Inspiration, Wisdom and Courage* (New York, 1957), pp. 465-466.

3. *Autobiography*, II, 568.

4. *Ibid.*

5. *Ibid.*, I, 81-86.

6. Lyman Beecher Stowe, *Saints, Sinners, and Beechers*, pp. 45-46.

7. *Autobiography*, I, 221.

8. *Ibid.*, p. 412.

9. E. E. Eells, *Sermon on Beecher*, p. 23.

10. [John Lyon Gardiner], handwritten note on the back of a MS copy of a sermon by Lyman Beecher of December 30, 1805, from the Beecher Collection, East Hampton Free Public Library: "Much of the respect & love which Dr. Beecher's people entertained for him arose in their infancy. His . . . behaviour to children gained their affections which he never lost, and much of the good he did was owing to this as a secondary cause. To children & young people he was particularly attractive, while by his own example he showed the respect due to the aged. . . ."

11. *Autobiography*, II, 119.

12. *Ibid.*, I, 525.

13. *Ibid.*, II, 118.

14. *Ibid.*, I, 219. Catherine Cebra Webb, "Diary," in Emily Noyes Vanderpoel, *Chronicles*, pp. 147-148: "I went to board in the family of Dr. Lyman Beecher . . . Miss Catherine Beecher and a Miss Burr, presided over the family." [Roxana was in her terminal illness at this time.]

15. *Ibid.*, pp. 148-150: "I had a room with two Misses Wakeman, who were also pupils at Miss Pierce's school. . . . There was a large sink in the kitchen, and a couple of basins, and we had to go there to wash—It was the only place—so of course we could not take much of a bath—which was a great trial to me."

16. *Autobiography*, I, 527.

17. *Ibid.*, p. 284.

18. *Ibid.*, pp. 265-267.

19. Lyman Beecher, *Instructions for Young Christians* (Cincinnati, 1834), p. 53: "If Christians would act for God with more decision, they would not need a microscope to make their graces visible."

20. Leonard Bacon, *Sermon at the Funeral*, p. 15.

21. Lyman Beecher, *A Sermon Addressed to the Legislature of Connecticut, at New-Haven, on the Day of the Anniversary Election, May 3rd, 1826* (New Haven, 1826), p. 6.

22. Lyman Beecher, *A Sermon, Occasioned by the Lamented Death*

of Mrs. Frances M. Sands, of New-Shoreham (Sag Harbor, 1806), p. 4.
23. Daniel Dorchester, *The Liquor Problem in All Ages* (New York and Cincinnati, 1884), p. 139. "Rum seasoned with cherries, protected against the cold; rum, made astringent with peach-nuts, concluded the repast at the confectioners; rum, made nutritious with milk, prepared for the maternal office; and, under the Greek name of *Paregoric,* rum, doubly poisoned with opium, quieted the infant's cries." *Ibid.*
24. Samuel Griswold Goodrich, *Recollections,* p. 69.
25. Daniel Dorchester, *Liquor Problem,* p. 139.
26. Samuel Griswold Goodrich, *Recollections,* p. 69.
27. Mason L. Weems, Three Discourses: 1. *Hymen's Recruiting Sergeant,* 2. *The Drunkard's Looking Glass,* 3. *God's Revenge Against Adultery* (New York, 1929). The original piece by Weems appeared in 1812. The thrust of the consideration is clearly indicated by the subtitle: *The Drunkard's Looking Glass, Reflecting a Faithful Likeness of the Drunkard in Sundry very Interesting Attitudes: With Lively Representations of the Many Strange Capers which he Cuts at Different Stages of his Disease.* At first, "When he has 'a Drop in his Eye': second, When he is 'Half Stewed'; third, When he is getting 'a Little on the Staggers or so'; And fourth and fifth, and so on, Till he is 'Quite Capsized,' or 'Snug under the Table with the Dogs,' and can Stick to the Floor without holding on."
28. Bill of Grove Catlin, tavern keeper, rendered to the First Ecclesiastical Society for entertainment of visiting clergy at the time of Lyman Beecher's installation in Litchfield, in the collection of the Litchfield Historical Society.
29. *Autobiography,* I, 177.
30. *Ibid.,* p. 245.
31. *Ibid.,* p. 246.
32. *Ibid.,* p. 247.
33. *Ibid.,* pp. 247-250.
34. *Ibid.,* p. 251.
35. *Ibid.,* p. 252.
36. Joseph E. Tuttle, "The Late Lyman Beecher, D.D.," *American Presbyterian and Theological Review* (April, 1863).
37. Esther Harriet Thompson, "Life in Old Litchfield." See also *Autobiography,* II, 22.
38. August F. Fehlandt, *A Century of Drink Reform in the United States* (New York, 1904), pp. 80-81.
39. Lyman Beecher Stowe, *Saints, Sinners, and Beechers,* p. 60, recounts Beecher's inability to work with Garrison on the matter of abolition because the journalist rejected the clergyman's realistic approach to the problem.
40. Eighth ed. (New York, 1829).
41. Catherine E. Beecher, "Song for the Youth's Temperance Soci-

ety of Cincinnati," *Western Monthly Magazine*, XXVII (March, 1835), 182.

42. Catherine E. Beecher, *Miss Beecher's Domestic Receipt-Book, Designed as a Supplement to her Treatise on Domestic Economy*, 3rd ed. (New York, 1856), p. 183.

43. ALS, Harriet Beecher Stowe, Andover, July 13, 1856, to Phillips and Sampson, Stowe Correspondence, Boston Public Library.

44. George C. Woodruff, *History of Litchfield*, p. 55.

45. Esther Harriet Thompson, "Life in Old Litchfield."

Chapter VI

In Extremis:
Confidence in the Face of Despair - 1810-1826

The experience of freedom abroad in young America stimulated thinking men to reexamine their theology. Older generations of Puritans had been tranquil, if not content, in acceptance of descriptive statements of God's relation to the world. Nineteenth-century churchmen sought to explain and, inevitably, to justify the creation as the work of an omnipotent, benevolent deity. Of numerous and varied theological reformulations, many focused on man's freedom. Typical and to a great extent normative of incipient Protestant liberalism was inquiry subsumed under the designation of the Moral Government of God. It was a compromise position, affirming God less as absolute sovereign (in which case he was logically responsible, and how could a good God be?) than as moral governor (who is ethical despite his problems and in no way compromises his character by his rule). In this perspective, free man as God's creation has power to choose—even to choose evil—, else true morality is foreign to the human condition. The defensible conclusion is that, granting the freedom of man, perhaps God could not prevent sin. For man, God had not decreed evil; he had only chosen good. The new theology was more compatible to free men. The practical situation was much as it had been.

Alexander Metcalfe Fisher (Yale University Art Gallery)

Although Harriet Foote was devoted to her brother-in-law, Lyman Beecher, she was so intransigent an Anglican that on visits to Litchfield she would walk straight past his *meeting house,* without so much as turning her head, to present herself at the true *Church,* where prayers were said and Scripture divided as, in her opinion, God intended that they should be. She was also tender of conscience. Therefore, when her niece and namesake lived briefly with her at Nutplains,[1] Aunt Foote, who instructed Harriet Beecher in the true faith as a matter of course, also made a valiant, though unsuccessful, effort, for Lyman's sake, to teach his daughter that marvel of words and wisdom produced by the Westminster Assembly and called—to the despair of many a postulant—the *Shorter Catechism.*

The young visitor was delighted with the Episcopal exercise that began, quite sensibly she felt, by asking a splendid question no one could miss: "What is your name, Child?" On the other hand, the Westminster catechism, which Congregationalists and Presbyterians employed in their search for understanding, plunged directly to the heart of an unsettling problem. "What is the chief end of man?" it inquired, and immediately answered in advice that was easy to memorize but vastly difficult to appropriate: "Man's chief end is to glorify God and to enjoy him forever."[2]

As Beecher all his life asserted this to be the solemn duty and high destiny of man, Harriet Foote, knowingly or not, pressed rightly in teaching the catechism as a kind of first lesson from Lyman. Its opening sentences reduce man's existence to distilled meaning: God is both Beginning and Goal.[3] This was the starting point of Lyman's creed—a fixed star in the light of which he viewed all that happened to him, or for that matter to anyone else. Nor did Lyman blanch at the implication Puritans drew from this premise-position: that any given event or circumstance was, therefore, potentially transparent to the everlasting mercy. If such doctrine de-

manded joyful affirmation of a universe that was sometimes
hard to the point of senseless cruelty, it afforded, too, an
impregnable fortress of comfort. The Calvinistic core of
Beecher's adamantine faith is particularly plain in two episodes at Litchfield. Both concern death; and as death—if
anything—brings men to honesty and essence, it is illuminating to look closely at Lyman standing in the aweful presence.
The first occasion was the death of Roxana.

Lyman had loved Roxana since he first saw her, at a
Fourth of July celebration in his Yale days, when Ben Baldwin had squired him to Old Guilford and introduced him to
the Footes.[4] She was engaged, and Lyman knew it; but an
immediate rapport between them dictated the action by
which, as Mary Chittenden later told Lyman, Roxana "freed
herself from that man." Beecher went directly to see her,
and, bold for the time, almost at once put his arm around her
and kissed her. "She did not object," then, nor on the next
morning, when he "moved up and moved up" as they sat
together on the sofa.[5]

Experience confirmed Lyman's swift intuition; and time
made it strong. To him, Roxana's love was unique, her death
a near-insupportable stroke. Its meaning for Lyman cannot
be measured by the cultic attitudes of her children. Catherine
wrote a doleful poem that the little Beechers memorized and
used to repeat in concert.[6] Henry Ward, only three when his
mother died, ascribed to Roxana that significance in his own
life which he believed the Virgin Mary held for "a devout
Catholic."[7] Lyman's tributes, usually restrained, and often
inadequate, afford a more reliable index to her superiority, as
well as to his devotion. "Oh, she was lovely truly."[8]

Roxana's watchful protection over her husband was self-
less and wise. If the strains of his violin disturbed the French
verb drill in her East Hampton schoolroom, she simply interrupted her teaching long enough to take the instrument away
from him with no other reproof than a twinkle in her eye.[9]
While he enjoyed sanctuary in Connecticut, arranging for
removal from Long Island, she fended off prying parishioners.[10] After the family arrived at Litchfield and discovered
the brutal cold of the Bantam hills, where ice storms came

sometimes in April,[11] it was Roxana who defeated the winter by building with her own hands a Russian stove, having but a picture for a guide, and only a workman to assist.[12] As Lyman went flamboyantly along his way, Roxana faithfully guarded his health and gladly bore his children, maintaining poise in a situation she neither misunderstood nor resented. In a witty note to Aunt Esther, Roxana insists that she would write more, were it not for her "circumstances, such as the weather extremely cold, storm violent, and no wood cut; Mr. Beecher gone; and Sabbath day, with company—a clergyman, a stranger; Catherine sick; George almost so; Rachel's finger cut off, and she crying and groaning with the pain."[13]

As there is no substitute for such an educated heart, there is no readiness to lose it. Beecher was not prepared for Roxana's death, but he was, however, prepared to have her die—an altogether different matter. He did not know how to live without her, nor did he wish to do so; but he stood ready to accept any dispensation from the hand of God, never doubting the ultimate charity of the darkest providence. The full majesty of his towering faith emerges in context of his loss of Roxana, whose excellence, after all, Lyman doubtless measured more accurately and missed more keenly than any other.

Roxana was known to be ill but six weeks. In mid-June she had described herself as "in good health."[14] She died of a quick consumption before the end of September.[15] There had followed days of "great emptiness" for Lyman.[16] "I am *alone; Roxana is not here.* . . . I do not murmur; I only feel daily, constantly, and with deepening impression, *how much I have had* for which to be thankful, and how much I have lost."[17] The redoubtable Col. Benjamin Tallmadge (a man who recognized character, even in a British spy) was quick to note and, with his customary candor, careful to record that Mr. Beecher seemed "to be wonderfully supported and comforted by the consideration that the Lord [had] done it." [18]

Beecher's belief that the universe was controlled by a single intelligent will (as opposed to the varied and capricious energies of chance) was more than a matter of simple arithmetic. If there were but one God, and he good, then all that happened must be subsumed under his benevolent character. That the goodness did not immediately appear was no proof of perversity in heaven, only a commentary upon man's inability to perceive. Roxana's death did not shatter Lyman's faith. As he would have put it, as indeed he did put it, God "governs the world in a manner above our comprehension," but "his administration is no less an object of confidence and joy, than if we knew the particular design of each event."[19]

In evidence of his faith, though not to prove it, Lyman married within the year. His large family and popular parsonage obviously wanted female oversight; and New England was quite accustomed to have her clergy marry as early as convenient, and as often as necessary. But by this action Lyman, in addition to admitting practical problems, gave fair report of his trust that God could turn misfortune to good account. When he left Litchfield at summer's end, the girls of Miss Pierce's academy said, somewhat spitefully, that Dr. Beecher had gone to Boston to "buy him a wife."[20] The fact was, rather, that like another mighty man before the Lord, when he realized that death was accomplished beyond recall, Lyman quit his fast, put away his sorrow, and turned again to face the insolent daylight with renewed faith in God.

It is true, though, that no bride was ever more ardently wooed nor more romantically wed than Harriet Porter, his second wife. Before he had known her for a fortnight, Lyman was assuring the auburn-haired belle of Portland that he stood in spirit watching nightly by her bed.[21] Distracted for her, and impatient of time, in the brief interlude between their meeting and their marriage, he "wandered from room to room,"[22] reading and rereading her "most precious letters."[23] His messages arrived by almost every post, and he begged her, when she answered, to have a care lest the sealing wax blot out her "beloved name."[24] Little wonder that he looked forward to the years with her as to the "most useful part" of his career,[25] and doubted not that she came to him "heaven-directed."[26] Thus did Lyman know a better resolution to his season of grief than that allowed to his daughter.

Catherine Beecher, who had her father's capacity for happiness, and was no whit less resilient than he, could not in his fashion capitulate to the stunning blow dealt her in the death of her fiancé, Alexander Fisher; but as she was a Beecher, she acted with an honest courage, becoming to her heritage. The young man's death was the second to throw Lyman's faith in stark perspective.

Alexander Metcalfe Fisher was a mathematician who deserved to be called a genius. Brilliant as a shooting star, and as quickly extinguished, he was only ten years of age when he fashioned for himself *A Practical Arithmetic,* because he judged the one supplied him to be inferior.[27] He was graduated from Yale at eighteen, the first scholar of his class, and soon began a teaching career at his alma mater that brought him to full professorship in his twenty-fourth year.[28] Erudite and elegant, he had, between times, written a Hebrew grammar,[29] studied the theology of his pastor, Nathanael Emmons[30] (that staunch Calvinist who thought one of the delights of heaven would be seeing "who is there"[31]), and produced, in addition to discriminating scientific items, a fictional *Journey to the Moon and Some of the Planets.*[32] His reputation as a musician rested upon solid accomplishment. And, marvelous to tell, with his achievements, this paragon also offered a most pleasing appearance.[33]

Catherine was a plain woman, angular and square-jawed, undistinguished by any physical feature except the fineness of her hair.[34] Much too wise to marry for looks, or for the "fascination of genius & the flattery of attentions,"[35] she was still human and could not have been displeased with the patrician Mr. Fisher, or his attentions to her. Samuel F. B. Morse's portrait of him shows an intense man with wide-set, intelligent eyes, the features aristocratic, almost delicate. The engagement of these oddly paired lovers, who were first attracted to each other by a common interest in writing poetry, delighted Lyman. Early in 1822 Fisher took passage on the *Albion,* bound for Europe to visit universities, interview philosophers, and purchase equipment for his physics laboratory at Yale. The wedding had been set for the following spring, at which· time he intended to return to New

England. On the twenty-second of April, a storm drove his ship onto the rocks of the southern Irish coast, and Fisher, with all the other cabin passengers, save one, was lost.[36]

Lyman was powerless to comfort his daughter. The years had prepared him, he said, to meet such sorrow with minimum "surprise and severity of disappointment,"[37] but, as it developed, Catherine's woe was neither shock nor frustration. She confronted the divine demand to submit in such form as to call into question not only God's possible caprice, but his injustice as well. Catherine was undone that so dear a life had been snatched away. That, however, she could have borne. The darker agony lay in the possibility (quite real for Catherine) that her lover's immortal soul fared worse than his physical body. Mr. Fisher, as friends and family knew, had sought conversion diligently, even desperately, to no avail. The survivor of the *Albion* had reported the last and dreadful moments of Fisher's life when, already wounded in a fall suffered on the lurching ship, he had stood, silent and bleeding, "his head down, & his countenance exhibiting deep & anxious meditation."[38] There was the off-chance that the miracle of grace had happened then; but Catherine and Lyman both knew this to be unlikely. According to the teaching of orthodoxy, therefore, he was most probably in hell. Beside himself because of his daughter's anxiety and hurt, Lyman was, nevertheless, clear in his statement of an awesome faith. She might, he granted, justifiably "indulge" in hope; but she could expect release only in submission to God.[39] Lyman refused to equivocate: "I cannot allow my heart to distrust or turn against my God," he wrote to his daughter. "I know that . . . what he does is right; and here I rest my faith and desire you to rest yours."[40] The distraught girl found no comfort in such counsel. "Oh Edward," she cried to her brother, "where is he now?"[41] No one could answer. Catherine's quest for certainty lasted for the rest of her life, and she hammered her creed into its sparse and final shape on the anvil of loneliness.

Characteristically, Catherine and Lyman admitted the public to their prolix and extended exchanges over theology. Lyman published his letters to his daughter.[42] For her part,

Catherine in succeeding years wrote often of the whole affair, always without embarrassment.[43] Meanwhile father and daughter, in commendably similar fashion, spent themselves so tirelessly in good works and worthy causes as to become a judgment upon the living and a death-threat to the shift-less.[44]

In *Common Sense Applied to Religion; or The Bible and the People,* written a full quarter of a century after Alexander Fisher's death, Catherine spoke her word to the universe and offered to orthodoxy her surrogate solution for its riddle. "There must be a dreadful mistake somewhere," she declared, "but I will trust and obey and wait quietly for light."[45] Yet Lyman's unshakable confidence that any mistake, if it existed, was surely man's shines even in the titles of his sermons.[46] He remained fundamentally without doubt, even in the face of his own death. When, as an old man, he was no longer sought after, and far gone in senescence, the stalwart warrior announced that had he the chance to fight the same battles of the past once more, he "would enlist again in a minute."[47]

Roxana's death occasioned a clear statement of his submission to the divine will. His failure to bring Catherine to a similar renunciation underscored the priority of God's sovereignty in his own life. It became as well a shaping influence in his compassion for the human plight, a force of such empathy in Lyman that, although he never turned his back upon the God of Calvin, he found himself tried for heresy[48] because of the way in which he explained the system to his fellow men who were attempting adjustment to the laws of Calvin's universe.

Understandably, Catherine was pathetic in her concern for Fisher's fate. By the standards of the time, however, her theological preoccupation and focus did not appear unbalanced. Forty years later the *Atlantic Monthly* (reviewing Lyman's *Autobiography*) judged it fruitless to inquire "whether a baby threw his bread and butter to the floor" because of taint from the old Adam or through a "surfeit of plumcake";[49] but in the early nineteenth century, America busied herself, as leisure and education would allow, with many such cobweb distinctions. Clergymen thought nothing of a long journey in a rickety, one-horse chaise for the sake of settling some nice point of celestial jurisprudence, or comparing their maps of the Infinite. And what they concluded in tedious dialectic they preached to parishioners who, lacking other or any entertainment, discussed the issues in the intervals of the plough and spinning wheel during the week that followed. Submission to the divine will was not for them an abstract matter; it was vital to their lives and related to their experience. "They had accustomed themselves boldly to challenge and dispute all sham pretensions and idolatries of past ages,—to question the right of kings in the State, and of prelates in the Church; and now they turned the same bold inquiries towards the Eternal Throne, and threw down their glove in the lists as authorized defenders of every mystery in the Eternal Government. The task . . . was that of reconciling . . . evil . . . with . . . Infinite Power and Benevolence."[50]

Samuel Hopkins, the renowned minister who often, for the hardness of his doctrine, preached to empty pews in Newport, but who enjoyed the respect even of the slave traders whom he denounced,[51] had defined the problem in the stark terms of willingness to be damned for the glory of God.[52] Common folk normally encountered this "impossible supposition"[53] in its existential form—the inability to experience conversion. If only God could initiate regeneration ("plainly taught" in the Bible, said Lyman[54]), was it possible to call God good, when this boon was denied many who sought it earnestly? Was it God's glory that lost souls demonstrated? Or—say it softly—something else? Such speculations pointed to sublime and dizzying heights that only the strongest, palm-crowned spirits attained.

Practically turned of mind, Lyman seldom found necessity to ask the Hopkins question, and had little enough patience with people who did. Once during a revival he overheard a young student from Andover put the fatal test to a potential convert. "Well, sir, would *you* be willing?" Lyman interrupted. "Yes, sir," the seminarian replied, "I humbly hope I should." "Then, sir, you *ought* to be," said the veteran, though he did take occasion afterward to "enlighten" the

boy to a "better theology."[55] This was but Lyman's way of
labeling the question as wrong-headed. As in his life he
continued to demonstrate, so in his formal statements he
insisted upon that unfaltering trust which, never making bid for
immolation, does not question or reject it when it comes.
"But is it my duty to be willing to be damned?" he asks, and
parries the thrust by admonition to love God so completely
as to be willing for him to dispose of all matters "just as he
pleases." Such a state is for Lyman by no means "synonymous with damnation. It is as different as heaven is from
hell."[56]

Despite inhibitions that, like walls of glass, too often
separate members of a family, there is still an instinctive
searching for essence among them that renders their comment about kindred significant, quite apart from any envy or
love it may express. Harriet Beecher Stowe peopled her
novels with her relatives, transforming their actions and attitudes into the matter of fiction. Less than sufficient, but
more than oblique, is the light thus thrown upon her sister
and father in relation to a sovereign's demand for submission
to the inscrutable. In Mrs. Stowe's writing Catherine appears
neither as the pontifical directress of education, nor yet as
the faintly ridiculous old lady, still dressing her hair in the
corkscrew curls of her youth.[57] Rather, as Mrs. Marvyn, she
is the intelligent and sensitive, faithful but unconverted member of Samuel Hopkins' flock, who, in sorrow over tidings
that her exemplary, though unregenerate, son has been
drowned, quotes Catherine's philosophy almost verbatim. "I
am quite sure there must be dreadful mistakes somewhere,"
says Mrs. Marvyn.[58] Portraits of Lyman are liberally scattered through the pages of Harriet's novels, and they introduce a new perspective. He is never more appealing, nor more
accurately drawn, than as Mr. Avery, the minister in *Oldtown
Folks.* Parson Avery's forte is logic, grim logic. Harriet pronounced "incredible, the ease and cheerfulness with which a
man in his study, who never had so much experience with
suffering as even a toothache would give him," could "arrange
a system in which the everlasting torture of millions is casually admitted as an item." But her picture is trustworthy, for

she is careful to add that, although Avery was "thoroughly and enthusiastically in earnest" about Calvinism "as far as Edwards and Hopkins" got it right, he was "busy in making some little emendations and corrections."

> [It] is to the credit of his heart [she writes] that these emendations are generally in favor of some original-minded sheep who can't be got into the sheep-fold without some alteration in the paling. In these cases I have generally noticed that he will loosen a rail or tear off a picket, and let the sheep in, it being his impression, after all, that the sheep are worth more than the sheep-fold.[59]

In the Unitarian storm that broke over Boston, both flock and fold were threatened. It was Lyman's joy and privilege to show his faith by courage and strength in that dark hour.

Notes to Chapter VI

1. Various of the Beecher children lived for a season in their early years with Roxana's family at Nutplains, near to Guilford. See Annie Fields, *Life and Letters of Harriet Beecher Stowe* (Boston and New York, 1897), pp. 15-22, for the account of Harriet's extended visit directly after Roxana's death.

2. *Autobiography*, I, 313.

3. James Benjamin Green, *A Harmony of the Westminster Presbyterian Standards with Explanatory Notes* (Richmond, 1951), p. 21.

4. *Autobiography*, I, 61.

5. MS written by Lucy Jackson White (daughter of Lyman Beecher's third wife), January 29, 1860, recording Lyman's reminiscences of his courtship, Beecher Collection, Stowe-Day Foundation.

6. *Autobiography*, I, 308-309.

7. Lyman Beecher Stowe, *Saints, Sinners, and Beechers*, p. 216.

8. MS of Lucy Jackson White, January 29, 1860, *supra*.

9. *Autobiography*, I, 146.

10. *Ibid.*, p. 182: "Deacon Tallmadge called . . . to inquire whether you did not repent of what you had done. I told him it was not . . . resolved on hastily. . . . He said that some people hoped . . . you would yet come back. I asked if people expected you would . . . if they did not comply with your proposals."

11. ALS, Lyman Beecher, Litchfield, April 3, 1818, to George A. Foote, Beecher Collection, Yale University. Henry Ward said of his father, "I have seen the time when we had to cut a twenty-five foot tunnel outward from the kitchen-door, carrying the snow through the

house; and such tunnels would sometimes remain a month before they would break down," in William C. Beecher and Samuel Scoville, *Henry Ward Beecher*, p. 68.

12. Catherine E. Beecher, *Educational Reminiscences*, p. 12. She also discovered a mistake in the presentation of a problem of perspective in an encyclopaedia and, of course, corrected the same. See also Esther Harriet Thompson, "Life in Old Litchfield."

13. *Autobiography*, I, 232.

14. *Ibid.*, p. 290.

15. Charles Edward Stowe, *Life of Harriet Beecher Stowe*, begins his work with a careful consideration of Roxana's death. The details are recounted in *Autobiography*, I, 215-221.

16. *Autobiography*, I, 300.

17. *Ibid.*, p. 334.

18. ALS, Benjamin Tallmadge, Litchfield, September 26, 1816, to John P. Cushman, Tallmadge Papers, Litchfield Historical Society.

19. Lyman Beecher, *A Sermon Delivered at the Funeral of Henry Obookiah, A Native of Owhyhee, and a Member of the Foreign Mission School in Cornwall, Connecticut, February 18, 1818* (New Haven, 1819), p. 3.

20. Emily Noyes Vanderpoel, *Chronicles*, p. 171.

21. ALS, Lyman Beecher, Durham, Connecticut, September 9, 1817, to Harriet Porter, Beecher Collection, Stowe-Day Foundation.

22. ALS, Lyman Beecher, Litchfield, September 18, 1817, to Harriet Porter, Beecher Collection, Stowe-Day Foundation.

23. ALS, Lyman Beecher, Litchfield, September 25, 1817, to Harriet Porter, Beecher Collection, Stowe-Day Foundation.

24. ALS, Lyman Beecher, Litchfield, September 16, 1817, to Harriet Porter, Beecher Collection, Stowe-Day Foundation.

25. ALS, Lyman Beecher, Litchfield, September 27, 1817, to Harriet Porter, Beecher Collection, Stowe-Day Foundation.

26. ALS, Lyman Beecher, Litchfield, December 22, 1817, to Nathaniel Coffin, Beecher Collection, Stowe-Day Foundation.

27. Lyman Beecher Stowe, *Saints, Sinners, and Beechers*, p. 79.

28. Franklin Bowditch Dexter, *Biographical Sketches*, V, 568.

29. Lyman Beecher Stowe, *Saints, Sinners, and Beechers*, p. 80.

30. Emmons, personally gentle, theologically grim, was pastor of Franklin, Massachusetts, Fisher's home town. Of the import of exposure to Nathanael Emmons another Franklin native, Horace Mann, observed: "I feel constantly, and more and more deeply what an unspeakable calamity a Calvinistic education is. What a dreadful thing it was for me!" George Allen Hubbell, *Horace Mann: Educator, Patriot, and Reformer, a Study in Leadership* (Philadelphia, 1910), p. 7.

31. *Works of Nathanael Emmons*, I, 122.

32. The MS is in the Fisher Collection of Yale University Library. The first pages are missing. More interesting as a curiosity than for intrinsic merit, the work, nevertheless, pictures a quasi-utopian situa-

tion in which all dress in the same fashion and speak a universal language.

33. Samuel F. B. Morse's portrait of Fisher hangs in Memorial Hall at Yale University.

34. Mae Elizabeth Harveson, *Catherine Esther Beecher, Pioneer Educator* (Philadelphia, 1932), p. 232, observes (as all portraits of Catherine illustrate) that she persisted to her days' end in dressing her hair in the manner she fancied showed it off to best advantage.

35. ALS, Catherine Beecher, Litchfield, [1821], to Louise Wait, Beecher-Stowe Collection, Schlesinger Library, Radcliffe College.

36. Franklin Bowditch Dexter, *Biographical Sketches*, V, 568.

37. *Autobiography*, I, 478.

38. ALS, Edward Beecher, Litchfield, October 29, 1822, to Catherine. Soon after Fisher's death Catherine had gone to Franklin, Massachusetts, for an extended visit with Fisher's parents, and there, according to her sister, she remained for "two years . . . taught his two sisters, studied mathematics with his brother, Willard, and listened to Dr. Emmons' fearless and pitiless preaching." Charles Edward Stowe, *Life of Harriet Beecher Stowe*, p. 25.

39. *Autobiography*, I, 478-479.

40. *Ibid.*, pp. 494, 516.

41. *Ibid.*, p. 479.

42. *Ibid.*, p. 478.

43. Mae Elizabeth Harveson, *Catherine Esther Beecher*, p. 236, tells of Catherine, past seventy, finally destroying the relics of the professor.

44. Catherine worked, literally, to within two days of the day of her death.

45. (New York, 1857), p. xxiv.

46. "The Government of God Desirable—A Sermon delivered at Newark, N.J., October, 1808, during the session of the Synod of New York and New Jersey," in Lyman Beecher, *Sermons Delivered on Various Occasions*.

47. *Autobiography*, II, 552.

48. The main focus of Beecher's heresy trial was upon the character and ability of natural man.

49. Unsigned review, vol. XV (May, 1865), xxxv.

50. Harriet Beecher Stowe, *The Minister's Wooing*, p. 333.

51. Samuel Hopkins, *Sketches of the Life of the Late Samuel Hopkins, D.D., written by himself; interspersed with marginal notes extracted from his private diary* (Hartford, 1805), p. 100.

52. Samuel Hopkins, *The Works of Samuel Hopkins*, 3 vols. (Boston, 1852), III, 59.

53. Samuel Hopkins, *A Dialogue between a Calvinist and a Semi-Calvinist*, bound with Hopkins, *Sketches of the Life. . . , supra*, p. 143.

54. Lyman Beecher, *Views in Theology* (Cincinnati and New York, 1836), p. 200. Beecher's *Views of Theology* (Boston and Cleveland, 1853) is volume III of his *Works*.

55. David Bartlett, *Modern Agitators*, p. 199.

56. "The Government of God Desirable," pp. 26-27.

57. A pupil who remembered Catherine's unsuccessful attempt to return in her old age to Hartford Female Seminary, which she had founded, described her: "Miss Beecher, standing alone on the platform, in her self-made black lace dress over pink paper cambric and her self-made shoes with soft soles and velvet uppers, and with her corkscrew curls bobbing up and down, would sing . . . in a faint quavering wreck of a voice." Quoted by Lyman Beecher Stowe in *Saints, Sinners, and Beechers*, pp. 134-135.

58. Harriet Beecher Stowe, *The Minister's Wooing*, p. 355.

59. Harriet Beecher Stowe, *Oldtown Folks*, pp. 223-226.

Chapter VII
Threatened Orthodoxy:
The Rise of Unitarianism — 1826-1832

American Unitarianism, primarily a phenomenon of New England, grew equally from the sentiment of laymen no longer able to accept the harsher doctrines of Calvinism and the effort of ministers concerned to reinterpret orthodoxy for their own day. Prime emphasis was on the nature and destiny of man. The liberal Christians (as they at first styled themselves) did not withdraw from the church and, accordingly, became objects first of suspicion and then of attack. The liberals opposed revivals. They defined religion in rational and practical terms. Open and general strife was precipitated in 1805 by the election of the liberal Henry Ware to the Hollis chair of divinity at Harvard. Subsequently traditionalists founded their own seminary (Andover) and their own publication (the Panoplist). The manifesto of the Unitarians was a sermon of William E. Channing, delivered in Baltimore in 1819 at the ordination of Jared Sparks, in which the preacher appealed to reason and renounced traditional views of the Trinity and the person of Christ. Channing founded the possibility of man's salvation in his response to the indwelling Spirit of God, the acknowledgment of the right he knows, and the achievement of the good of which he is able.

Nathaniel William Taylor (Yale University Art Gallery)

Toward the close of the year 1825, Lyman grew restive to depart Connecticut. His work sagged;[1] his debts soared; and he himself was settled into such a state of melancholy and malaise as he had rarely known.[2] The keenness of his disenchantment is somewhat obscured by the scribes who recorded it. When the Beecher children came to construct a semblance of autobiography from the letters and sermons their father had saved and sorted for fifty years, they were grown affluent and famous, and could easily afford the luxury of focusing only upon the charm of Litchfield, and of romanticizing the meager dimension of their life on North Street. This characteristic appears in their remembrance of how their father's salary was partly paid.

A minister in those days was as a rule engaged for a specified stipend and his firewood. The adult Beechers recalled this patronizing arrangement in terms of that wonderfully unique institution of New England, the minister's woodspell. On a fine winter's day (chosen by canny Yankee prescience of a time when the snow would be right and the sledding at its best) parishioners converged upon the manse from all directions, bringing each a load of firewood, which was at once a gift for the glebe and an indication of a good Christian's stout axe arm.[3] At the parson's board that day there would be doughnuts and sharp cheese, and hearty slices of rich loaf cake, refreshments prescribed by rigid protocol.[4] Until the temperance excitement made both host and guest uncomfortable with the courtesy, the visitor also had a mug of steaming flip, a great favorite in the Litchfield hills, which was made by lacing spicy, homebrewed beer with rum, and stirring it with a red-hot flip iron until the draft became bubbly and aromatic.[5] There were singing, and laughter, and innocent rivalry over the comparative excellence of the great stacks of oak and shag-bark hickory. Lyman was at his best on such occasions, "adroit in detecting and admiring the special merits of every load as it arrived."[6] The gala atmosphere, though, did not cancel the genteel peonage the wood-spell preserved. Lyman was not deceived.

His reminiscing children delighted even in the nuisances of Litchfield. Noisy, ubiquitous rats had "romped all night" through the parsonage, and "gnawing and sawing" as if "they had set up a carpenter's shop,"[7] made sleep all but impossible and neurosis all but certain. Yet when they were delivered of the noxious vermin, the Beechers invested them with inoffensive, even winning, personality.[8] Or there was Dinah Atwell, a poor, demented creature, who was self-appointed tithing-mistress of the Litchfield meeting house and all the solemn assemblies gathered there. She used to frighten young children half out of their wits when she interrupted the constant combing of her bushy gray hair to swoop down from her lofty perch upon any prodigal who dared thwart her zeal to keep the dogs out and the boys in.[9] On reflection, Beecher sons and daughters found her terror amusing, her eccentricity quaint.[10] At the actual time of removal to Boston, Lyman's fourth child, Mary, who had married Tom Perkins, wrote from Hartford that she was sad to think of the family leaving the orchard and the mowing lot; she said that she cherished Litchfield and was certain she should never love another place so much.[11]

Lyman's regret was not so naive, nor his love so unalloyed. Finance is admittedly the fulcrum upon which his "Request for Dismission" turns,[12] but he was moved by neither greed nor ambition. The fact is, he could no longer match his income to the extending need of his family. His inchoate restlessness fed upon this knowledge.

Seven children had been born into the Beecher home since Lyman settled at Litchfield. Roxana had borne three of them: Harriet, destined for fame; Henry Ward, the family's natural actor; and the accident-prone Charles, forever bandaged and bruised. Harriet Porter, the second wife, was herself quickly mother of three, with as much Beecher blood and as many Beecher traits as any of Lyman's other progeny: Frederick, the child of her heart, early born and soon dead; Isabella, a toddler when the family left Connecticut; and

Tom, only an infant. While necessity had multiplied and living grown dear in the parsonage, Lyman had remained (as he did for the rest of his life) the lovable, childlike pensioner on heaven, who could give away money for a worthy cause without even bothering to count it,[13] or answer the practical questions of a middle-aged man whom he was urging into the ministry with a calmly infuriating "The Lord will provide," and then shout, "JEHOVAH JIREH, don't forget Abraham."[14]

Faith, however, is no medium of exchange; nor is self-sacrifice negotiable. Lyman in his last year at Litchfield was alerted to a circumstance that demanded specie as well as trust. He must have money or withdraw George, his third son, from college. Having gladly denied himself "in equipage" and allowed his "fences to fall into decay," he was stubbornly unwilling to sacrifice the education of his children (by which he, of course, meant his sons), and unable to secure it without additional income.[15]

Lyman's sons were promised for the ministry before they decided for themselves. Their mothers had given them to God, and Lyman intended to assist (goad, if need be) to their proper goal, these boys who were born for the gospel.[16] Edward's future appeared predictable and auspicious in 1825. His conversion, slow to come, had been solid on arrival; and his scholarship was unquestioned.[17] The proud possessor of a Phi Beta Kappa key, Edward longed for a watch to wind with it. (Lyman snorted at such "foppery."[18]) William, less successful in society or schoolroom, was disposed to fits of the family curse, dyspepsia; but as he found himself "completely down in the dumps" just when too many parties were coincidental with assignments in the second volume of Euclid, it may well be that his illness was not, as he supposed, exclusively physiological.[19] Still, his was by no means a case to abandon as hopeless. As Lyman understood matters, William's worry over "want of feeling" for God was strong indication that feeling was exactly what his oldest son *did* have.[20]

All things considered, Edward and William were as good as in the ministry already. But there were the others. Lyman was not intimidated by looming expense. Neither was he misled. With lack of money standing presently before him like an arbitrary hurdle he must somehow clear, Lyman was unshaken in his confidence that all his sons would become ministers. They did. Long afterward the youngest Beecher son, James, not yet born when the family removed from Litchfield to Massachusetts, gave shrewd appraisal of the situation, just at a time when he had so successfully completed a voyage as officer on a clipper ship as almost to insure a career at sea. "Oh, I shall be a minister," he said. "That's my fate. Father will pray me into it."[21] Far from shrinking at the prospect of preparing so many for such labor, Lyman was eager, and, had there been more sons to give, would gladly have accepted heavier responsibility. His disposition is transparent in words spoken when he considered the early outcropping of genius in one of his gifted daughters. Said he, ruefully, "Wished Harriet was a boy."[22]

Lyman did not hold Litchfield guiltless in the difficulty of his family finance and enforced departure. Roxana's death had been induced, he felt, by her "undue exertion" in accepting boarders in her effort to compensate for his insufficient salary. Yet his words of farewell, though unambiguous, are without rancor, and his honesty is intact. "You have done for me what you promised," he told his parish, "and more."[23] Five years later he had become captious. Resentful of having "spent the best years" of his life in Litchfield, at nothing better than "a dead lift," he complained of having been compelled to hold conferences in "that old West school house, dark and dirty, lighted with candles" begged from neighbors and "stuck up on the side walls with old forks" because the congregation was too niggardly then to buy "half a dozen tin things."[24] Lyman could never revert to the scene "without shuddering."

That he should leave Litchfield was much clearer to Lyman than where he should go. Heaven, as ever, came to his rescue. The "rumors" he had sensed "floating . . . from Boston" materialized into a firm call from a visible congregation,[25] and Lyman quite properly regarded it "as a providential indication of the divine will"[26] that the newly formed

Hanover Society of that city asked him to become their pastor. So it was that Lyman Beecher, in his fifty-first year, removed to Boston, where, for the next six years, he was more concerned with heretic than with heathen. When for the first time "he rode up to the door of [the] new and elegant church, with his wife, in a poor country chaise covered with white cotton cloth," the curious adolescents waiting for a glimpse of the pastor found horse and driver "both alike, very unattractive." Their faces communicated what breeding forbade them "to say, 'Well, we are sold this time!' "[27] They were not, as they soon learned, and they made themselves captives to Lyman's rustic charm. He was no less bound to them. "Oh, how well it went! 'Twas the best church I ever saw," he said.[28]

> The people of Boston [wrote Timothy Dwight] are character-istically distinguished by a lively imagination; an ardour easily kindled; a sensibility soon felt, and strongly expressed; a charac-ter, more resembling that of the Greeks than that of the Romans. They admire, where graver people would only approve; detest where cooler minds would only dislike; applaud a performance, where others would listen in silence; and hiss, where a less susceptible audience would only frown. This character renders them sometimes more, sometimes less, amiable; usually less cau-tious; and often more exposed to future regret. From this source their language is frequently hyperbolical; and their pictures of objects, in any way interesting, highly colored.[29]

Dwight's description, if true, may well explain why Beech-er was happier and more successful in his third pastorate than in any other. One of his staunchest admirers said that "he was never at his best, even in the pulpit, after leaving Bos-ton."[30] His radical likeness to such people is immediately clear, his affinity with them obviously an affair of the heart.

Whether Boston was an Athens in 1826 depends upon definition. For those of her fifty thousand residents who spent their time in nothing else than "to tell or to hear some new thing," there was no lack of novelty. During the nine-teenth century Boston lost her preëminence, but not her prominence, as a seaport. When the Beechers lived there, clippers and cutters still arrived daily, spilling ideas and information over the city as they crowded it with travelers and immigrants.[31] In the shops one could select from "a choice collection of Perfumery, recently received from Paris,"[32] purchase American-made wall paper[33] or playing cards manufactured in Massachusetts.[34]

Bostonians, however, were interested in more than the modish or the novel. The Plymouth Rock of elite American choruses was the Handel and Haydn Choral Society of Boston, founded in 1815, and serious and self-confident enough to request Beethoven to compose a work especially for them, a compliment the master declined for the sake of other commissions.[35] New England's literary renaissance was not yet the wonder it became, but there were signs that the winter was over and past. Here and there sporadic beauty was grown to full flower, as in "A Forest Hymn," written by a country doctor's poet-son who had already published "Thanatopsis."[36] The Boston Athenaeum, a library for a generation, began now to function also as an exhibiting museum.[37] Although the city was still puritan enough to darken her playhouse on Saturday—the eve of the Sabbath—it was possible to attend professional productions at the Federal Street Theatre, and, before the year was out, at the grand, new Tremont as well. There was often less than Shakespeare on the boards, but there was sometimes that.[38] A minor point of pride with Bay sophisticates was the satisfaction that pedestrians were not threatened by runaway stock. The streets of Boston, unlike those of Philadelphia and Baltimore, "were not perambulated day and night by swine."[39]

At about this time a British visitor in Massachusetts, noticing the numerous Unitarian churches in Boston, confessed himself unprepared to see them "in all the dignity" and with the "towering spires and peals of bells" that he associated with more traditional houses of worship.[40] Had he but known, many Unitarian structures looked like orthodox sanctuaries for the quite simple reason that—until recently—they had been. The change was an outward symbol of the woe that had called Lyman to the city. By his puritan standard Boston's glory was departed, and the true Church's rightful place was usurped by another. The transformation had happened in the following fashion.

In Massachusetts, Unitarianism had become a rock to split on in 1805 when orthodox churchmen lost control of Harvard through the appointment of the liberal Henry Ware as Hollis Professor of Divinity.[41] The action was at once taken as a dark portent and understood for all its dismal import for the tradition[42] by Jedediah Morse, minister at Charlestown, and thus automatically member of the Board of Overseers of Harvard College.[43] When Lyman Beecher arrived in Boston, Morse had been warring for more than a generation in the struggle to clarify the line of demarcation between Trinitarians and their foes.[44] The contest, fought with that special fierceness Americans reserve for clashes over politics and religion, had irreparably shattered congregational and family unity. In the subsequent rash of "Reviews," and "Answers," and "Appeals," and "Replies" that afflicted New England, the question of who owned the church property was a constant irritant. Though admittedly of less importance than the doctrine of Christology, it was often of much more immediacy. When a congregation was splintered into opposing factions, as often happened, it was necessary to decide who should have the key to the church-house door. Moreover, property usually included gifts that had accumulated through many years. Money and principle were at stake in no small measure.

Matters were complicated by the relationship between *church* and *parish*, two distinct, but not separate, organizations. The *parish* comprised the male voters in any town who were taxed to support the church. Legal authority was vested in the parish. *Within the parish* was a smaller, select group, both men and women, who had "owned" the covenant—a challenge rarely met: they were *the church*. Because of their elevated spiritual status, church members, as a group, were accustomed to expect, and usually to receive, deference in matters exclusively religious. An exception was the clash that had hastened Lyman away from East Hampton, when the church was willing to raise his salary, but the truculent parish was not. Normally, however, the parish left ecclesiastical matters in the hands of the church and endorsed their decisions, especially regarding the choice of a minister. An affair that did not work out in this way made a test of a church squabble at Dedham, Massachusetts, and put a humbled orthodoxy on guard.

Altercation had arisen in Dedham regarding the call of a new minister. Over the loud protests of the church, the parish had selected a liberal man who smelled of the heresy from Cambridge, where he had been prepared for the pulpit. The majority of the church members, disagreeing with and taking umbrage at the action, withdrew and formed a new church. They also claimed all the property the former organization had controlled. The minority of the church, thus dispossessed and deserted, feeling much put upon, but strengthened by the supporting sentiment of the parish, proceeded to reorganize the fragment of the church that had remained and sued at law to recover what they regarded as their stolen property. No one missed the crucial nature of the litigation. After argument and appeal the matter was settled once and for all by a decision of the Supreme Court. The orthodox were quite taken by surprise. The court held that "where a majority of the members of a Congregational Church separate from a majority of the Parish, the members who remain, though a minority, constitute the Church in such Parish, and retain the rights and property belonging thereto."[45] So it came about that in many a Massachusetts town, though the limits of the parish remained constant, the designation of the meeting house was altered, and—tragic in Lyman's eyes—the old faith was cast aside.

When Beecher became minister of the Hanover Church, he was no stranger to Boston, nor Boston to him. From his Connecticut fastness he had earlier seen the Unitarian "wolf coming," and "thought surely" someone would "lift up his voice; but on he came and all was silent."[46] This was not exactly the case, for the contest was hotly debated, although, it is true, as often in pamphlet war as in pulpit witness. The unfolding drama excited Lyman. It was like "fire in [his] bones."[47] When Bostonians in 1823 invited him to come assist in a revival at the Park Street Church, that "Gibraltar of orthodoxy,"[48] he had leaped to go. Folk in Litchfield, thinking him unequal to the trip,[49] were pleased to have him return strangely refreshed.[50] They might have guessed it would be so. Preaching to great throngs "composed of *all Denominations,*" as he did in Park Street,[51] was the breath of Beecher's nostrils. It was also his strategy: "The Unitarians can not be killed by the pen," he said, "for they do not live by the pen. They depend upon action, and by action only can they be effectually met."[52] Lyman's sermons were acts, events even. Action ever, and sometimes antic accompanied him into the pulpit, but his appeal transcended the intoxication of cadence. There was the time when Lyman, overcome with the feeling of having preached poorly, sat dejected in the corner of the carriage as the family made their way home from meeting. He keened over his failure and wished aloud that he might recall what he had said and try it another way. "Why, Father," interrupted Henry Ward, "I thought you preached real *loud.*" "Yes, boy, that's it," said the doctor. "When I've nothing to say I always holler!"[53] In the defense of the faith of the fathers against the upstart Unitarians, though, Lyman had much to speak for and was ready, as he said, to "tear passion to a tatters."[54] Beecher was happy in the Park Street revival, and Boston was amazed. It was the same when, three years thereafter, he came to the city to remain.

As had happened before, and as would happen again, Beecher at Hanover Church stepped into a place for which he was second choice. Enthusiastic enough in their call to him,[55] the Hanover Society had preferred to have Dr. Payson of Portland.[56] Happily, in time they owned Beecher as their man. Dr. Payson, of course, could "preach and pray as well as any man that ever lived," wrote Calvin E. Stowe, Lyman's son-in-law—

> but as to laying out extensive plans of aggression beyond the limits of his own congregation, attending councils, making speeches at public meetings, writing essays and reviews, watching over theological discussions, taking care of all the young men he could drum up for the ministry, organizing the labor of others, setting everybody at work, in short wheeling any number of different heavily laden wheel-barrows all at one and the same time, this is what Dr. Payson could never have done; but this and more is what Dr. Beecher did during all the six years he labored in Boston.

His years in Boston were "the busiest, the most laborious, the happiest, and visibly the most successful" of his life.[57]

According to Beecher's children, "Calvinism," when their father assumed the Hanover pastorate, suffered as a "dethroned royal family wandering like a permitted mendicant in the city where it had once held court" while "Unitarianism reigned in its stead."[58] To a beleaguered orthodoxy, Lyman was "as one of the old Puritan fathers risen from the dead."[59] If he did not successfully achieve a palace revolution, he kept border brigandage at a minimum and effectively restricted heresy's domain to the kingdom of Boston.[60] After his day in Boston it was possible to give serious reading to the waggish observation that Unitarianism was a belief in the Fatherhood of God and the brotherhood of man, in the neighborhood of Boston.

Notes to Chapter VII

1. *Autobiography*, II, 32-33.
2. *Ibid.*, pp. 40-41.
3. Harriet Beecher Stowe, *Oldtown Folks*, pp. 478 ff.
4. *Autobiography*, I, 326.
5. August F. Fehlandt, *A Century of Drink Reform*, p. 21, gives the recipe for a flip: " . . . home brewed beer with an infusion of spirits, sweetened and seasoned with sugar and nutmeg, and warmed with a red-hot poker." See Alice Felt Tyler, *Freedom's Ferment: Phases of American Social History to 1860* (Minneapolis, 1944), p. 309.
6. *Autobiography*, I, 326.
7. Harriet Beecher Stowe, *Poganuc People*, p. 177. See William C. Beecher and Samuel Scoville, *Henry Ward Beecher*, p. 63, for Henry Ward's observation: "We never could estimate how many populated our old house."
8. Lyman Beecher Stowe, *Saints, Sinners, and Beechers*, p. 40; "A Song of Remembrance," Beecher Collection, Stowe-Day Foundation.
9. Esther Harriet Thompson, "Life in Old Litchfield."
10. "A Song of Remembrance," Beecher Collection, Stowe-Day Foundation.
11. ALS, Mary Beecher, [Hartford], February, 1826, to Edward, Beecher Collection, Yale University.
12. *Autobiography*, II, 39-46.
13. David Bartlett, *Modern Agitators*, p. 194, tells of Beecher con-

tributing to a missions collection money he had been instructed to spend for a coat.

14. James C. White, *Personal Reminiscences*, p. 25.

15. *Autobiography*, II, 45.

16. Shortly before Roxana died she "dedicated her sons to God for missionaries, and said that her greatest desire was that her children might be trained up for God." *Autobiography*, I, 295. Harriet Porter regarded her marriage to Lyman Beecher as a response to God's call to her. See ALS, Harriet Porter, Boston, September 16, 1817, to Lyman Beecher, Beecher Collection, Stowe-Day Foundation. Her "intense positive religious and moral" instruction created "deep though vague religious yearnings" in the children. Harriet Beecher Stowe, *Men of Our Times*, p. 507.

17. *Autobiography*, I, 431-432, 459-460, 475, records some—but by no means all—of the chapters in the history of Edward's difficult conversion.

18. *Ibid.*, p. 423: "I have no objection to your wearing a watch when you have earned and paid for one."

19. ALS, Lyman Beecher, Litchfield, February, 1824, to Catherine, Beecher-Stowe Collection, Schlesinger Library, Radcliffe College.

20. *Autobiography*, II, 26.

21. Lyman Beecher Stowe, *Saints, Sinners, and Beechers*, p. 384.

22. *Autobiography*, I, 524.

23. *Ibid.*, II, 43.

24. *Ibid.*, p. 250. Alain C. White, *History of Litchfield*, pp. 29 ff., makes it clear, however, that stoves, or any other "conveniences," were not considered important by the congregation. In this connection he has an instructive description of the Sabbath Day houses, built for the convenience of worshipers from a distance.

25. *Autobiography*, II, 33.

26. *Ibid.*, p. 43.

27. James C. White, *Personal Reminiscences*, pp. 4-5.

28. Julius A. Palmer, *Hanover Church, Boston* [reprinted from the *Congregational Quarterly* (April, 1872)], p. 18. Palmer was an organizing member of the church and observed its whole history.

29. Timothy Dwight, *Travels*, I, 508.

30. James C. White, *Personal Reminiscences*, p. 10.

31. In mid-eighteenth century, Boston was a town of 15,000 population. The town received a charter and became a city in 1822. "Boston," *Concise Dictionary of American History*, Wayne Andrews, ed. (New York, 1962). In 1820 Boston had 43,940 inhabitants; in 1830, 62,163. Census Office, *Census for 1820* (Washington, D.C., 1821); Census Office, *Enumeration of the Inhabitants of the United States* (Washington, D.C., 1831). A part of this growth was surely accounted for by the "Celtic" wave of Irish immigrants which rose from 54,338 in 1821-1830 to 207,381 in 1831-1840. "Immigration" in the *Concise Dictionary, supra.*

32. *American Traveller*, February 2, 1830.

33. Timothy Dwight, *Travels*, IV, 481.

34. *Ibid.*, p. 486.

35. Frank Jewett Mather, Jr., Charles Rufus Morey, and William James Henderson, *The American Spirit in Art*, vol. 12 in *Pageant of America* (New Haven, Toronto, and London, 1927), p. 322.

36. Fred Lewis Pattee, *Century Readings for a Course in American Literature* (New York, 1926), pp. 250 ff.

37. Frank Jewett Mather, Jr., *et al.*, *American Spirit in Art*, p. 16.

38. Oral Sumner Coad and Edwin Mims, Jr., *The American Stage*, vol. 14 in *Pageant of America* (New Haven, Toronto, and London, 1929), pp. 77, 87.

39. James Boardman, *America and the Americans* (London, 1833), p. 283.

40. *Ibid.*

41. Conrad Wright, *The Beginnings of Unitarianism in America* (Boston, 1955), pp. 274-280.

42. Jedidiah Morse, *The True Reasons on Which the Election of a Hollis Professor of Divinity in Harvard College Was Opposed at the Board of Overseers, Feb. 14, 1805* (Charlestown, 1805).

43. William B. Sprague, *Annals*, II, 249-250.

44. James King Morse, *Jedidiah Morse: A Champion of New England Orthodoxy* (New York, 1939), p. 24, and *passim.*

45. Earl Morse Wilbur, *A History of Unitarianism in Transylvania, England, and America* (Cambridge, 1952), p. 432.

46. *Autobiography*, I, 448.

47. *Ibid.*, II, 53.

48. Charles Beecher, "Life of Edward Beecher," unpublished MS, p. 36. The original manuscript copy is deposited in the Illinois College Library, Jacksonville, Illinois. It was presented to the college in 1950 by John Beecher.

49. ALS, Benjamin Tallmadge, Litchfield, April 12, 1823, to J. P. Cushman, Tallmadge Papers, Litchfield Historical Society.

50. ALS, Benjamin Tallmadge, Litchfield, May 29, 1823, to J. P. Cushman, Tallmadge Papers, Litchfield Historical Society: "His services were highly acceptable to the people of Boston, & his handling the Subjects on which he preached, with great Dexterity, he drew hearers & a crowded auditory...."

51. *Ibid.*

52. *Autobiography*, I, 449.

53. Esther Harriet Thompson, "Life in Old Litchfield."

54. *Autobiography*, I, 437.

55. Minutes of the August 24, 1825, committee meeting of the Hanover Church, *supra.*

56. Calvin E. Stowe, "Sketches and Recollections," p. 229.

57. *Ibid.*

58. *Autobiography*, II, 110.

59. James C. White, *Personal Reminiscences*, p. 7.

60. Sidney E. Mead, "Lyman Beecher and Connecticut Orthodoxy's Campaign Against the Unitarians, 1819-26," *Church History*, IX (September, 1940), 229: " . . . revivals offer one of the most fruitful explanations of the fact that Unitarianism hardly spread beyond the Boston area."

Chapter VIII
Boston Prophet:
Traditional Answers
to New Questions – 1826-1832

Congregational clergymen, attempting to destroy Unitarianism and revitalize Calvinism, moved steadily (if unconsciously) away from the tradition they professed. While tenaciously affirming the divinity of Christ and the Trinitarian formulae, they modified the system at critical points. Nathaniel Taylor, professor of didactic theology at Yale, gave impressive and influential statement (allegedly Calvinistic) of New England's growing liberal sentiment. Styled Taylorism, or the New Haven Theology, his thought did not please strict conservatives. Yet new theology was nascent, even in the ranks of the orthodox. In a scheme where God was increasingly understood in terms of benevolence rather than arbitrary justice, man enjoyed the liberty of a free agent: though still personally responsible for his own guilt, man found the benefit of the atonement within easier reach than formerly; and grace, now resistible, was in greater supply. Vigorously and widely proclaimed, the compromise gospel lacked distinction and vitality to achieve decisive victory in Boston. Unitarianism enjoyed no spectacular growth, but there was no lasting renaissance of orthodoxy.

Hanover Church

Lyman Beecher thought in military metaphor when he considered the struggle to guard the faith. Unitarians, therefore, were the enemy. Their progress was onslaught against God, their humiliation a victory for heaven.[1] When, through courtesy or curiosity, Unitarians thronged his Park Street revival, Beecher shouted that "the moment" had come "to charge as Wellington did at Waterloo when he saw the Guards of Napoleon fall into confusion."[2] Reading Lyman's account of the warfare is "like walking over an ancient battle-field, silent and grass-grown, but ridged with graves, and showing still by its conformation the disposition of the troops which once struggled there in deadly contest."[3]

Beecher was more nearly the field marshal of the campaign than the chief of staff. The commander was his first friend and dearest idol, Nathaniel William Taylor, Dwight Professor of Didactic Theology at the new Yale Divinity School, a man for whom, according to Harriet Beecher Stowe, her father entertained "an unbounded and romantic attachment."[4]

In the holy war, whether he was seeking to demolish an encampment or simply to fell a single soul who sat like "a partridge on a dead limb, watching," as the doctor tried "to get a shot at him,"[5] Lyman's ammunition was theology. Common fame had it that his theology differed little, if at all, from Dr. Taylor's, and identified the creed of the two men;[6] but this was considerably more than Lyman himself was willing to do.[7] The popular mind, though, was set. "Beecherism," a term infrequently heard, had sometimes an overtone of the facetious.[8] But it was possible in Lyman's day to speak of "Taylorism" and be soberly understood to intend that modification or (depending upon one's prejudice) clarification of Edwardean Calvinism achieved in Connecticut[9] which Lyman Beecher argued and preached from Boston to Cincinnati and back again.[10] No one saw this more clearly than Bennet Tyler, the East Windsor watchdog of orthodoxy, who published anonymously a series of letters describing the origin and progress of the liberalism that was in due course styled "the New Haven Theology." Though misleading at tender points,[11] Tyler correctly charged that Beecher was "in high degree responsible for the spread" of Taylorism, and for its "favor in the eyes of the community."[12]

What the public designated "Taylorism," however, was not the exclusive creation of the man whose name it bore. It had evolved from the common effort of two friends during the harrowing years in which they stood together in the thick of battle. Chiefly concerned not to build a system, but to capture souls, Beecher and Taylor fought to present orthodoxy in a form young America would be powerless to resist. Accordingly, Lyman spoke with reason, and he never granted, practically, that able arguments would not shatter any skepticism. (Destiny would have been different with Byron, he sighed, if only the poet could "have talked with Taylor and me."[13]) The attempt thus to commend the tradition to a new generation made it necessary for Taylor and Beecher to reinterpret the theology of Jonathan Edwards. Long before Beecher left Litchfield, Taylor arrived there on one occasion, expressly "to talk about Edwards." Keenly disappointed to find Lyman absent, he wrote and left for him an illuminating letter suggesting a plan by which they might mend those matters that Edwards had ignored (or marred) and between the two of them "change the current of theological sentiment."[14] It is transparent from the letter that this was not their first such speculation about Edwards, and that it would by no means be the last.

Calvin E. Stowe said that his father-in-law "checked" Taylor and, unfortunately, prevailed upon him to keep closer to Edwards than Taylor was inclined to do. In undignified figure, though sensible to the spirit of combat, Stowe contended that Beecher sent "Taylor into the ring against the most practiced pugilists with one hand tied behind him."[15] Perhaps he did. In any case, deciding what part of the resultant system is Beecher's and what part is Taylor's is difficult, if not impossible. The separation is vastly complicated by their personal relation, which allowed their contemporaries to mistake (or exploit) expressions of loyalty for statements of faith. Lyman, without the author's permission, changed manuscript copy Taylor had sent to the *Spirit of the Pilgrims,* omitting, rearranging, substituting words that had been carefully written for Pharisees who would surely dissect every picayune. Taylor, though regretful, was "not disposed to censure" his older friend, considering their "long intimacy" and Beecher's purpose, which was but to give "additional illustration" of Taylor's views.[16] Nor would Beecher say aught against Taylor. Hard pressed in the warfare of the West, when he strove to secure the citadel of Lane Seminary and to preserve his own professional reputation, Lyman published a letter in the *Cincinnati Journal* acknowledging that much difficulty would be resolved if he would "formally and publicly denounce Dr. Taylor." Lest any might misread his position, Beecher added: *"I will not do it."*[17]

The association of these friends had begun when they first met in Timothy Dwight's study. Taylor, a divinity student, was amanuensis to the weak-eyed president of Yale, and Beecher was still minister at East Hampton. The carefully groomed Taylor (who seems to have been born a reproach to "unpolished shoes and unkempt hair"[18]) mistook the "rather small, plain-looking man" asking to see Dwight for some neighboring farmer, "come to arrange with the doctor for his winter supply of potatoes," and he interrupted his writing only long enough to offer the visitor a chair.[19] Taylor stopped to listen, though, as Dwight and Beecher talked, and before the interview had ended, a union was effected between Lyman and Nathaniel that outlasted their lives.

In his youth, "Nat Taylor, fair beyond compare / The pride of all Yale College O—"[20] had charmed a generation by his "boyish beauty and amiableness" of disposition.[21] As a Congregational minister, grown handsome, and touched by fire, the Reverend Nathaniel William Taylor so awakened and captivated New Haven that, even as the War of 1812 cheapened currency and inflated prices, his parish erected for him on the green a stately church modeled after London's pleasing St. Martin-in-the-Fields.[22] With growing dignity and reputation he had moved from the pastorate to professorship at Yale. The rise of Unitarianism was for him—no less than for

Lyman, his comrade at arms—a call to battle stations, and he enlisted to endure with valor.

Lyman, who was brought to Massachusetts to fight Unitarians, had engaged Boston heretics more than once before he came to Hanover Church. He first directed missiles in formal barrage against them when in September of 1817 he accepted an invitation to preach at the ordination of Sereno E. Dwight as pastor of the Park Street Church.[23] The sermon he chose for the occasion he had delivered earlier under the exacerbating circumstance of the departure from East Hampton.[24] When he arrived in Litchfield he found that Connecticut was no longer, as in former days, "quiet as a clock," but echoed rumblings of the Unitarian controversy.[25] Lyman, therefore, worked on the sermon, polishing and expanding it, with the result that when he went up to preach it at Boston, the city heard the gospel as she never had before. The "old men were in a glorification," and even those "not given to praising let out."[26] Entitled "The Bible a Code of Laws," this excoriation of lassitude and apostasy was just the ammunition for a stunning blow against the enemy in Boston. There was a "sensation all over the city."[27] At Beecher's funeral, Leonard Bacon recalled, less than accurately, that it was "a direct assault" that struck the "most defenceless quarter."[28] Effective it doubtless was, but it was adroitly indirect. Though speaking freely of paganism and popery (old iniquities to which Beecher frequently dealt blows in passing), the sermon, strangely, does not once use the word "Unitarianism." Rather, Lyman's technique is to make strong statement of the truth and then warn that any who are guilty of deviation call plagues upon their heads and barter for wormwood their portion of the Tree of Life. The distance between Lyman's creed thus described and the Unitarian position escaped few who sat under his spell that day in the Park Street Church. Making a connection Beecher did not supply, the congregation could easily conclude that as the true path, along which alone lay hope, was so plainly not the way of the Unitarians, there must, sadly, be no salvation with them. Thus Unitarians, though unnamed, stood convicted of criminal error, refusing to accept the truth themselves, and offering false security to others.[29]

The conclusion, incidentally, sustained the current epithet, "Brimstone Beecher,"[30] and detracted nothing from the popular designation of Park Street Church as "hell fire corner."[31] "If there be a place in the world of despair of ten-fold darkness, where the wrath of Almighty glows with augmented fury, and whence, through eternity, are heard the loudest wailings, ascending with the smoke of their torment:—in that place," thundered Beecher, "I shall expect to dwell, and there, my brethren, to lift up my cry with yours should we believe lies, and propagate deceits."[32]

Having discharged his volley, Lyman retreated to Connecticut and did not descend on eastern Massachusetts again for two years. Life in Litchfield town continued as feverishly happy as ever. In this interim Lyman wooed and married Harriet Porter,[33] received an honorary degree from Middlebury College,[34] and packed Edward (the family scholar) off to Yale.[35] Beecher felt like "a bottleful of new wine, all in ferment."[36] Once he "attacked" (his word) an old barn with a saw and such vigor that in two hours' time he sundered it from beam to base and brought the roof crashing down upon Culver, the hired man.[37] Reveling in the garden, with its potatoes knee-high about the elm tree, and "raspberries set so thick you [could] not see between them,"[38] Beecher sporadically directed his energy to such projects as planting cabbages or hauling stones from the meadow. But pleasant distractions and domestic crises did not blunt Lyman's vigilance nor lay the Unitarian threat. "My soul is moved within me," he wrote, "that so many of the temples in Boston and around should be only splendid sepulchres, where the spiritually dead sleep, never to awake till they meet at the judgment seat that Saviour whose divinity and atonement they deny."[39] Meanwhile Beecher and Taylor maintained constant interchange, and watched the Unitarian development with sleepless eye. As an old woman, Taylor's daughter still remembered how Lyman used to come boiling out of the Bantam hills and burst "into the house, speak to no one," and rush, unannounced, "up the back stairs" to her father's study.[40] Together they planned and prayed.

When, therefore, in 1819, Elias Cornelius, who was to be installed as associate pastor of the Tabernacle Church in Salem (within the very sight of the Boston front), asked Beecher to preach at the ceremony, the warrior was quick to seize the opportunity to return to the siege. Lyman would have accepted in any case. Cornelius had been a staunch friend since the days when he had lived in the Beecher home at Litchfield while studying theology with the doctor. But with the swarming Unitarians of Boston "silently putting sentinels in all the churches, legislators in the hall, and judges on the bench," as Lyman later said, and even infiltrating the ranks of "physicians, lawyers, and merchants,"[41] there was a stirring challenge in the call to arms. Moreover, the Dedham case (currently in litigation) was dramatizing the insidious ability of Unitarians to rip out walls that divided saints from strangers. It was a setting for a sermon.

Again Lyman trained his artillery obliquely, and taxed the Unitarians not with snatching property from rightful owners, but with doing violence to the sanctity of the church.[42] By their rationalization of conversion, they obliterated the distinction between the elect and the world. Yet the Church, he reminded them, embraced the regenerate alone. Parishes were not meant to control nor to become churches, "much less to *destroy* them."[43] Succeeding generations found the sermon tedious. For Beecher's fellow soldiers it was incandescent, and for Cornelius, new reason to rejoice. "When I heard the echo of your trumpet" as you "leaped upon the battlements of Zion and sounded the alarm," he exulted, hope and joy "thrilled through my heart."[44]

Four years afterward, in "The Faith Once Delivered to the Saints," Lyman distinguished bluntly between the true church and "that irreligious, immoral and voluptuous" community of the Unitarians.[45] The proud and thunderous deliverance defined and defended Calvinism (and lauded Edwards who had "been to error what the mounds and dykes of Holland [had] been to the sea"[46]). Ironically, this "huge

bomb thrown right into the camp" of the adversary[47] delighted the Unitarians, not, to be sure, because it wounded
them beyond recovery, but because the occasion, unlike
earlier encounters with Lyman (when they were left little
course except to retire to their tents), allowed them to
outflank Beecher by confessing that *his* orthodoxy "might
also be adopted by all Unitarians."[48]   Coming from a "reputed Calvinist," the sermon was nothing short of remarkable, said a Unitarian critic, for its "decidedly *anti*-Calvinistic
bearing; expressly denying some" distinctive features of Calvin's system, "distinctly asserting none," nor even implying
"them in such a manner, as to make it obvious to a common
reader."[49]   In candor the reviewer added, "We thank him for
it."[50]

So it was that Lyman Beecher arrived at Hanover Church,
already a byword as the scourge of Unitarians, but already
suspect as too closely linked with Nathaniel Taylor, and thus
a renegade from loyal Calvinists. The assessment of the man's
theology awaited the tortuous procedure of his heresy trial;
meanwhile he appeared faithful to an established image. In
his Boston years Lyman's sermons simply restated old
themes. He fought Unitarianism as he always had fought it.
Storming the same fortress, and charging a familiar foe, he
achieved a modest victory: Unitarianism did not die; but
neither did it thrive. The price Lyman paid for halting the
advance, however, was a dear one. Public controversy had
exposed his spontaneous witness to cold analysis. Increasingly he was plagued by enemies from the orthodox camp,
sometimes making formal accusation (and sometimes whispering slanderous rumor) that it was he who was heretic, and
the Beecher-Taylor theology, ruinous error.

In the delicate balance of the universe there were also
afloat benign rumors, which, though they blurred somewhat
the sharp profile of the bold prophet, endeared him to the
hearts of a generation who accepted the legend of his foibles
as a quasi-benediction for their own. Beecher, who had not
been able by prayer or revivalism to bring Boston to her
knees, eventually found the city at his heels. His person

triumphed where his prophecy had failed. Boston began to create her own mythology of his charm, which, like all myth, was grounded in history.

So energetic that he used at odd intervals to race to the cellar of his Copp's Hill residence and furiously to shovel from one corner to another the load of sand he kept there for the express purpose of relaxing constitutional tension,[51] Lyman (probably honest in saying that he could not live a week without "jimnastics"[52]) sometimes ranged the neighborhood searching for the release his taut system demanded. An enthusiastic woodcutter, Beecher set his saw as carefully as he adjusted the articles of his creed, and kept it conveniently in his study, where it was half-concealed in the heap of council minutes, incomplete manuscripts, and sermons. Without a garden in Boston, he often longed for physical exercise and coveted the work that from his window he saw regularly laid out for the itinerant sawyers. He was especially envious when his own woodpile was reduced to a state of discouraging orderliness. Once, impulsively, he grabbed his saw and rushed to assist one such worker who, as it happened, was bitterly prejudiced against Beecher (without ever having met him) because the doctor was a teetotaler. The dayman endeavored to discover from his helper (whom he had seen come from the Beecher residence) just what kind the doctor was. "Tough old chap, ain't he?" Lyman "guessed" he was "to them that try to *chaw him up.*" As the men worked and talked they warmed so each to the other that Lyman consented to sell his saw to the itinerant. When the workman, calling the next day to close the bargain, discovered the identity of his new friend, his embarrassment melted before Lyman's unaffected openheartedness. "Oh," said the doctor, "you're the man that wanted to buy my saw. Well, you shall have it for nothing—only let me have some of your wood to saw, when you work on my street."[53] The journeyman became one of Lyman's stoutest constituents, concluded that "old Beecher" was a "right glorious old fellow," and would thereafter hear no word against him. It was just this simplicity and imperturbable good humor that

transformed Beecher from ogre to patron in the popular
Boston mind. Captured by his charm, they did not quarrel so
hotly with his creed. This was more than clear in the consequence of the Hanover Church fire.

"About one o'clock yesterday morning," wrote a reporter
for the February 2, 1830, issue of the *American Traveller,*
"we were aroused from sleep by the watchman's appalling
cry of fire." The sight of Dr. Beecher's church "wrapt in
flames was," he confessed, "one of the most grand and
sublime spectacles" he had ever seen: "an immense volume of
fire was rolling high up from its tower—the whole city was
brilliantly illuminated" and the thickly falling snow was like
"a shower of spangles and silver."[54] More than beauty,
however, marked the night. The firemen came promptly, but
they did nothing.[55] Resenting Beecher as a spoilsport who
was against lotteries,[56] and who had stopped the selling of
grog from booths on the common,[57] they took occasion to
punish and humiliate him by standing idly by and watching
as the church building collapsed. They also sang, bleating out
doggerel inspired at the moment: "While Beecher's church
holds out to burn; / The vilest sinner may return." Presently
tell-tale blue flames and an unmistakable redolence in the
winter air led to the discovery that the merchant who had
leased some of the basement rooms of Hanover Church had
used them to store an excess stock of whiskey.[58] The firemen were hilarious. Anybody but Beecher (quite innocent, as
it happened) would have been embarrassed beyond endurance. Not he. The next morning, with ashes still smouldering
and the mob making rustic jokes about "old Beecher" and his
"spirit fire," several of Lyman's lugubrious friends assembled
at Pierce's book store, saw the doctor actually "skipping"
down the street and, unbelievable, "gay as a lark." "Well,"
said Beecher, beaming, "my jug's broke; just been to see it."
His gloomy companions could only laugh with him, and feed
on his hope.[59] They did; and so did Boston.[60]

Time and again acid criticism turned in this way into warm
acceptance. The city that had feared him when he arrived
because she knew he "had been a man of war from [his]

youth and had shed much blood"[61] lived to claim him as her
own, a David whom she loved more for the music and
laughter of his heart than for his having killed giants.

Beecher never forgot his role as a soldier in the army of
God. Awaiting the final clash—and never doubting that it
would come—he continued to fight by Taylor's side while he
lived, and to defend his memory and message after his younger friend outran him in the race for glory. One of Lyman's
last cogent utterances, in a lucid interval that shattered,
however briefly, the dark senility of his last years, was a
passionate affirmation of faithfulness under fire: "I have
fought a good fight."[62] Indeed, it was Beecher's quaint
conceit that he and Taylor might strike a final blow for God,
even in death. He said that he wanted to be buried "where it
would do the most good." That place, he decided, was as
near to Taylor as physical circumstance would allow. Young
men, he predicted, "will come and see where Brother Taylor
and I are buried, and it will do them good."[63]

Halfway down Cedar Avenue in New Haven's Grove Street
Cemetery, there is a lot fenced with iron pickets, dominated
by a gray shaft of granite on which is inscribed the legend of
Nathaniel Taylor—how he lived and how he died,
and how he loved the law of God. Hard by the monument,
below and to the right, a stone slab carved with a plain cross,
and bearing only a name and dates, marks Lyman's grave.
Before he died Beecher had purposed in his heart to mix his
dust with Taylor's, and it was the decision of Nathaniel
Taylor's widow and of Beecher's wife that these friends
should not be divided in their death.[64]

Notes to Chapter VIII

1. *Autobiography*, I, 435-451, 538-563.
2. *Ibid.*, p. 539.
3. Review of Beecher's *Autobiography*, *Atlantic Monthly*, XV (May,
1865), 631.
4. Rebecca Taylor Hatch, *Personal Reminiscences and Memorials*
(New York, 1905), p. 31. Mrs. Hatch was Nathaniel Taylor's daughter
and, of course, knew and associated with the Beecher family.

5. *Autobiography*, II, 73.

6. Lyman Beecher, letter published in *Cincinnati Journal*, May 11, 1837. Also see *Autobiography*, II, 119-143.

7. Samuel J. Baird, *History of the New School, and of the Questions Involved in the Disruption of the Presbyterian Church in 1838* (Philadelphia, 1868), p. 186, quotes the Rev. Asahel Nettleton (a prominent revivalist of the period who, nevertheless, disapproved of Nathaniel Taylor's theology): "Dr. Beecher, at that time, did not fully agree with Dr. Taylor, and they were often, as I expressed it, 'like two cocks, by the gills,'—Dr. Taylor clear over the mark and Dr. Beecher so far over that I could agree with neither." See [Bennet Tyler], *Letters on the Origin and Progress of the New Haven Theology* (New York, 1837), p. 8.

8. *Autobiography*, I, 385.

9. E. H. Gillett, *History of the Presbyterian Church*, II, 481.

10. Beecher's confession of orthodoxy, which, according to Leonard Bacon, put Unitarians on the defensive, was *The Faith Once Delivered to the Saints: A Sermon Delivered at Worcester, Mass., Oct. 15, 1823, at the Ordination of the Rev. Loammi Ives Hoadly, to the Pastoral Office over the Calvinistic Church and Society in that Place* (Boston, 1823).

11. Zebulon Crocker, *The Catastrophe of the Presbyterian Church in 1837, Including a Full View of the Recent Theological Controversies in New England* (New Haven, 1838), pp. 269-281.

12. [Bennet Tyler], *Letters on New Haven Theology*, p. 93.

13. *Autobiography*, I, 530.

14. *Ibid.*, p. 384.

15. Calvin E. Stowe, "Sketches and Recollections," p. 228.

16. "Dr. Taylor's Reply to Dr. Tyler," *Spirit of the Pilgrims*, V (December, 1932), 677.

17. May 11, 1837.

18. Theodore T. Munger, "Dr. Nathaniel W. Taylor—Master Theologian," *Yale Divinity Quarterly*, V (February, 1909), 236.

19. Rebecca Taylor Hatch, *Personal Reminiscences*, p. 27.

20. *Ibid.*, p. 8.

21. S. W. S. Dutton, "A Sketch of the Life and Character of Rev. Nathaniel W. Taylor, D.D.," *Congregational Quarterly*, II (July, 1860), 246.

22. Oscar Edward Maurer, *A Puritan Church and its Relation to Community, State and Nation: Addresses Delivered in Preparation for the Three Hundredth Anniversary of the Settlement of New Haven* (New Haven, 1938), pp. 93-95.

23. *Autobiography*, I, 350.

24. *Ibid.*, pp. 350-351.

25. *Ibid.*, II, 165.

26. *Ibid.*, I, 351.

27. *Ibid.*

28. Leonard Bacon, *Sermon at the Funeral,* p. 17.

29. Lyman Beecher, *The Bible a Code of Laws: A Sermon Delivered in Park Street Church, Boston, September 3, 1817, at the Ordination of Mr. Sereno Edwards Dwight, as Pastor of that Church; and of Messrs. Elisha P. Swift, Allen Graves, John Nichols, Levi Parsons, & Daniel Buttrick, as Missionaries to the Heathen* (Andover, 1827), p. 31: "The view we have taken of the Scriptures as containing a system of divine Laws, illustrates the obligation to believe correctly, the fundamental doctrine of the Bible, and the criminality of error on these subjects."

30. Walter Balfour, *A Letter to the Rev. Dr. Beecher, Boston* (Boston, 1829), p. 36. The sobriquet is written on the last page of the pamphlet.

31. The circumstance of such designation is variously given, and the more frequent description was "Brimstone Corner." The historic record of brimstone actually being stored there seems to have been a parable of the brand of sermons often prophesied. See H. Crosby Englizian, *Brimstone Corner: Park Street Church, Boston* (Boston, 1968), pp. 14, 55n, 209. Also see *Atlantic Monthly,* XV (May, 1865), 631.

32. Lyman Beecher, *The Bible a Code of Laws,* p. 37.

33. *Autobiography,* I, 362-363.

34. Franklin Bowditch Dexter, *Biographical Sketches,* V, 248.

35. *Autobiography,* I, 375.

36. *Ibid.,* p. 373.

37. *Ibid.,* p. 410.

38. *Ibid.,* p. 411.

39. *Ibid.,* p. 408.

40. Rebecca Taylor Hatch, *Personal Reminiscences,* p. 29.

41. *Autobiography,* I, 449.

42. Lyman Beecher, "The Designs, Rights and Duties of Local Churches," *Sermons Delivered on Various Occasions,* pp. 184-185.

43. *Ibid.,* p. 195.

44. *Autobiography,* I, 441.

45. Lyman Beecher, *The Faith Once Delivered to the Saints,* p. 8.

46. *Ibid.,* p. 42.

47. Leonard Bacon, *Sermon at the Funeral,* p. 18.

48. *The Christian Examiner and Theological Review,* I (1824), 2.

49. *Ibid.,* p. 1.

50. *Ibid.,* p. 3.

51. *Autobiography,* II, 113.

52. ALS, Lyman Beecher, Boston, February 3, 1827, to Catherine, Beecher-Stowe Collection, Schlesinger Library, Radcliffe College.

53. Calvin E. Stowe, "Sketches and Recollections," p. 231.

54. This edition of the *American Traveller* is in the Boston Public Library.

55. James C. White, *Personal Reminiscences,* p. 5.

56. *Ibid.*, pp. 13-14, gives account of Beecher's fight against the lotteries. See also *Cincinnati Journal*, February 18, 1831.
57. Julius A. Palmer, *Hanover Church, Boston*, p. 22.
58. *Autobiography*, II, 228.
59. Calvin E. Stowe, "Sketches and Recollections," pp. 230-231.
60. James C. White, *Personal Reminiscences*, p. 13, writes of Irish laboring men digging on the site of Hanover Church and pretending to have discovered Beecher's jug.
61. *Autobiography*, I, 543.
62. *Ibid.*, II, 557.
63. *Ibid.*, p. 555.
64. Rebecca Taylor Hatch, *Personal Reminiscences*, pp. 32-33. When Chauncy Goodrich had offered, "Brother Beecher, there is room in *my* lot in the cemetery, if you wish to be laid in New Haven," Lyman had replied, "I wish to lie beside Brother Taylor and in *his* lot." The last time he called on Mrs. Taylor before his death, he pointed toward the cemetery but did not speak. Both Mrs. Taylor and Mrs. Beecher understood.

Chapter IX

An Exclusive Gospel:
Old Prejudices in a Young Republic - Interlude

The exclusive character of religion in young America stubbornly persisted in national life. Most obvious in relation to slavery, the protean manifestation also surfaced as discrimination against Indians and as intolerance toward Roman Catholics. Early effort to convert Indians often gave way to the temptation to exploit them. Warfare between whites and Indians augmented racial alienation. Attitudes of such missionaries as John Eliot, though not unique, were exceptional, and Puritans bequeathed to the republic a disposition to consider Indians inferior. Indian missions flourished sporadically after 1800, but society perpetuated anti-Indian prejudice. Feeling against Roman Catholics, present in the colonies, reappeared in the 1830's as nativism that insisted upon favoring those born in America as against immigrants. In reaction to increased immigration of Catholics, nativists, equating religion with nationality, were strongly anti-Catholic, and produced both periodical literature (for example, The American Protestant Vindicator*) and organization (*The New York Protestant Association*). Both prejudices had religious dimensions: they assumed identity of America's rightful destiny with Protestantism. The presence of either prejudice in individual or group indicates not the essence of Protestantism but the interpenetration of culture and religion.*

Lyman Beecher (Stowe-Day Foundation)

Official decision regarding the measure of identity between Beecher's creed and Taylor's had to await a heresy trial in Cincinnati. Meanwhile Boston misjudged Lyman's theology by missing completely the larger—even universal—quality of his thought, partly because it was expressed in rustic idiom. The Bay City confused the crockery with the soup, as it were, and thus dismissed one who by reason of his tough-minded individualism was at a radical level akin to Boston's frontier of the intellect.

Lyman Beecher still said "creetur" and "natur" when he moved to (and, for that matter, when he departed) Boston.[1] As a homespun prophet he enjoyed no easy access to society in the Charles Basin. Litchfield had not risked the luxury of castes, for, as in any small town, survival itself demanded a measure of democracy. Boston, though, was a city of more than fifty thousand, with a recognized elite. As it happened, the Brahmins were all Unitarians—"the literary men . . . the trustees and professors of Harvard College . . . [and] the judges on the bench."[2] These proper and privileged folk, though relentlessly discriminating, did not occupy themselves exclusively with the cultivation of lofty minds. There were those who in their castle-homes dined well, waited on by oriental servants, and amused by the sight of peacocks, strutting through the gardens.[3] Sometimes they forsook reading to play at "draughts and chess,"[4] or to attend great balls where they danced cotillions on floors specially "painted with arabesques."[5]

Beecher was ill fitted for this burnished life. Moreover, he disapproved of it. The Boston metamorphosis that was bartering Sparta's strength for Athens' grace offended him. His astringent denunciations from the Hanover Street pulpit did not, however, distract Bostonians from a life they enjoyed and defended. *The Christian Examiner* (Unitarian, intellectual, fashionable) recommended the merits of wine, openly acknowledged that hard liquors might on occasion be "beneficial or even necessary,"[6] and refused to "condemn cards."[7] Only by the narrow margin of his charming eccentricity did Beecher escape classification with the Philistines who considered the pips of the deck the "dialect of the evil one, and the theatre ... his temple."[8] Men of Boston, though, Unitarian or not, were powerless to resist the appeal of a Beecher, homeward bound from Quincy market, waving awkwardly to friends as he dashed along, bearing in one hand a silk handkerchief full of oysters, and clutching in the other a live and angry lobster.[9] They also found it difficult to take such a man seriously as a theologian, and sometimes, all but impossible to avoid identifying the essence of Lyman's religion with either his towering wrath or his childlike enthusiasm.[10] Having at first regarded Beecher with frosty composure, Boston, in the end, hardly noticed him at all, save as a character. Barely had Beecher turned to the West when a rowdy farce, *Departed Spirits, or the Temperance Hoax,* lampooned him and other teetotalers from the Boston stage.[11] Unitarians eschewed the vulgar piece; but they rejected it because they deplored coarse entertainment,[12] not because they agreed with Lyman Beecher that the theatre would "beguile unstable souls ... to death [and] hell."[13] Indeed, pressed on the point, they might have accepted the actor's caricature as accurate.

Indicative of the Beecher whom Boston remembered, and of how she judged him, is an episode of Lyman's visiting a neighboring church. Having concluded his sermon and taken his seat, suddenly (by what quixotic spirit the record does not say) he was moved to testify during another's discourse. He began to snatch at the preacher's coattails, whispering repeatedly in a clear voice, "Get done as soon as you can: I must speak again," until the pulpit was once more his, at which time he erupted in "rocket ... after rocket [and] bombshell ... after bombshell" in a display never before equalled "by the Doctor himself."[14] Such behavior endeared Beecher to the heart of the orthodox, a fiercely loyal clan in Boston; but it confirmed the urbane, Unitarian establishment in the conviction that Beecher was more amusing—even lovable—than significant. The judgment is at best inaccurate, at worst an indictment of Boston's provincialism, and in any case a vindication of Dr. Channing's observation that a man who betrayed in his "brogue or uncouth tones his want of cultivation" could not take the place "to which, perhaps, his native good sense entitled him."[15] The fact is that, for whatever reason, fashionable Boston did not discover (and so could not appreciate) Beecher's sense of mission to the world, a sense of mission too dynamic and too imaginative to be contained in any conventional institution, or expressed by any shibboleth, even Boston's.

It was not, however, solely the fault of Boston that she misjudged Lyman. Sometimes his perspective was distorted or obstructed by the beam of prejudice. On those occasions neither saint nor clairvoyant could have perceived so much as a spark of prophet's vision beneath the surface of Lyman's crusty insularity. The circumstance is clear in the history of the Foreign Mission School at Cornwall, Connecticut; and there is added paradox in the panic of a seer, disconcerted at the impending realization of an erstwhile goal.

The school at Cornwall owed its life to the appearance in New England of the Sandwich Islander Henry Obookiah, an odd combination of mimic and mystic, and the "first Polynesian explorer of Connecticut who has left an account of his experience with the natives."[16] Orphaned on his native Owyhee by a bloody tribal encounter in which his parents were "slain before his eyes," Obookiah barely eluded a warrior who speared his younger brother. The wretched youth achieved doubtful sanctuary with a greedy witch doctor who sought to make the lad a shaman like himself, and would have done so, had not the boy bought his freedom with a pig.[17] The spare words laconic friends cut into the marker above Obookiah's New England grave scarcely hint at the drama of his story, save in reference to the miracle of God's redeeming grace. The inscription declares simply that "His arrival in this country gave rise to the Foreign Mission School, of which he was a worthy member," and testifies that though "destined for a Pagan Priest," he "became a Christian."[18] Lyman knew the whole romance. So, too, did the Connecticut clergy. They marveled at it.

Obookiah had contrived to reach America by shipping as cabin boy with New Haven's Captain Brintnall. During the voyage he stopped in the Seal Islands, where he met a certain Russell Hubbard, "friend of Christ," and Yale man, who taught him English letters from the pages of a spelling book. Once in the States, the Polynesian melted Yankee hearts, and received hospitality and instruction by New Englanders from college president Timothy Dwight to the students of Andover Seminary. The opportunity to practice on a live heathen charmed American Puritans, who were, moreover, vastly reassured by Obookiah's reaction to their ministry. He "silenced the . . . common objection" that foreign pagans were "too ignorant to be taught," and even made it impossible any longer to doubt that they "had souls as well."[19] The Foreign Mission School at Cornwall, a spontaneous outgrowth of the enthusiasm for Obookiah and the desire to multiply his kind, was founded in 1817 "to afford hospitable asylum to unevangelized youth, of good promise" and to train as missionaries those "providentially brought to . . . [New England's] shores."[20] Within a year Obookiah was struck down by typhus fever.[21] His death intensified the zeal of the school sponsors.

Lyman, grieved by the loss, but determined that the foothold in the promised land should not be forfeited, rode over from Litchfield in the bleak February chill that he might preach the funeral sermon. It was wrong, he said, to mourn Obookiah or to wish him back. "Who would dare to stop the song which he sings . . . or to rob the angels of their joy," the preacher asked.[22] Although conceding that no one would have ordered the events thus, Lyman confessed that in the dark providence of his death, he heard Obookiah saying "more audibly than ever, 'Go forward.' "[23] Connecticut Christians readily heeded the summons Beecher interpreted. Shortly young men from Polynesia, Malay, China, Japan, Portugal, and New Zealand—to say nothing of many from American Indian nations—were happily studying in the school situated under the shadow of Colt's Foot mountain.[24]

The enterprise lasted scarcely ten years. Theodore Gold, who should have known, reported that the school was "a decided success, as the original plan was concerned," but added that the project was abandoned when it became possible to educate natives. "on their own ground."[25] Litchfield's Isaiah Bunce, sub-acid editor of the *American Eagle*, grumbled early about the Cornwall endeavor. But then he was distrustful of the whole missionary movement, and snorted at the rash of benevolent "cent" societies and Dorcas groups currently afflicting New England and dedicated to what he considered the indefensible duty of clothing savages. What, he asked, of the "Female Bed-Bug Society; Mrs. Sally Pillow, president; Miss Amelia Bedcord, secretary?"[26] Yet the school survived derision and calumny. Now and again an unworthy person like "Mrs. C." arrived at Cornwall, ostensibly to serve, but eager only to exploit the situation.[27] That "low-minded, frivolous" woman carried about a cage of live birds and a shawl box wherever she went, and was brazen in her complaint over the burden of "morning and evening devotions."[28] Bunce, however, lacked substantial focus for his attack until the winter of 1823. In that year John Ridge, an Indian and former student of the school, married Sarah Northrup, the steward's daughter, and so caused "much agitation in South Cornwall." Wise folk, while distinguishing between "things . . . lawful" and things "expedient," regretted the marriage, because they foresaw "great evil in the church and society" thereby.[29] Emily Fox, local poetess, lamented Sarah's fate and wailed that John had "snatch'd her from her mother's breast" and taken her to "a little, small wigwam / And nothing allowed her for a bed, / But a dirty blanket."[30] The truth seems to have been that Sarah was willing and John well-to-do.

There was romance enough to render the matter fascinating to Cornwall, but too much novelty to make it tolerable. Although the school continued, thereafter it languished. Students communicated regularly with their sponsors in letters of pious cant.[31] Fledgling missionaries wrote poems with names like "The Wandering Pilgrim," copied them in their notebooks, on pages adorned with water colors of lakes and hemlocks. These informative, though leaden, compositions preserve impressive statistics in pedestrian couplets:

"The languages now are thirteen / Twelve nations are likewise seen."[32] But the shadow of disgrace lay heavily upon the school. The agents, of whom Lyman was chief, knew it well, and they forbade students "visiting or marrying in the white families";[33] but the gesture was feeble, for the matter was already out of hand.

What had happened was no "cause of wonder" for Isaiah Bunce. He considered it but the inevitable "fruit of the *missionary spirit*" arising from the "conduct of the clergymen at that place [the Foreign Mission School, of course] and its vicinity." The agents and the superintendents were responsible. Reluctant to publicize "the name of the female thus throwing herself into the arms of an Indian," Bunce said that he would "hesitate not to name those believed to be either mediately or immediately the cause of the unnatural connection." Nor did he. They were "Rev. Dr. Lyman Beecher, Rev. Timothy Stone, Rev. Charles Prentice, Rev. Joseph Harvey, and Rev. Herman Daggett."[34] Further, he challenged an indignant public who "said that the girl ought to be publicly whipped, the Indian hung, and the mother drown'd" to "trace the thing to its true cause," and see whether the men named, or their system, had not planned "the transaction as a new kind of *missionary machinery.*"[35]

In the spring of 1825 alarm became violence, with the news of another untoward marriage soon to be celebrated. Harriet Gold, impeccable of heritage, was engaged to marry Elias Boudinot, a Cherokee. The match especially incensed Cornwall because, as few had suspected it, many were outraged by lovers guilty not only of impropriety, but also, critics said, of the duplicity of "so long concealing from the public view the intended design."[36]

There was a demonstration on the green. Harriet was burned in effigy, and cursed that she might see her children "fall by each other's tomahawks" and herself die by the "scalping knife of her husband."[37] Bunce, though prepared for such a development because he considered missions inappropriate and impractical, defended Harriet when she was called "lewd, disgusting, filthy."[38] "Foolish, weak, or infatuated," surely he granted she might be, but "not in the least to blame."[39] He contended that Harriet, living in an atmosphere charged with religious emotion and dominated by a mother "poisoned all but to death"[40] by missionary zeal, could not have done otherwise than she did, and only endeavored to act in accordance with the "will and approbation of the Agents, her *Brahmins.*"[41] Bunce's denunciation of these culprits was as caustic as any prophet's condemnation of sinners. He indicted the Missions Board in Boston as an "adulterous offspring of mistaken piety and spiritual pride," which had been "dandled in the lap of Mammon till that nuisance and monster at Cornwall had sprung from its loins."[42]

Men of missionary zeal in Lyman's day often appeared pathologically impatient for that time when "the elements" would be "melting . . . the earth . . . on fire" and "all its pleasant and magnificent things . . . sinking into ruin."[43] The millennium, even so, was a blessing more desirable in prospect than in proximity, although the nicety of such distinction usually escaped ardent preachers. Longing for the day of the Lord and pressing the cause of missions to hasten the time, they were, nevertheless, reluctant to depart the lofty security of status or to risk life at the radical level of a kingdom come. When, therefore, their evolving gospel seemed to permit or demand a restructured society they changed their word, or their tactics, or both. In this respect Lyman was no different from the rest. Indeed, he could be more successful than most in tacking with the winds of prejudice and provincialism, because he was quick to see the advantages of giving little to gain much.

On June 17, Lyman Beecher attended a meeting of the Agents of the Mission School. In a solemn document those men confessed that although they had indeed, after "actual inquiry and thorough investigation," assured the community that "no repetition of marriage . . . between any [student] . . . of the Foreign Mission School, and any female of the vicinity was to be expected," another such marriage was in fact imminent. Moreover, Harriet and young Boudinot had "carried on by secret and covered correspondence" a "negotiation for marriage" that was now "a settled engagement."

As honest men they felt they had no alternative except to condemn "those engaged in or accessory to their transaction, as criminal," insulting to the Christian community, indifferent to the interests of the school. The agents begged the public not to "associate in their just censure," those who had striven to prevent the evil. "Let the blame fall where it justly belongs," they pleaded, and promised "vigilance and decision for the future."[44]   Lyman's signature was first on the document. Harriet and Elias married in March of 1826.[45]   The school closed its doors the following year.

Beyond all cavil, Lyman was in this context less God's daring prophet than a captive priest, intent on nothing so much as upon preserving the status quo. The Cornwall chapter, however, is not the only one in which Lyman appeared unsophisticated. His provincial anxiety was not restricted to Indians. Uneasy in the face of social upheaval, he was panic-stricken at the prospect of America's multiplying population of Catholics. So loudly and so effectively did he trumpet his fear that he was—at least in one instance—even blamed with inciting to riot.[46]

In the summer of 1834, Beecher, some time since settled in Ohio, had come again to Boston. Characteristically, he was begging for a worthy cause. Lyman's old teacher, Timothy Dwight, had called the West a "heaven design'd ... example bright."[47]   Equally as enthusiastic, Lyman was "led to speak of the character, wants, and dangers of the great [Ohio] valley," so as to "kindle the interest" of New Englanders and "draw forth their liberality."[48]   This meant warning Easterners of the danger of popery. Oblivious apparently of the boatloads of Catholic immigrants spilling daily onto the wharf of Boston, Beecher appealed to Massachusetts to send men and money to save Western pioneers lest predatory Jesuits capture the land and lay it in the thrall of a foreign prince.

On Monday night, August 11, an angry mob stormed the Ursiline convent of Mount Benedict, just across the Charles River from Boston, and with almost no warning, set fire to the walls. All, even the sick, were evacuated safely. And two stalwart nuns managed to rescue the chapel tabernacle with its treasure of the blessed sacrament, carry it into the garden, and hide it "in a bed of asparagus."[49] But the building was destroyed. Moreover, mischief was set afoot. Rowdy fellows roamed the streets for days, and only with difficulty were surly Irish laborers from the railroad camps outside Boston prevented from attacking the city.[50] Catholics blamed Lyman, and charged that the churls had been "goaded on by Dr. Lyman Beecher,"[51] but Lyman insisted that the sermon "to which the mob ascribed" was preached before his presence in Boston was generally known, and on the very evening of the riot, some miles distant from the scene, and that probably not one of the rioters had heard it or even "knew of its delivery." Nevertheless, the convent was burned, and just at the season when Lyman was alerting Massachusetts to danger from the "despotic character and hostile designs of popery."[52]

Measuring Beecher by nothing more complex than concern to conquer Catholics, or protect his own vanity, is naive. Prejudice was incidental to his character, not integral to his passion. His was a vision of Christianity that, at its clearest, had vast ramifications. Just for this reason, therefore, he was distressed that the grand achievement for missions at the Cornwall School should be, even slightly, retarded by an ill-advised marriage, and, similarly, he was impatient with lazy Protestants who were too apathetic or niggardly to meet the challenge of the West. He did, indeed, view interracial marriage with shocked disapproval; but his heart was fixed on evangelizing the world. He did, indeed, deplore Rome, and fear her power, but what he sought was not to ensnare Catholicism, but rather to hasten the victory so compelling that it should not be frustrated, and most certainly not by "the Romish church."[53] Moreover, however Beecher might sporadically betray a distorted value, he was his own man, an individual more likely to combat popular opinion than to conform to it. Lyman was still strange to his new parish of Litchfield when he had asked the priggish Rev. Mr. Stone of nearby Cornwall about the best spots for catching trout. His neighbor, "erecting his form to its highest altitude and looking down with contempt said, 'Mr. Beecher, fishing is not respectable here.' 'I intend to make it respectable,' " replied Parson Beecher,[54] and so he did: for convention as such he cared not a fig.

It was the same with cultural rite as with personal habit. Boston had known a different kind of musician before Lowell Mason arrived to revolutionize music in the city. With novel and effective techniques for introducing music "in the public schools, Mason impressed himself indelibly on the democracy of his times."[55] Organizing oratorio societies and composing engaging tunes for hymns, Mason also impressed himself on church music in Boston, and, for that matter, on Protestant religion in America. It might have been supposed that Beecher would have agreed with Father Taylor's feelings about musical novelty in the church. Taylor, notwithstanding his own dramatic flair in the pulpit,[56] thundered disapproval, bitterly rejecting newfangled doings of choirs, and scorning those who with "profane lips dared to imitate the groans of Christ upon the cross." He castigated those "infidels with instruments . . . [who] mimicked the blast of the angel's trumpet."[57] Not so Beecher. "His full belief that the millennium was coming . . . that the Church was just about to march with waving banners to final and universal dominion, imparted to music, as it had to theology, an entirely new spirit."[58] Mason enjoyed free rein in Beecher's church, selecting hymns he considered appropriate for the service, although now and again, Lyman, when he needed a moment's breather in the midst of preaching an especially strenuous sermon, was likely to look up over the heads of the congregation and call to the choir loft, "Mr. Mason, sing Old Hundred."[59] By Lowell Mason's hand Boston first heard the "heavy double diapasons" resonant enough to "vibrate" the "pews, doors & window sashes."[60] The musician, remembering Beecher's part in bringing him from the secular career of bank-clerk in Savannah to the artistic celebrity of the Boston scene, said that it was Dr. Beecher who had "laid the train," that all he himself had done was "to apply the fuse."[61]

When evangelistic fervor informed his unconventionality, Lyman could render the commonplace transparent to the eternal, heedless of any wrath he thereby called down upon his own head. Undecided whether to brand him a knave or a fool, those who saw no further than Beecher's idiom at times dismissed him as a rustic with more animation than insight. Determined critics, however, easily discovered the points at which the doctor was vulnerable. Dr. Ebenezer Porter, president of Andover, accused him of tampering with the gospel "to render it palatable to men."[62] Quite innocent of this charge, Beecher was, nevertheless, so confident of the intrinsic power of the gospel to convince (if only it were cogently stated) that he never stopped trying to interpret the good news: he knew the futility of preaching, save in terms of torn garments and grains of mustard seed. Sermons needed "horns," he said, for men to lay hold of.[63] Far more characteristic of Lyman than the implicit Pharisaism of his openly confessed inability to believe infidels sincere[64] is the account that scandalized his generation of how he received into his Boston church a woman who was "as much of a Universalist as were Revs. Ballou and Streeter,"[65] because he believed that beneath their surface differences both he and the woman stood supported by a common ground.

The point is not whether the story is apocryphal (as it well may be) but that, since all legend roots in truth, Beecher is rightly identified with sentiment wholly at odds with every canon of Calvinistic anthropology. Doubtless he recognized his proper classification no more accurately than did his contemporaries. Gloomy as Jude regarding the extent of man's sinfulness and the inevitability of his failure, Lyman still argued man's "power to the contrary,"[66] and in no small measure contributed to the growing optimism that informed American religious evaluation of the human condition. Disowned by reactionaries of his time, Lyman was too often regarded by liberal peers as a provincial with a theology as outmoded as his dress.

Theodore Parker spoke of Lyman's father as "Blacksmith Beecher," who, "grim all over with soot," was in 1780 "forging axes 'dull as a hoe,' and hoes 'blunt as a beetle' " that were "yet the best that men had in Connecticut in those days." "What," he asked, if "lumberers and farmers had come together, and put it into their Saybrook Platform,[67] that to the end of time all men would chop with Beecher's axes and dig with Beecher's hoes, and he who took an imperfection therefrom, his name should be taken from the lamb's book of life, and he who should add an improvement thereto, the seven last plagues should be added unto him!" Plainly such madness was unthinkable, yet it was of similar folly, or worse, that Parker accused Lyman; for he taunted him with attempting to impede humanity's advance. "In 1830, in Boston," he continued, "Minister Beecher, grim with Calvinism, . . . was making a theology—notions of man, of God, and of the relations between them. His theological forge was in full blast in Hanover Street, then in Bowdoin Street, and he wrought stoutly thereat, he striking while his parish blew. But his opinions were no more a finality than his father's axes and hoes." "Let Blacksmith . . . and minister . . . hammer out the best tools they can . . . but let neither . . . say . . . 'I am the end of human history, the last milestone on the Lord's highway of your soul.' Depend upon it mankind will not heed such men. . . . Progress is the law of God."[68] The implied censure is ill spoken. The fact is that Beecher was readier than most to abandon old tools and shape new ones. He dreamed of the past; he eulogized it; but he lived, with an almost obliterating genius, in the immediate present. Concerning man's ability Lyman voiced an increasingly popular estimate that was open to the future, and as different from the anthropology of Calvinism as chalk from cheese. A vignette from national politics illuminates the essential point at which Lyman disagreed with the establishment.

Sectional interests were taking ominous shape in 1832. Planters quarreled with industrialists over protective tariff. Frontiersmen, eager for free land, resented Senator Foot's attempt to control its distribution. The clear-eyed De Tocqueville had warned that there was "no sure barrier" against tyranny in America[69] and observed that "habits [could be] . . . formed in the heart of a free country" that might "some day prove fatal to its liberties."[70] Seventeenth- and eighteenth-century political philosophers, almost exclu-

sively concerned with "transfer of power from king to people," had assumed that democracy was intrinsically splendid,
and always better than monarchy.[71] They grew rhap-
sodic about self-government. Naively they ignored the possibility that men—even though in the majority—might be less
than good. Now that the powerful character of popular
opinion was emerging in stark dimension, the notion of it
frightened perceptive members of minority groups. It
appeared that there was inherent illness in democracy. A
unique therapy for the disease was offered, not by a theologian or a missionary, but by a statesman-politician who,
ironically, was a Unitarian and therefore, theoretically at
least, committed to an optimistic view of man and the extent
to which man's innate sense of morality and rectitude
might be trusted.[72] That danger of majoritarian tyranny in
Jacksonian democracy which De Tocqueville rightly anticipated,[73] John C. Calhoun essayed to cure by devising a
system of nullification. Unfortunate in its focus, the concept
was actually a plan to safeguard the rights of minorities
against, if you will, the social outcropping of human depravity. But Beecher, who, as a Calvinist, should have set
small store by man's moral ability, chose to forget or bypass
the fatal weakness and, with bold and daring confidence in
the human race, looked for a millennial kingdom, the coming
of which man's effort hastened, if indeed it did not insure.

Alas, seeds of such a dream could no more flourish in the
rocky soil of Calvinism than Lyman's spirit could thrive in
the stifling atmosphere of convention. Thus the opportunity
to go West (simultaneously escaping Boston, as it happened)
seemed to Lyman heaven's expedient to bring him to a
climate where his ideas could live. It was a double blessing.
Although Cincinnati was a city, there were more forests than
fences in Ohio. Nature had ever been Lyman's milieu. Once
in his youth the surf and the salt air had restored him to
health. Always he had drawn strength from the soil, taking
his problems into the garden where he would frequently
interrupt his weed-pulling with the cry, "Now I've got it,"
and rush for pen and paper.[74] Thus he turned westward in
the faith that God's miracle would attend him. That miracle,

which had somehow never happened in East Hampton, or in
Litchfield, or in Boston, would surely come to pass in Eden.
"I have responded to the call of Providence," he said, "the
great causes which are to decide the destinies of this nation
are to be found in the West. The great conflict of our
political independence, was on the other side of the moun-
tains; a more important conflict is now to be sustained . . . on
this side. Here is the vast territory—the exuberant soil— . . .
the great rivers—the teeming millions—."[75]
What Lyman discovered was not majesty, but pettiness.
There were abrasive problems of administering a new and
struggling school, with rebellious students, and tergiversating
sponsors; there were domestic griefs that lacked too often
any dignity to raise them to the level of tragedy; and there
was abusive personal attack that brought him before the bar
of a church court, accused of heresy. A less resilient soul
would have collapsed. Lyman endured.

Notes to Chapter IX

1. *Autobiography*, I, 14.
2. *Ibid.*, II, 110.
3. Van Wyck Brooks, *The Flowering of New England, 1815-1865*,
rev. ed. ([New York], 1937), p. 8.
4. *The Christian Examiner*, NS, III (May, 1830), 209.
5. George B. Emerson, Manuscript "Journal," Massachusetts Historical Society.
6. *The Christian Examiner*, NS, IV (November, 1830), 242-243.
7. *Ibid.*, NS, III (May, 1830), 209.
8. *Ibid.*, p. 203.
9. *Autobiography*, II, 565.
10. Theodore Parker, *Autobiography, Poems and Prayers*, Rufus
Leighton, ed. (Boston, n.d.), p. 296, writes of Beecher after having gone
through one of his protracted meetings: "I greatly respected the talents,
the zeal, and the enterprise of that able man, who certainly taught me
much, but I came away with no confidence in his theology; the better I
understood it, the more self-contradictory, unnatural, and hateful did it
seem. A year of his preaching about finished all my respect for the
Calvinistic scheme of theology."
11. John B. Gough, *Autobiography and Personal Recollections*
(Springfield, 1870), p. 83. Gough was a reformed drunkard and former

actor who foreswore alcohol and devoted his energy to the cause of temperance.

12. *The Christian Examiner*, NS, III (May, 1830), 219.

13. Lyman Beecher, "Resources of the Adversary and Means of their Destruction—A Sermon Preached October 12, 1827, before the American Board of Missions, at New York," in *Sermons Delivered on Various Occasions*, p. 272. An item in the *American Traveller*, January 26, 1830, reports the recent appearance of Booth in *Hamlet*, played in an "original and peculiarly happy manner."

14. H. P. Hedges, "Anecdotes."

15. William E. Channing, *Works* (Boston, 1891), p. 19.

16. Ralph Henry Gabriel, *Elias Boudinot, Cherokee and His America* (Norman, 1941), p. 35.

17. [E. W. Dwight], *Memoirs of Henry Obookiah, a Native of Owhyhee, and a Member of the Foreign Mission School; who died at Cornwall, Conn. Feb. 17, 1818, aged 26 years* (New Haven, 1819), pp. 5-12.

18. Obookiah's grave is still tended by Cornwall residents who know his story and honor the tradition.

19. [E. W. Dwight], *Memoirs of Obookiah*, p. 99.

20. *Ibid.*, appendix; Ralph Henry Gabriel, *Elias Boudinot*, p. 50.

21. [E. W. Dwight], *Memoirs of Obookiah*, pp. 118-119.

22. Lyman Beecher, *A Sermon Delivered at the Funeral of Henry Obookiah*, p. 36.

23. *Ibid.*, p. 34.

24. Theodore Gold, ed., *Historical Records of the Town of Cornwall, Litchfield County, Connecticut* (Hartford, 1877), pp. 29-31; Adam Hodgson, *Letters from North America, Written During a Tour in the United States and Canada*, 2 vols. (London, 1824), II, 288 ff.

25. Theodore Gold, *Historical Records*, p. 29.

26. *The American Eagle*, June 30, 1823.

27. Oscar P. Bollman, "The Foreign Missions School of Cornwall, Connecticut," unpublished STM thesis of Yale Divinity School, 1939, pp. 64-65.

28. *Ibid.*, p. 65.

29. Theodore Gold, *Historical Records*, p. 85.

30. *Ibid.*, p. 34.

31. Three ALS, William Botelho, Jr., Chinese student at Cornwall, November 15, 1823, to Rev. William Jenks, Cornwall Collection, Connecticut Historical Society.

32. "The Cornwall Seminary," an original poem in the copy book of a student of the Missions School, Cornwall Historical Society.

33. *The American Eagle*, July 25, 1825.

34. *Ibid.*, March 22, 1824.

35. *Ibid.*

36. Theodore Gold, *Historical Records*, p. 85.

37. *The American Eagle,* August 29, 1825.

38. *Ibid.*

39. *Ibid.*

40. *Ibid.* Bunce charged that the agents were "destitute of common sense," that they must have supposed that missions students "would lose all *sexual* feeling" upon coming to Connecticut, and that the ministers' "plan was at best but a half witted one."

41. *Ibid.*

42. *Ibid.,* July 25, 1825.

43. Lyman Beecher and D. T. Kimball, "Missions Will not Impoverish the Country," in *Missionary Papers* ([Boston, 1833]), pp. 3-4.

44. Statement of the agents relative to the closing of the school, Cornwall Historical Society.

45. Ralph Henry Gabriel, *Elias Boudinot,* p. 91.

46. James Truslow Adams, *New England in the Republic 1776-1850* (New York, 1926), pp. 334-336.

47. Timothy Dwight, *Greenfield Hill,* II, in Vernon Parrington, ed., *The Connecticut Wits* (New York, 1926), p. 220.

48. *Autobiography,* II, 333.

49. Peter Condon, contributor, "Letter of Sister St. Augustine Relative to 'The Burning of the Convent,'" in United States Catholic Historical Society, *Historical Records and Studies,* Vol. LV, Parts I and II (New York, 1906), 223.

50. Alice Felt Tyler, *Freedom's Ferment,* p. 371.

51. Peter Condon, "Letter of Sister St. Augustine," p. 221.

52. *Autobiography,* II, 334. Beecher cannot be blamed exclusively for the Charlestown fire. In repeated notices of the disaster, the Boston press is singularly devoid of reference to him, and, moreover, offers partial explanation of the event in the detailed account of a vicious rumor (preceding and coincident with the burning of the convent) of the disappearance of a resident from the religious house in question. *The Daily Morning Post,* August 9, 1834, under the heading "Mysterious," reported that a young woman, known to be unhappy in the convent, was called for and not found; but on August 10, the paper announced that "the reported disappearance of a nun from the Convent at Charlestown is untrue." A letter from Edward Cutter, published in the *Post* of August 12, strongly suggests that there had been anti-Catholic turbulence in the area for some days. In a story on the fire, carried in the August 13 edition, the *Post* declared: "It is well known that for some days past a groundless rumor has prevailed in Charlestown and in its vicinity, that a young lady by the name of MARY HARRISON or MARY ST. JOHN HARRISON placed in the Catholic Convent, as a candidate for the veil, has been secreted or abducted, through the machinations of the controlling agents of the establishment, and was not to be found by her friends." References to the fire

(accounts, lists, rewards, outrages, etc.), frequent through issues of August 25, do not mention Beecher. See also the *Daily Evening Transcript* for the same period, in which Beecher is mentioned only in an August 18 report of how he (along with other clergymen of the city) had preached on the day before "from texts applicable to the events of [the] last week."

53. Lyman Beecher, *Views in Theology*, pp. 234-235.

54. H. P. Hedges, "Anecdotes."

55. Charles and Mary Beard, *The Rise of American Civilization* (New York, 1927), I, 801.

56. Taylor was the model, at least in part, of Herman Melville's Father Mapple, the sailor-harpooner turned chaplain to seamen. See *Moby Dick*, Chapters VIII-IX.

57. Gilbert Haven and Thomas Russell, *Father Taylor, the Sailor Preacher* (Boston, 1904), p. xvii.

58. *Autobiography*, II, 150-151.

59. *Ibid.*, p. 153.

60. E. E. Eells, *Sermon on Beecher*, p. 13.

61. ALS, Lowell Mason, Orange, New Jersey, January 15, 1863, to Henry Ward Beecher, Beecher Collection, Yale University.

62. *Autobiography*, II, 162.

63. Esther Harriet Thompson, "Life in Old Litchfield."

64. Lyman Beecher, *Lectures on Political Atheism and kindred subjects; together with Six Lectures on Intemperance*, Vol. I of *Works* (Boston, 1852), 174.

65. Scrap Book "S," p. 158, Bostonian Society, Old State House; see also the *Independent*, March 26, 1863.

66. The phrase, of course, is Nathaniel Taylor's distinctive description of the human relation to inevitable sin, for discussion of which see Sidney E. Mead, *Nathaniel William Taylor 1786-1858, A Connecticut Liberal* (Chicago, 1942), pp. 187-191.

67. An assembly of Congregational ministers and lay delegates, meeting in Saybrook, Connecticut, in 1708 by order of the Connecticut legislature adopted a platform that was a practical combination of Westminster doctrine and Congregational polity. See Clifton E. Olmstead, *History of Religion in the United States* (Englewood Cliffs, 1960), p. 90.

68. Theodore Parker, *The World of Matter and the Spirit of Man*, pp. 147-148.

69. Alexis de Tocqueville, *Democracy in America*, Phillips Bradley, ed., 2 vols. (New York, 1946), I, 262.

70. *Ibid.*

71. Charles S. Sydnor, *The Development of Southern Sectionalism 1819-1848* ([Baton Rouge], 1848), p. 212.

72. Charles M. Wiltse, *John C. Calhoun*, 3 vols. (Indianapolis, 1944-1951), I, 268-269.

73. George E. Probst, *The Happy Republic: A Reader in Tocqueville's America* (New York, 1962), pp. 361-370.

74. James C. White, *Personal Reminiscences*, p. 36.

75. *Cincinnati Journal*, January 4, 1833, in the report of Beecher's inaugural address as president of Lane Seminary.

Chapter X
Lane Seminary:
A Western School of the Prophets – 1832 -1833

Puritan colonists never considered the possibility of any except an educated ministry. They founded Harvard, first college in America, because they dreaded to leave the church an illiterate ministry when their own generation died. Educators of the era assumed that entering students would bring a thorough knowledge of Biblical content. The curriculum provided for instruction in the original languages of the Scriptures, as well as courses in theology, ethics, and philosophy. Those who sought additional work in divinity presented themselves at the home of some distinguished minister and, if accepted, studied under his direction (after the fashion by which professional education was secured in other fields), often living as a member of the minister's family, until such time as the tutor considered his apprentice a fit candidate for ordination. Although the Dutch Reformed Church established a theological seminary in 1784 by electing John Henry Livingston of New York to a professorship of theology not connected with any college, the first permanently located seminary was that founded by the Congregationalists at Andover, Massachusetts, in 1807. Presbyterians led the way in the West, establishing Western at Pittsburgh, 1827, and Hanover (later renamed McCormick and moved to Chicago) in Indiana, 1830. Under the Plan of Union, Lane Seminary was jointly sponsored by Congregationalists and Presbyterians.

Cincinnati, 1837 (Cincinnati Historical Society)

Cincinnati was better prepared for Lyman than he for her. Only a short while out of the wilderness, the city achieved queenly estate quickly, coming in less than forty years from mean cabins and muddy paths to "handsome streets [and] . . . public buildings."[1] A decade before Lyman's arrival in the river town a European visitor remarked the numerous "gay carriages and elegant females" there, and noted that the "spacious taverns [were] crowded with travellers from a distance."[2] Although her self-conscious inhabitants looked indulgently on odd Tunkers, thronging the market to sell "fat mutton and fine flour,"[3] Cincinnati was not so cosmopolitan as to be impervious to the heathen ways of pagans, nor so civilized as to suffer them gladly; but, increasingly subjected to speculators and celebrities, she was fast becoming adroit at absorbing both. Cincinnati could listen without commitment.

Frances Wright, the enchanting Scotswoman of proper background who advocated free love and lectured in public, had descended upon the city in 1828 with a resulting "effect," which, according to Mrs. Thomas Trollope, "can hardly be described."[4] Serene Cincinnatians considered it shocking, indeed, that this handmaiden of Beelzebub, who boasted "gold within her purse, / and Brass upon her face,"[5] should mount the rostrum. (Even Catherine Beecher did not herself deliver the addresses that she wrote on female education, but sat, as composed as any Beecher could, and as every lady ought, while some appropriate gentleman spoke her words.) The brazen Fanny, however, quite stunned the natives, who attended her appearance in great numbers, with her "mischievous sophistry" about equality of man and "glowing anathemas upon the artificial institution of marriage," all the more scandalizing because at the very season a minister in Cincinnati extolling the "inestimable importance of connubial constancy" found himself "preaching to empty pews."[6] Probably no one expected anything else from the woman who had already accused revivalists of making "the ignorant foolish, and the foolish insane."[7] Cincinnati was thrilled, but not converted. Miss Wright departed, and people on the Ohio continued to marry and say their prayers. In the end, Cincinnati prevailed, if, indeed, there was a victory; for the fiery Frances was in a measure domesticated by the city she denounced. Much later, long since having conceded the failure of an interracial experiment with communitarian life in Tennessee, Frances Wright, estranged and bereaved, returned to Cincinnati to spend the last and relatively irenic years of her life.

Had Lyman been as perceptive as he was courageous, he might have discovered wisdom in the episode. As a cultural outpost of New England, Cincinnati was more than ready to entertain new ideas and fresh prophets, and, in point of fact, was already acquainted with the continental intellect. Ephraim Peabody, who channeled the influence of Goethe and Coleridge to the frontier through the pages of the *Western Messenger,* that "exotic . . . Boston flower blooming in the Ohio valley,"[8] came to Cincinnati before Lyman. But Cincinnati, however accustomed to novel, even startling, ideas, questioned orthodoxy more comfortably than she deserted it. Likely to tame rather than to follow, the Western Queen served Fanny Wright as she had others—heard her and went home. Listening to exhortation for recreation was one thing, but racing after an upstart was something else again, especially if the raw notions threatened the expanding commerce of the city.

Before he settled in the West, Lyman went reconnoitering to Ohio. Catherine traveled with him: Catherine, who of all his children was most akin to his own mind-set and spirit.[9] Like agents of Jehovah spying out a promised land, father and daughter climbed Walnut Hills, two miles north of the city, and, standing in a grove of beech and oak trees, considered the future.[10] Beecher had not yet accepted the invitation to become first president of Lane Seminary, but he was pleased with what he saw in Cincinnati, including the inevitable ordeal that lay ahead, should he remove to the West. Conceiving a war against "deep-laid conspiracy" and errors of "genuine scarlet dye,"[11] Lyman instantly recognized the struggle to outflank Rome and other unchristian enemies as his kind of conflict—a contest to take the western prize for the Lord. Tender enough about contending with fellow ministers, he was keen for strife with the unquestioned enemies of truth.[12] When circumstances forced choices between brothers, therefore, Lyman temporized, and, consequently, endeavoring to keep the peace among squabbling theologians, sometimes hastened and exacerbated catastrophe he strove to forestall. But he flourished on combat with the Philistines, and as the western encounter, as he saw it, was to be 'twixt angels and demons, Beecher would be "perfectly fearless," and quick to deliver "a hard blow" with tranquil conscience.[13] Valor in this place would have to wrestle with Satanic powers. Lyman was ready.

Catherine also was enthusiastic. As for the land, she said that she had never seen a place "so capable of being rendered a Paradise." Natives assured her that people had to leave the hilltops if ever they meant to "be sick and die." Almost she believed them.[14] More significantly, Catherine, discerning what was at stake, knew how her father would decide, and stood ready to support his choice. A paladin as well as a prophetess in this instance, she was prepared for struggle and confident of victory.

The location of Lane Seminary was high on a hill, out of sight, but not beyond knowledge, of the river. From this point it was possible to pass "through the fields," along the "top of a ridge," and reach an "old & lofty bluff," from which one could see "the city, spread out . . . like a map," with the river marking the boundary between "the hills, & the opposite shores of Kentucky, varied, bold and cultivated."[15]

The turgid waters of the Ohio, however, separated more than Kentucky and the hills. Here was the boundary between slave state and free. Already events were moving toward the tragedy of war, inexorably as river currents to the sea. And as waters in flood time overflow their banks and destroy ancient landmarks, so rising sentiment was shattering old structures in Cincinnati where free blacks congregated in numbers, and where runaway slaves from Kentucky found sanctuary, if they were lucky. But the old barriers that were dissolving had not yet disappeared; and the new patterns, though emerging, were not yet firm. Thus it came about that Lyman, often sensitive to the tide of the future, did not comprehend all that he saw, and came trumpeting salvation of sinners, acting on the assumption that no urgency superseded that to save souls. The fact is that Lyman regarded Catholicism as a prime target in the West, at a time when politics and geography made abolition an inescapable focus of concern. Moreover, a moderate attitude toward slavery was difficult, if indeed possible. For many the question was not whether the nation could survive, but whether Christianity could bear social application. Lyman, preoccupied with evangelism, took inaccurate measure of student intensity over the plight of the blacks. Consequently, seminarians passed astigmatic judgment on a president who seemed unmoved by their passion. Meanwhile, ecclesiastical watchdogs, suspecting Lyman's orthodoxy, awaited occasion and opportunity to strike him down.

For Lyman, the obvious and necessary service to the West was the training of young ministers to win the territory. Reform would surely follow revival, but revival must precede reform. The immediate and practical obligation was to transform plans and prayers into the live students and solid bricks of a seminary. Believing he could do this, Lyman returned to Boston, announced his decision, and brought his family West. It came about, though, that Lyman, once he was there, found himself beset on two fronts—slavery and orthodoxy—when he had volunteered for another. Rome did not prove so formidable an enemy as he had feared. Moreover, Cincinnati did not lionize him, nor students listen. The guardians of faith only bided their time. But although the promised paradise never materialized, the hope that it would did not fade at once.

Lane Seminary had "originated with two Baptist brothers" from the State of Maine who migrated and became "Merchants of New Orleans," but were, in October of 1828, at Cincinnati, searching for a project in which to invest "surplus funds . . . to promote the interests of the Redeemer's King-

dom."[16]   Generously abandoning a plan to underwrite a
theological school for their own sect at the West, Ebenezer
and William A. Lane, when they learned that "preliminary
steps" had been taken in another direction,[17] donated the
sum of four thousand dollars (substantial for the times)
"toward the establishment of a Presbyterian Seminary." As
modest as he was obliging, Ebenezer, uneasy in the intelligence that the bill of incorporation was to designate the
school as "The Lane Seminary," wrote, firmly expressing for
himself and for his brother as well, "aversion to any honor of
a worldly nature." Unsuccessfully, he urged the Trustees to
change the name to "some other more appropriate."[18]

American shrewdness periodically manifests itself in the
attempt to circumvent taxes and perdition at a single stroke,
and to buy immortality in the bargain. Men who have fleeced
their neighbors have, now and again, returned a portion of
the booty as endowed institutions—schools, museums,
orphanages—reasoning, no doubt, that for the gift's sake,
heaven will forgive and the world forget all former offense.
And, indeed, it often happens in just this way. Theological
seminaries are not entirely free from such heritage, for the
names of enemies of the people have sometimes been graven
over their doorways as sponsors of the kingdom. But it is
erroneous and unjust to suggest that all or even most schools
dedicated to the training of ministers came thus to life. In the
early nineteenth century there were, as there are now, men
who though not free from a touch of spiritual arrogance were
of honest commitment to lofty goals. The brothers Lane
appear to have been such. The skimpy details that are available point to their unaffected goodness, indicating, as the
Cincinnati Journal declared, that they were "actuated by the
pure principles of benevolence."[19]

Land for the western seminary was given by the Kemper
family, long advocates of both education and religion. The
Rev. James Kemper, Presbyterian, had begun his ministry in
Cincinnati in 1791, and shortly, with his family of ten
children, took up residence in what was then an entire
wilderness, to which he gave the name Walnut Hills.[20]
Assisted by his sons, he made the first footpath between that

place and the town of Cincinnati. Later his children bought acreage adjoining their father's, and the family became large landowners in a desirable area.

Hobbled by inadequate schooling, James Kemper had for some years yearned to spare others similar disadvantage,[21] by founding, preferably nearby, a theological seminary for godly, though indigent, youth. "As early as 1825, the General Assembly of the Presbyterian Church," considering the rapid increase of population in the Mississippi valley, "declared it expedient to establish a Western Theological Seminary," and, undaunted by the incongruity of Calvinists presuming to structure anything without flaw, appointed a committee, Gen. Andrew Jackson, chairman, to "perfect a plan," and determine a "suitable location."[22] Father Kemper, a commissioner, pleaded the cause of Walnut Hills in the 1826 Assembly, but that body, although by a narrow choice, rejected his proposed site. Even so, Kemper, and others with him, continued to long for a school close at hand.[23] When he learned, therefore, that the Lane brothers had resolved to give money to "educate pious young men for the gospel ministry,"[24] he and his household gladly deeded to the Seminary first sixty acres (north of Elnathan Kemper's farm and east of Montgomery Road),[25] and thereafter an additional fifty acres (south).[26]

The gift of Kemper land and Lane money was originally conditioned upon the Trustees' pledge to make the Seminary a manual labor institution.[27] The attempt to vitalize academic life by systematic doses of physical industry (an experiment begun by M. de Fellenberg at Hofwyl, Switzerland[28]) was introduced to America at the Oneida Institute, in Whitesboro, New York. It was immediately popular, highly regarded by a democratic constituency committed to the right of the indigent to education, and reassuring to the residual puritan disposition that continued to doubt the validity of any virtue apart from hard work.[29] Moreover, resourceful Yankee minds recognized a sound compact in the arrangement.

Lyman's decision to remove to the West had not turned upon the proposal of self-help for students, but the cause of manual labor was one he would have accounted for righteousness in weighing the prospects of Lane. Strangely diverse and often at serious odds theologically, the Beechers exhibited an almost uniform and surely adamant affinity for confusing hardihood with orthodoxy. None of them manifested the penchant more than Lyman, who confessed himself unable to last in his work as much as a week without the daily hours of exercise in his "wood house & in jimnastics," and, of course, the endless walks.[30] So forsworn was Lyman against lassitude that he continued well into maturity to spend himself with the sand in his cellar, or, whenever it was possible, to saw and stack great piles of wood.[31] Such rituals were quasi-devotional for the man who grappled with garden stumps in order to sharpen his theological perceptions.[32] Never so deep in letters that he failed to hear the whirring of birds' wings, Beecher used to rush from his study with a loaded gun and attack the waves of pigeons that plagued the Cincinnati manse. The best spectacles, he said, let one look through the uppers to shoot birds, and see through the lowers to write metaphysics.[33] Generally unable to hold the other Beechers to his own orthodoxy, Lyman was more than successful at enlisting his children into the ranks of Christian athletes.

As a college student, Charles Beecher wrote a poem judged "heathenish" and unworthy of "Dr. Beecher's son," because the infidel hero of it killed his father and himself; but in the very letter that boasted of his liberation, the rebel Charles reported with serious enthusiasm that for exercise he had in his room a "slack rope" he could "put up or take down," and on which, of course, he regularly practiced.[34] Catherine urged calisthenics for the curricula of female academies, and Harriet, frail and miserable, dutifully shivered in the icy baths of the Brattleboro water cure—all, in part, through dedication to Papa's ideal of soul and body developing together. Once the idea was introduced, it seemed in every way right to Lyman that fledgling ministers should witness and strengthen their faith through physical labor. What better or more natural place of beginning than a farm? There was one at Lane from the start.

Students planted and harvested and thus supplied the table while they earned their keep. Soon the orchard boasted apples of variety and excellence: Winter Red, London Pippin, and Smith's Cider.[35] The Trustees, heady with early success, made provision for "additional and various forms of mechanical employment. . . . A part of the students were organized as a printing association; and another portion as a company for the manufacture of furniture" and brooms.[36]

For certain isolated students the arrangement was successful. Some earned "the whole of their annual expenses,"[37] which, in those years, were $70. For the most part, however, the plan failed. The Lane administrators were reluctant to admit that the scheme would not work, when "Cincinnati, the commercial emporium of the West," offered market for anything "raised on the farm or made in the mechanic shop."[38] Their numerous resolutions concerning stewards and superintendents, keeping of accounts, and such matters as "the purchase of tools" and the "sale of milch-cows" attest the stubborn conviction of the Trustees, who did not give in "until it became too evident that the students, if they were not eating their own heads off, were devouring the institution, leaf and stalk."[39]

Envisioned as a permanent arrangement, there was also in the first days of the Lane dream a preparatory school, grandly designated the Literary Department, an ill-advised experiment begun on November 18, 1829.[40] Five years later, at the request of both "faculty and the committee," it was "brought to a close."[41] Difficulty with labor and curriculum, however, was relatively minor. There lay in Lane's future an ordeal indicative of that metamorphosis of religion in America which became recognizable in the nineteenth century and was more nearly an altered essence than a changed appearance. The clash underscored the distance serparating what custodians of churchly traditions thought religion should be, and what zealots were determined to make it. The distress was beyond the clairvoyance of Lane's founders and patrons in the halcyon autumn of 1832, when Lyman was on his way to Ohio, and all was hope in his heart and in theirs, or even in the following spring, although by that time the signs of the storm were already visible. In March of 1833, James Kemper confided to his diary, "All is well that ends well. After long labor and much expense, I have a Literary and Theological Seminary at my door."[42] The matter was not so simple as the satisfied comment suggests. History must take account of circumstances Kemper ignored.

Shortly there appeared in the community, if not indeed at Kemper's door, one Theodore Weld, a relentless prophet of anti-slavery who combined "moveless severity" with "deep wild gloom."[43] Familiar to Cincinnatians as a spellbinding orator, Weld, who had visited the Queen City more than once, had returned to cast his lot permanently with Lane, careful all the while to show himself as a partisan of the enslaved blacks.

Weld, thoroughly accustomed to the activism that keepers of their brothers must discharge, was modestly insistent on anonymity. Only twenty-eight, he had already been unsuccessfully sought as secretary for the American Society for Promoting the Observance of the Seventh Commandment, [44] and had been pressed (though against his will) into the post of general agent for the Society for Promoting Manual Labor in Literary Institutions.[45] He was known, too, as a mighty man for temperance. Tireless in self-immolating zeal, he was, when he enrolled at Lane, totally committed to the cause of abolition, a passion that by that time dominated him above all else and continued to do so until emancipation was accomplished.

Weld first came to the Seminary at a period when the school would have been better off with less land and more money, for at that time the institution "existed only in name—without professors, without students, without funds or buildings," and the prospect was "dark enough to stagger the strongest faith."[46] Curiously, it was in large part because of the dismal face of the future that Theodore had been won for Lane.

Confronted with the possibility of giving up the land and abandoning the enterprise, F. Y. Vail, a member of the despondent board of Lane, volunteered to seek Eastern support, and set out to do so. Naturally enough, while he was in

New York City, he called upon that wealthy, generous, and pious silk merchant, Mr. Arthur Tappan, for, after all, it "was owing to him chiefly that the appointment [of Dr. Beecher as president] took place."[47] Together with his brother, Lewis, Arthur had directed Vail to Theodore Weld, who was, at the very season, searching for a suitable site to establish a Manual Labor School where virile Christianity could come into its own.[48] As quick as the Tappan brothers to recognize in Weld a natural leader for men without Moses, Vail urged him to consider locating among the "rising millions of the West," where he might build a "national, model institution."[49] "We only need to have your plan and efforts identified with our own," Vail pleaded, in order to attract "the influence of New York."[50] Weld was convinced.

No one was happier for the prospect of a Beecher-Weld association than Arthur Tappan. Such a company was security that invited support of Lane as wise investment in the kingdom; and indeed the venture earned early dividends. Knowledge that students in growing numbers looked favorably toward Lane was presently enlivened by the intelligence that a significant group from the Oneida Institute had chosen the new seminary for their theological education. Always generous, and now more confident, Tappan "encouraged the trustees in the enterprise, and held out to them the expectations of liberal pecuniary aid."[51] Returns might well be tenfold.

Tappan had provided more than an arena where soldiers of Christ could wrestle with enemies of the faith; he had unwittingly guaranteed a field of battle where strife would divide saints over the Christian's role in a slave society. When Lane finally opened her doors Arthur Tappan was an enlisted abolitionist, but he had not always been. The history of how he came to be such makes plain why, in the inevitable disagreement between Lyman and Theodore Weld, Tappan left the president to strive alone.

Arthur Tappan was originally one of the "warmest friends" of colonization, for he believed the movement would be an effective force to Christianize Africa. Disillusion began with his discovery of the brisk trade in "ardent spirits, tobacco, powder and balls" that flourished between Liberian colonists and their American sponsors. Driven to question whether "this splendid scheme of benevolence was not a device of Satan, to rivet still closer the fetters of the slaves," Tappan reached a grave conclusion about colonization that he published with customary forthrightness: "I now believe," he wrote, "that it had its origin in the single motive to get rid of the free colored people, that the slaves may be held in greater safety."[52] Characteristically, he moved at once toward the formation of a national Anti-slavery Society, a goal accomplished on December 4, 1833. The transition, begun after Tappan's first endorsement of Beecher, crystallized well before Theodore Weld arrived in Cincinnati as a student. Arthur Tappan's new position, identical with Weld's, was intrinsically hostile to the program of the colonizationists, whose endeavors Beecher regarded as tolerable both to abolition and to Christianity. Thus, guileless though he was, the philanthropist had effectively set the circumstances that brought Weld and Beecher into a proximity that—for all their forbearance and charity—precluded coëxistence within the narrow confines of Lane Theological Seminary.

Lane actually began operation as a theological seminary in December of 1832, when Lyman was inducted as president.[53] Before that time, staff was slight and housing meager. "During the summer of 1830" a building afterward known as the Boarding Hall had been "completed and brought into service."[54] But on the very eve of Beecher's arrival another structure "one hundred feet long, and four stories high" with "single rooms for upwards of one hundred students,"[55] had "not a rafter nor a shingle," only "naked walls."[56]

For that matter, Lyman and his family were in little better state for living accommodations than were the students. Temporarily, they resided in the "most inconvenient, ill-arranged, good-for-nothing, and altogether to be execrated affair that ever was put together ... built without a thought of a winter season," by a landlord who probably "acted up to the light he had, though he left little enough of it for his tenants."[57]

Lack of comfort, however—to say nothing of lack of elegance—never daunted so oak-hearted a prophet as Lyman, and even less the Spartan students who were fast gathering in Cincinnati. More than one of them came down from the Oneida Institute, bringing respect for asceticism and practical experience in austerity.[58] Two candidates for the ministry, "wishing to preserve their invaluable manual labor habits," instead of taking the stage "to Cincinnati, traveled to the head of the Alleghany" river, "hired themselves out on a raft, and besides performing an important missionary service amongst their new associates, earned $20 each to aid them in their future efforts for self-support."[59]

Records of Lane students singing and roasting oysters in the evening, or eating great slabs of pie with their knives, because it "would have been hard on the fork,"[60] are authentic, but atypical. They tell of the students who came to Lane after the first wave of the self-appointed avengers of the Lord descended upon Cincinnati, or of those who remained after the passionate vanguard had departed to another theater of war. The original students, some of whom in a sense of greatest urgency were already on location awaiting the arrival of faculty and president while Lyman was still in Boston, were both dedicated and sturdy. They dispensed "with tea and coffee and all articles of luxury," pledging themselves to "live on principles of Christian simplicity and economy."[61] They were citizens of eternity and, pending permanent residence in the New Jerusalem, sojourners only perforce in Vanity Fair. Nevertheless, they endeavored to narrow the gap between the world they lived in and the world they loved.

They renounced the "buckram refinement" and "dandy airs . . . affected by clowns who set up as gentlemen,"[62] and condemned women who hung "Gold and precious stones" about their "ears and bosoms," and crowned the whole with ostrich feathers.[63] Whatever else such censure reveals, there is a plain indication of raging spirits. It was at about this time that George Hastings, writing of a soirée attended by Lane men, reported that the affair went "swimmingly, considering how horribly stupid a parcel of Theol. Students can make a party."[64] He was quite wrong, of course, for Beecher's boys, though deadly serious, were anything but dull. Adroit in stimulating energies for bringing in a kingdom, and contemptuous of sloth or any weakness, they typically dismissed one spiritual laggard with the judgment that it would be appropriate for him to return home and use his time to "crack nuts and kill raccoons."[65] But orthodoxy was not unalloyed at Walnut Hills. There was the student who professed himself an agnostic, although it is just possible that he succumbed to the swiftness of the race. His "desperate rush into infidelity" appeared to the faithful as an attempt to "paralyze his conscience."[66] For the most part, though, students were durable: as they had not come by default, they dissipated neither time nor energy. Others they judged even more severely than they judged themselves. Having left Oneida because (among other reasons) they disapproved the character of at least some of the faculty, certain of the zealots who converged upon Lane demanded professors who were "obligated to teach or starve,"[67] thinking thus to guard against any compromise of rigid standards. (An instructor at Whitesboro had been so profligate as to lie "abed in the morning," and before walking slowly to class, to brace himself, not with soul-strengthening exercise, but with tea or coffee.[68]) Alerted to the possibility of appointment to the faculty of one whom they considered undesirable, the students said flatly that he would "never cross the threshold" as an instructor, and moved effectively to see that he did not.[69]

Few and intense were the passions of the prophet band. They loved God and hated the devil, which, for them, meant that they abominated soft living, strong drink, infidelity, and, in due course, slavery—above all, slavery.[70] Understandably, they accepted Theodore Weld as a patron saint.

Weld, son of a parsonage, and advocate of genteel religion, came to ardent faith through the violent agency of Charles Grandison Finney, the lawyer turned revivalist with such reckless disregard for conventions that he alarmed even Lyman Beecher. In a classic pattern, Weld's commitment followed a vituperative abuse of Finney that he could not sustain in face-to-face confrontation. A Mrs. Clark, Weld's aunt and Finney's great friend, tricked Theodore into coming to hear Finney preach. The revivalist, advised by the well-intentioned woman, delivered a scathing, personal attack against the young man, holding Weld "up on his toasting-fork" for more than an hour. Weld repaid him in compounded coin before an astonished audience at the corner store. And then, contrite, he sought out Finney in order to apologize. When the two men met, the tension resolved in deeply acknowledged kinship. They fell first into each other's arms, and then together sank to their knees, "sobbing and praying, . . . sobbing and praying."[71] The fire thus kindled within Theodore Weld burned fiercely for many years. Fused with anti-slavery zeal, it became the ruling passion not alone for him, but also for those drawn to follow Weld with such fervor that his spirit became their spirit, and his God their God. Of such adamantine and lustrous ardor were the former Oneida Institute students who moved toward Lane in the late spring and summer of 1832. For his part, Weld recognized his influence over them, and accepted it as providential.

Theodore Weld, the darling of the rebels, traveled to Cincinnati as deck passenger on a river boat, which meant that he paid nothing, but was obliged to "find [himself] . . . sleep on deck, and help 'wood.' "[72] He had recently spent time in New York with the Tappan brothers and others prominent in anti-slavery movements, and he was now convinced of the strategic significance of the West in the irrepressible conflict.

> I knew of a number who were coming from the Southern States to Lane [he wrote] besides many of the Oneida Institute boys. . . . When I went through the West and South, and saw the situation at Lane Seminary, I was satisfied that was the place for us. I developed . . . my views on slavery, and my intention to improve the excellent opportunity to introduce anti-slavery sentiments, and have the whole subject thoroughly discussed.[73]

Lyman, though unaware of plain omens that augured a troubled future, never doubted Weld's significance: "In the estimation of the class," he said, Weld "was president. He took the lead of the whole institution. The young

men . . . thought he was a god."[74] They did. His arrival to
enroll in Lane seemed to his devotees a clear answer to their
earlier cry, "Lord have mercy on the great West."[75] It did
not yet appear that they must choose between Lyman and
Theodore. To be sure, the trustees were, in the eyes of the
students, *"very fallible men,"*[76] but Lyman, initially, they
approved as one not "merely coming to do the drudgery and
eat the bread," but ready to "throw his body and soul" into
the cause.[77]

Notes to Chapter X

1. Timothy Flint, *Recollections of the Last Ten Years, Passed in
Occasional Residences and Journeyings in the Valley of the Mississippi
from Pittsburg and the Missouri to the Gulf of Mexico, and from
Florida to the Spanish Frontier; in a Series of Letters to the Rev. James
Flint, of Salem, Massachusetts* (Boston, 1826), p. 38.
2. Morris Birbeck, *Notes on a Journey in America* (London, 1818),
p. 70.
3. Timothy Flint, *Recollections*, p. 40.
4. Frances Trollope, *Domestic Manners of the Americans*, Donald
Smalley, ed. (New York, 1949), p. 69.
5. Everett Webber, *Escape to Utopia* (New York, 1959), p. 161.
6. "Oliver Oldschool," letter to the *Cincinnati Chronicle and Literary Gazette*, August 30, 1828.
7. Frances Wright, *Views of Society and Manners in America*, Paul
R. Baker, ed. (Cambridge, 1963), p. 113.
8. E. Venable, "Early Periodical Literature in the Ohio Valley," p.
15, quoted by Avis Baker, "Cincinnati as a Western Outpost of Boston
Liberalism," unpublished master's thesis (Chicago, 1914), p. 34.
9. ALS, Lyman Beecher, Boston, December 1, 1829, to Catherine,
Beecher-Stowe Collection, Schlesinger Library, Radcliffe College. A
part of this letter is published in the *Autobiography*, II, 157, but the
following significant sentence is omitted: "This you must not show to
any one for I only think on paper what I would not say but to you."
10. *Autobiography*, II, 266-267.
11. Review of Beecher's *Plea for the West* from the *New York
Observer*, reprinted in the *Cincinnati Journal*, July 3, 1835.
12. Calvin E. Stowe, "Sketches and Recollections," p. 228.
13. *Ibid.*
14. *Autobiography*, II, 267.

15. ALS, G. W. Perkins, Walnut Hills, August 17, 1838, to his wife, Beecher Collection, Stowe-Day Foundation.

16. *Cincinnati Journal,* September 8, 1829, notice in answer to a query "Where is Lane Seminary?"

17. John Vant Stephens, *The Founding of Lane Seminary* (Cincinnati, 1941), p. 5.

18. *Ibid.,* p. 6.

19. September 8, 1829.

20. MS, "Faculty Book," Lane Collection, Cincinnati Historical Society, p. 1.

21. John Vant Stephens, *Founding of Lane,* pp. 2-3.

22. E. D. Morris, *Leaves from the Early History of Lane,* in *Our Monthly* (Cincinnati and Philadelphia, January, 1870), p. 42. The paper was originally read at the fortieth anniversary of the founding of Lane Theological Seminary, celebrated in connection with the reunion of the Presbyterian Church, at Walnut Hills, November 26, 1869. See also E. H. Gillett, *History of the Presbyterian Church,* II, 351.

23. *Ibid.*

24. John Vant Stephens, *Founding of Lane,* p. 4.

25. E. D. Morris, *Leaves from Lane,* p. 42.

26. *Catalogue of the Officers and Students of Cincinnati Lane Seminary; together with a Brief View of its Present Condition, Advantages, and Prospects* (Cincinnati, 1832), pp. 12-15. See also John Vant Stephens, *Founding of Lane,* p. 5.

27. E. D. Morris, *Leaves from Lane,* p. 44.

28. *Cincinnati Journal,* December 15, 1829.

29. Benjamin P. Thomas, *Theodore Weld: Crusader for Freedom* (New Brunswick, New Jersey, 1950), p. 18. Thomas refers to manual labor programs in America that antedated that at Oneida: "At Andover Theological Seminary the trustees built a workshop to accommodate seventy-five students. Maine Wesleyan Seminary had a farm of 140 acres as well as a shop. Theological schools at Auburn, New York; Wilmington, Delaware; Maryville, Tennessee; and Danville, Kentucky, fell in with the plan, as did colleges such as Bowdoin, Waterville (now Colby) and Middlebury, and academies like the Woodbridge School at South Hadley, and Phillips at Andover. In all these schools, however, manual labor was optional; at Oneida it was compulsory." *Ibid.*

30. ALS, Lyman Beecher, Boston, February 3, 1827, to Catherine, Beecher-Stowe Collection, Schlesinger Library, Radcliffe College.

31. *Autobiography,* II, 113.

32. *Ibid.,* p. 306.

33. *Ibid.,* p. 516.

34. ALS, Charles Beecher, Bowdoin College, December 4, 1833, to Lyman, Beecher-Stowe Collection, Schlesinger Library, Radcliffe College.

35. Invoice for apple trees purchased for Lane in 1834, Lane Collection, McCormick Theological Seminary Library.

36. E. D. Morris, *Leaves from Lane*, p. 44.

37. *Cincinnati Journal*, January 6, 1832.

38. *Ibid.*, December 15, 1829.

39. E. D. Morris, *Leaves from Lane*, p. 45.

40. *Ibid.*, pp. 43, 45.

41. *Fifth Annual Report of the Trustees of the Cincinnati Lane Seminary* (Cincinnati, 1834), p. 7.

42. E. D. Morris, *Leaves from Lane*, p. 45.

43. Theodore Weld, [New York], March 1, 1838, to Angelina Grimké, Gilbert H. Barnes and Dwight Dumond, *Weld-Grimké Letters*, II, 577.

44. William Brown and D. Fanshaw, New York, March 17, 1834, to Theodore Weld, *ibid.*, I, 130. The society succeeded Arthur Tappan's American Magdalen Society, an organization dedicated to the rescue of prostitutes.

45. Benjamin P. Thomas, *Theodore Weld*, p. 26.

46. *Autobiography*, II, 240.

47. Lewis Tappan, *The Life of Arthur Tappan* (New York, 1870), p. 225.

48. *Autobiography*, II, 314.

49. *Ibid.*, pp. 320-321.

50. *Ibid.*

51. Lewis Tappan, *Arthur Tappan*, p. 225.

52. *Ibid.*, p. 129.

53. E. D. Morris, *Leaves from Lane*, p. 45.

54. *Ibid.*, p. 44.

55. *Catalogue* for 1832 *(supra)*, p. 15.

56. S. W. Streeter, [Cincinnati, August, 1832], to Theodore Weld, in Gilbert H. Barnes and Dwight Dumond, *Weld-Grimké Letters*, I, 83.

57. Charles Edward Stowe, *Life of Harriet Beecher Stowe*, p. 64.

58. Gilbert H. Barnes and Dwight Dumond, *Weld-Grimké Letters*, I, 17n.

59. *Third Annual Report of the Trustees of the Cincinnati Lane Seminary* (Cincinnati, 1833), p. 15.

60. A. T. Rankin, "Recollections of Lane," MS, Lane Collection of McCormick Seminary Library.

61. *Third Annual Report*, p. 9.

62. Charles G. Finney, July 21, 1831, to Theodore Weld, quoted in Benjamin P. Thomas, *Theodore Weld*, p. 24.

63. ALS, Willard Jones and Benjamin Burge, Cincinnati, February 23, 1837, to Peter Washburn, Lane Collection of the Cincinnati Historical Society.

64. ALS, George H. Hastings, Cincinnati, April 7-May 5, 1837, to Elizabeth C. Lyman, Beecher Collection, Connecticut State Library.

65. C. Waterbury, A. Duncan, and S. W. Streeter, [Cincinnati, December], 1832, to Theodore Weld, in Gilbert H. Barnes and Dwight Dumond, *Weld-Grimké Letters*, I, 93.

66. *Autobiography*, II, 317.

67. E. Weed, [Cincinnati], August 2, 1832, to Theodore Weld, in Gilbert H. Barnes and Dwight Dumond, *Weld-Grimké Letters*, I, 78-79.

68. S. W. Streeter, [Cincinnati], August 4, [1832], to Theodore Weld, *ibid.*, I, 82-83.

69. E. Weed, August 2, 1832, letter to Theodore Weld (*supra*).

70. *Autobiography*, II, 313.

71. *Ibid.*, p. 312.

72. *Ibid.*, p. 315.

73. *Ibid.*, p. 314.

74. *Ibid.*, p. 321.

75. Asa A. Stone, Whitesboro, [N.Y.], November 1, 1832, to Theodore Weld, in Gilbert H. Barnes and Dwight Dumond, *Weld-Grimké Letters*, I, 87.

76. E. Weed, August 2, 1832, letter to Theodore Weld (*supra*).

77. Calvin Waterbury, Cincinnati, August 3, 1832, to Theodore Weld, *ibid.*, I, 81.

Chapter XI
Rebels and Martyrs:
A Conflict Over Abolition — 1834-1835

The American Colonization Society, founded 1817, hoped to solve the problems of slavery through suppressing slave trade, assisting in the manumission of slaves, and, characteristically, deporting free blacks to Africa. Aided by local organizations, churches, and government agencies, the society transported 6,000 Negroes to Liberia between 1821 and 1867. Colonization was regarded both as an anti-slavery measure, and as a safeguard to slavery that removed troublesome free blacks from society. Abolitionist opposition to colonization became formidable after 1830, by which date antislavery activity (dormant since the invention of the cotton gin) began to enjoy new life. Abolitionists agitated for immediate emancipation gradually accomplished. Colonizationists called abolitionists unrealistic, and accused them of using words so as to confuse the public. Abolitionists indicted colonizationists with being anti-black. After 1835, with growing numbers of legislators who were abolitionists, slavery became a dominant political issue; and from 1850 to 1865, the history of abolition was the history of the nation.

Lane Theological Seminary, 1844 (Cincinnati Historical Society)

Life at Lane was "exuberant and glorious," wrote Lyman's son Charles, and immediately qualified his judgment with the telltale phrase, "while it lasted."[1] So much was true; for the storms that broke early over the school at Walnut Hills were not those that insure that the air will be washed and the winds stilled for a fine, tranquil summer: they promised a bleak winter of despair. Caught in the perverse tendency of events to cluster, Lyman suffered as loss displaced crisis, and ordeal swallowed up sorrow. Overlapping in time, and simultaneous in demand, were the forces of distress and grief that, coming to a head before Lyman's appearance at Lane, descended upon him almost as soon as he reached Ohio. Within scarcely more than a year, the seminary students (whom Lyman fondly called his boys and considered children) disowned and deserted him; fellow clergymen whom he felt to be his brothers brought him to trial for heresy; and his wife died. Bereavement Lyman could bear. He had already haggled with death more than once, and, though he had lost in the engagement, steadfastly refused to quit the struggle. As for theological disputation, it was an astringent for his depleted energy and divided mind. Besides, he generally won his doctrinal duels. The stroke for which he was unprepared was the rejection by the students.

On the fifteenth of October, 1834, twenty-eight of them asked to be dismissed. Eleven others followed suit the next day. Another resigned independently on the seventeenth.[2] The exodus continued until of the forty students originally in theology, only three remained, and but five of the sixty in the literary department from the preceding year. Eight prospective students forsook Cincinnati after talking with the dissidents.[3] Lyman was left in bleak isolation to preside over a near vacant seminary, and to consider how a debate over abolition had brought on such a disaster.

It was indeed slavery that had undone him, for, however the seminarians had arrived at Walnut Hills, it was as active abolitionists (and because they were) that they departed. Students argued that faculty and trustees denied them freedom of speech,[4] but their actions acknowledged a prior conflict with the establishment.

When Lane students, in passionate commitment to immediate emancipation, turned their backs upon Cincinnati and fled the restrictive environment of the seminary for the free air of Oberlin College, Lyman was as astonished as if a sheep had bitten him. Dr. Beecher was, of course, aware of the threatening shadow that slavery cast, not just over Ohio, but across the whole land. No one with eyes and ears, living in Cincinnati of the 1830's, could ignore the "uneasiness and bitterness" that were both cause and content of the "irrepressible conflict." Steamboats, their decks crowded with "chain gangs of slaves," moved constantly past the wharves, bearing their living cargo to be sold down the river.[5] Residents who avoided the water front, doubtless to shut out such shattering exposure to slavery, could read in local journals typical expressions of rumbling black sentiment that, while not ungrateful for what "had been done for colored children in Cincinnati," still insisted that "much more good might" and must be accomplished.[6] Fugitives from bondage, who were hunted or sheltered in Ohio, kept sympathy and hatred alive,[7] and Lane students, sitting in easy judgment, identified the president of the seminary with the enemies of abolition, and, by extension, of Negroes. The fact is, rather, that Lyman, certainly not hostile to blacks, was so obsessed with the proclamation of the kingdom that he proved oblivious (not indifferent) to the tragic implications of slavery. Moreover, his free, resilient spirit rendered him incapable of psychological projection into any situation of servitude. James Bradley, a Negro student at Lane who had "purchased his own body,"[8] was noticeably tender regarding status in Cincinnati, and, from either timidity or caution, declined to attend a soirée at the president's home. Beecher, when he learned of it, confessed that "if he had thought of his feeling so, he would have gone to him personally, and told him he *must* come."[9] Surely he would have, and no doubt the good doctor would have persuaded Bradley, for Beecher had a way with people, as effective with blacks as with any, when their paths crossed under circumstances that forced him to see them as souls. There was that occasion when Lyman had preached to two thousand Negroes at once, and at the time he "came down to them and upon them" in a way to make them clap their hands and cry "Amen! Amen!" and then "jump up etc.," in obvious rapport. "That's good," they had chanted. "That's preaching!"[10] The episode is authentic, but hardly typical. According to his son-in-law Calvin E. Stowe, Beecher, "without being conscious of it," retained "not a little of the old Connecticut prejudice about blacks," and never particularly gave his attention to matters of slavery, because "his mind had been wholly absorbed by other themes."[11] He simply did not, perhaps could not, understand. The unconsciously patronizing perspective from which he assessed the discord, when even he could no longer ignore the slavery-induced tensions at the school, is obliquely reflected in a visitor's comment regarding Lane's Negro cook. Cliché though it is, the word probably expressed popular sentiment there, and assuredly it was inoffensive to non-rebellious members of the seminary community. Of Julia Harrison, who distributed gratuitous exegesis along with ginger cake, a transient at Walnut Hills remarked, "her spirit was pure, and her life Christian," even though "her face was black."[12]

Through the effort of Theodore Weld, a born catalyst, the troubled community at Lane moved ineluctably toward confrontation over the matter of immediate emancipation. Dedicated, and brave to the point of daring, he was, nevertheless, not a foolhardy man, and operated with almost instinctive cunning. Vastly knowledgeable of the slave's plight, and as articulate as a Beecher, he began by introducing Lane students to the facts. Members of a small cell group who "sympathized together" in the "abhorrence of slavery selected each his man to instruct, convince and enlist in the cause." Thus, wrote Weld, "we carried one after another."[13] Meanwhile it was no secret that Weld openly cultivated intimacy with the blacks of the city. From his first appearance in Cincinnati he identified himself with Negroes.

> If I ate in the City [he recalled], it was at their Tables. If I slept
> in the City it was in their homes. If I attended parties, it was
> *theirs—weddings—theirs—Funerals—theirs—Religious   meetings—
> theirs—*Sabbath Schools—Bible classes—theirs. During the 18
> months that I spent at Lane Seminary *I did not attend Dr.
> Beecher's Church once.* Nor did I ever attend any other of the
> Presbyterian Churches in the City except brother Mahan's, and
> did not attend there more than half a dozen times. . . . The white
> Methodist I attended only once. . . . I was with the colored peo-
> ple in their meetings by day and by night.[14]

Cincinnatians took note of this association with the blacks,
although, in truth, Weld was sufficiently odd in appearance
to have commanded attention quite apart from any qualification as a fanatic. He looked a mess, seems to have known it,
and cared not a whit that it was so. Until his beard grew to
painfully irritating length (or unless his friends insisted), he
never bothered to shave. Nor was that the worst: "Now as to
my hair," he said, "I don't comb it once a year. Every
morning I put my head all over into cold water half a dozen
times, then frictionize it with the stiff hair brush after wiping
it dry and then let it straggle in all directions like the quills of
a porcupine."[15]

Yet Weld's attraction rested, finally, upon character, not
eccentricity. Under his numinous influence people acknowledged the uncommon ability, the incandescent passion, and,
above all, the integrity that called forth disciples, wherever
he went, whatever his cause. His procedure was both practical
and necessary. Conversions to the fight for emancipation had
to be accomplished with deliberation, and one by one. Abolition was by no means universally endorsed at Lane. To begin
with, most students were ill disposed to attack the peculiar
institution, and some, in the early days, actually owned
slaves. One had "come to seminary relying upon the hire of
his slaves to carry him through his theological course."[16] The
American Anti-Slavery Society had been but recently
formed. "Lundy and Garrison, like bulls rampant, were fret-
ting the Northern welkin with their roar," and Lane students,
never having doubted that slavery was *a* problem, had now
seriously to consider the possibility that it just might be *the*
problem. "I suppose," one of the rebels later recalled, "there

was a general consent in the institution that slavery was somehow wrong and to be got rid of," but there was not at first "a readiness to pronounce it a sin."[17] After Theodore Weld's blistering attack upon slavery, *sin* seemed a paltry word to describe so shameful a wickedness.

The setting for his public denunciation was a series of gatherings arranged at first for students of the seminary to engage their faculty members over questions of abolition and colonization. The encounters were termed *debates,* were widely reported as such, and have subsequently been thus described. More nearly they were extended sessions of discussion and inquiry among students, regarding the fact and theory of slavery in America. When it came Weld's time to speak, he "held the floor for eighteen hours. His speech was a thesaurus, giving the origin, history, effects, both upon the despot and the victim, of slavery."[18] Theoretically at least the contest was between the colonizationists, who worked to establish colonies in Africa for free Negroes, and abolitionists, who pressed for "gradual emancipation immediately begun."[19] What occurred was a "nine evenings' annihilative onset upon slavery, followed by a unanimous vote in favor of immediate emancipation. Nine evenings more devoted to the colonization scheme resulted in its rejection, with but a single vote in its favor."[20]

Eventually, and quite rightly, the followers of Weld were called rebels. Exposure to Weld's charisma focused their zeal narrowly upon slavery, and with great intensity; but they were not callow youngsters, susceptible to any wandering Lollard. They were in dead earnest about their vocation; and they were staggeringly confident. By the time that Lyman came to the seminary, most of the students had been preaching, or, as they said, "prophesying," in the "waste places about Cincinnati" for more than a year. Settled men (at least six of them were "heads of families"), some had already dedicated "themselves to foreign missions."[21] Their average age was twenty-seven. For many of them the seminary career was but a tedious necessity set between them and the fields they felt elected to harvest. Providentially they found in the case for abolition both opportunity and obligation to blast

the power of salvation into the city, without tarrying for any.
Inspired by Weld, the rebels grew impatient of anything short
of instant millennium. Their tolerance quickly fell below that
point at which they could brook paternalism, and paternalism was exactly what they observed in Lyman. Paternalism
and vacillation.

The outcome of the debates enormously reassured the
abolitionists, for they had achieved a stunning victory. "Eight
months ago," Theodore Weld wrote to Lewis Tappan, "there
was not a single immediate abolitionist" at Lane. Some of the
"most influential and intelligent" students were from slave
states. The colonization society was thriving then, "and aboli-
tionism was regarded as the climax of absurdity, fanaticism
and blood."[22] But having won by words, the frondeurs now
set about implementing their faith through works.

> I must tell you something more [Weld continued in his letter to
> Tappan]. We have formed a large and efficient organization for
> elevating the colored people in Cincinnati—have established a
> Lyceum among them, and lecture three or four evenings a week,
> on grammer [sic], geography, arithmetic, natural philosophy,
> etc. . . . and we are about establishing one or two more. We are
> also getting up a library for circulation. . . .

Two Lane students had withdrawn to commence a school for
the blacks, and "besides these" there were "three large Sabbath schools and Bible classes" and elaborate plans for a
"SELECT FEMALE SCHOOL" to serve Cincinnati Negroes.[23] Pointing out that more than three-fourths of the
almost three thousand blacks in the city were emancipated
slaves who had secured their own freedom, Weld concluded
that Cincinnati was "the best locality in the Union to act
upon slavery by a spectacle of free black cultivation."[24]

Prosecuting such activity, however, carried with it the
occupational hazard of appearing to encourage and participate in the practice currently described as "amalgamation."
Dr. Beecher endeavored to caution the missionaries regarding
their idea of "social intercourse according to character, irre-
spective of color," a principle, as Beecher's son Charles
pointed out, "as dangerous as it is just." Knowing how the

city would react to the inevitable accusation, Lyman "con-
versed with Weld repeatedly." "Said I," he recalled, "you
[will] . . . defeat your own object. . . . If you want to teach
colored schools, I can fill your pockets with money; but if
you visit in colored families, and walk with them in the
streets, you will be overwhelmed."[25] Lyman might as well
have spoken to the wind. Just as he feared, Cincinnatians
were alarmed by what they saw, and angered by what they
imagined. "The most influential citizens openly talked of
sending up an organized mob to demolish the buildings, and
drive Faculty and students from the ground. The Faculty
took the alarm, called the students together" and warned
them "that they were now too far in advance of public
sentiment."[26] Gossip about the Lane students was "extensive in the city," and "reports multiplied."[27] There were,
among other rumors, tales that one student had spent the
night in the home of a Negro family; that a member of the
seminary community boarded with another; that students
walked brazenly in public with Negro women; and that
seminarians left their cards "for colored girls."[28] Students
who in the debate had repeated with more sincerity than
documentation the gruesome episodes that had occurred
"down river," or "in the tidewater," or "out west,"[29] were
shocked to discover themselves now the victims of excited
imaginations. Then and later they denied all charges techni-
cally and the more sensational of them categorically: "[I]f
any member of the Seminary had, at any time, walked with a
colored young lady either in the city or out of it, no one of
us had any knowledge of it."[30]

By the time that Beecher's prediction came true, however,
the seer was out of the city—traveling in the East seeking
endowment, and attending anniversaries. Ironically, it was on
this trip that he had assured Lewis Tappan "in express
words" that he would "insist on the recognition of free
discussion" among the students.[31] Never consciously
threatened by the prospect of encounter, Beecher had at first
promised to participate in the debates himself.[32] He changed
his mind and sent Catherine as his representative only under
the cautionary counsel of others. With an eye to the prosper-

ity of the seminary and the circumstances that seemed to affect endowment, he was quite willing to forego an evening's forum for the sake of strengthening the foundation. Had he followed his inclination, he would have been prominently there, no doubt remembering how masterfully President Timothy Dwight had bested students at Yale, and probably imagining that he could play some such splendid role at Lane. Alas, he sadly misjudged both the fervor of the students and the reaction of his sponsors. In his absence, nervous trustees, at first apprehensive, and then thoroughly alarmed, reached the mad decision to forbid further discussion by the students. They could hardly have been more ill-advised with respect to the strategy they employed, for the time for effective action was already past, if, indeed, it had ever existed.

In special session on August 20, while Lyman was away from Cincinnati, the executive board passed some amazing resolutions that proved them as ignorant of human nature as they were desperate for peace. What they in effect attempted was to guarantee that Lane would stand aloof from the slavery controversy. They announced that the chief duty of students was academic and that it was therefore improper for them to become involved in extraneous causes, especially those "upon which able men, and pious Christians differ." [33] Such folly, the board members held, would "unsettle the judgment, and unfit the mind for genial and useful intercourse with mankind," and inundate the community with "a heated torrent of unextinguishable rancor."[34] The committee called for the dissolution of the anti-slavery society (and for that matter of the colonization society as well), pointing out along the way that students had organized without faculty permission. But most startling of all (and most inflaming to the students), they obtested legislation to prohibit abolitionists from "delivering public addresses or lectures" at the seminary or elsewhere, or making "public statements . . . when assembled at their meals, or on ordinary occasions, without approbation of the faculty." Moreover, the committee members besought the trustees to establish control of the students' coming and going from the seminary, to regulate their participation in any effort that would "excite party animosities, stir up evil passions among themselves or in community, or involve themselves with the political concerns of the country."[35] And—in conclusion—to enforce the foregoing, they asserted the right of the trustees to dismiss any students who failed to comply with these regulations. Although such Draconian legislation would simply have made explicit what disciples of gloom had already demanded as the only dike against the madness at Lane, those who sat with the executive board made it plain that they were only asking for, not enacting, the laws. Even so, it did not help that they published what they had resolved. Three months earlier, Weld had charged the press with attacking the students. He accused James Hall, editor of the *Western Monthly,* of misrepresenting student activity in the Lane debates, and reproached him for seeking to "muzzle discussion upon the subject of slavery." At that time Weld had proclaimed in sentiment less alloyed than his metaphor, that it was too late to "stop the stars," or "puff out the sun," because the nation was already "shaking off its slumbers to sleep no more."[36] Now the anti-slavery press pounced upon the matter and cried that the Lane administrators would restrain free speech.[37]

In the crisis at the seminary, currents of prejudice and principle swirled about two distinct yet inseparable issues: the choice of abolition or colonization as *the* Christian solution to slavery; and the extent to which students might freely speak and assemble. As matters stood in the summer of 1834, generally, the students—egalitarian, outspoken—were set against the faculty and administration—conservative, proprietary. As it became manifest during the long, sweltering days that all in the Lane community would have to choose sides, Beecher was increasingly suspect in the eyes of the abolitionists. Charles Stuart, Weld's mentor and a powerful advocate of emancipation, heard "with pain" of Lyman's "detestable" sympathy for the colonizationists, and labeled it "one of those hallucinations to which the greatest minds are as liable as," he added waspishly, "the feeblest."[38]

As for the Christian's proper posture, Lyman denied any legitimate conflict "between the Colonizationists and the Abolitionists. I am myself both," he confessed, "without perceiving . . . any inconsistency."[39] Naive or expedient, the stance was not one forced upon Lyman by immediate exigency. Months before the debates he had declared that a final decision between abolition and colonization was "not essential to the successful efforts of each in behalf of the slave." [40] What difficulty there was arose from a "headlong, reckless purpose . . . and an affected, childish pity." Consequently, duty and reason called for the union of factions, since both worked for one purpose—the liberation of Negroes, which, though an admirable goal, was no end in itself, but finally "connected with the emancipation of all," not only from slavery, but from "religious and political delusion, from ignorance, degradation, vice, immorality and debasement." It was all part of "that grand achievement by which, the whole family is to be carried forward to the acme of perfection," affecting "millions born and unborn, and their eternal salvation in the life to come."[41] The upsurge Lyman often attained by such lofty wingbeats as these did not bear him to so high an altitude that the world and its problems were lost to his sight. More precisely, it was just because of his expansive view that Lyman could honestly regard a fragment of history (or any disturbance within it) as paltry when measured by the splendid vision of millennium. In the present instance he judged compromise neither an embarrassment to God nor a reproach to man.

Such spiritual blindness (and abolitionists could regard Lyman's attitude as nothing less) shocked Weld's disciples. They were now ready to conclude that any who walked in the company of colonizationists stood more likely on cloven hoof than on feet of clay. Even so, they waited with studied patience for Beecher's return. Asa Mahan, pastor of the Sixth Presbyterian Church in Cincinnati, and the one member of the board decidedly in sympathy with the rebels, wrote frantically to Beecher, "informing him of . . . the peril of the Seminary," and urging him "to hasten home and prevent the dismantling of the Institution."[42] But Beecher did not hurry home, at least not for a while. More like Jonah fleeing to Tarshish than St. Paul pressing toward Macedonia, he stopped at Columbus and "from thence turning north" (rather than west) spent "about two weeks in the town of Granville," [43] action Beecher justified somewhat casually to Theodore Weld, who, as it developed, had also written the absent president. "I did not hasten home on the receipt of your letter," the president explained, "because I could not do but one work at a time; and I did not answer it because, being absent and unacquainted with the necessary facts, I could say nothing without jumping in the dark." [44] More concerned than he sounded, Lyman was obviously irritated, and regarded the turbulence as an unnecessary tempest which could have been avoided with a modicum of intelligence and consideration. "Every mind is a sieve and every mouth a trumpet and every pen a telegraph," he complained. [45] Though not at this time laying the blame on Weld (as he later did), Lyman reminded Weld that it was a breach of etiquette and a betrayal of confidence that things said in the sanctity of the Beecher home had been "telegraphed and blazoned on from pillar to post to Cincinnati." [46] Nevertheless, Lyman insisted that the Lane rebels were a "set of glorious good fellows," whom he "would not at a venture exchange for any others." [47] He begged them to be patient until his return: "[P]ray much, say little, be humble and wait." [48] The Trustees might have been wise to follow the same counsel, but they did not, and, in the absence of the president, proceeded formally to enact the proposed and hated laws. Lyman, returned, discovered a situation "gone too far to afford much prospect of a change." Years later, Beecher reconstructed the affair as mischief past redemption. "I found all in a flurry," he recalled. "If I had arrived a little sooner I should have saved them; but it was too late." [49]

Certainly grace was in short supply by the time Lyman appeared. Yet whenever Beecher had come, his laissez-faire attitude toward slavery would have enraged the students, and his insistence upon faculty regulation of free discussions would have seemed insufferable. His position differed little from that of the other faculty members (save for Morgan [50]) or from that of the trustees (save for Mahan), and students rejected it, more bitterly disappointed because earlier they had loved Beecher deeply.

When it became apparent that the legislation would stand, the students cried tyranny. Huntingdon Lyman, one of the revolutionists waiting out the summer in Cincinnati, wrote to James A. Thome, another firebrand, and told him of the final decision. "Who that has an opinion and a soul will enter L. Sem now?" he wailed. "Who can do it without degrading himself?"[51] What he actually asked, of course, was whether anyone with soul, already there, could long remain. The rebels made swift and characteristic answer.

On the opening day of the fall term, students assembled in the chapel, "sent a committee . . . to the Faculty, with a request that some of the latter should . . . expound . . . the new code of laws which had just been enacted. This was done." Members of the faculty committee were Beecher (now discredited in student eyes), Stowe (also suspect as a turncoat), and Biggs (unpopular even before the debates).[52] "Then another committee was sent to inquire whether the students would be permitted to discuss among themselves the character of the new code." They were told that the only question for a student at Lane regarding the regulations was whether he would "acquiesce . . . and act loyally under them." Persistent, the students sent yet another committee and asked if they might "discuss among themselves the propriety of their continuing in the Seminary while subject to such laws." On learning the prompt denial of this request,

one of the leading students now arose, and remarked, that one privilege remained to them, namely, to say, by rising to their feet, whether they would, or would not, continue members of the Institution under existing circumstances. For himself, he would say, that the most solemn convictions of duty to his God, his conscience, his country, and the race, constrained him to say, that he could not longer continue a student of Lane Seminary. He should, therefore, ask of the Faculty an honourable dismission; and he would request every student present, who was of the same mind and determination with himself, to signify the same by rising and standing upon his feet. The mass of the students promptly arose; a very small minority, among whom was a son of Dr. Beecher, looking on with consternation. Each of the seceding students asked and received of the Faculty an honourable dismission, and "went out, not knowing whither he went."[53]

Five miles from the seminary the refugees found shelter in "a deserted brick tavern."[54] A friend provided fuel, and the ever generous Arthur Tappan, when he heard of the exodus, sent them money for "hiring a building . . . buying . . . books [and] . . . paying for their board."[55] Estranged from Lane, but still pledged to the ministry, the rebels determined to found their own theological school. Thus, Cincinnati boasted two "Lane" seminaries: "one at Cummingsville, full of students" but lacking endowment and faculty, and one at Walnut Hills, with everything a school could ask except students.[56] Unwilling to admit defeat, Beecher persuaded the Trustees to revise the hated laws, and then searched out "the most discreet and sober" of the rebels, and appealed to them. He told them how sad Lane was for the rift, and said that they, too, were "apt to be sad." The dream could still be recaptured, if all might give but a little. It was of no use. Some of the students "worked like beavers" to effect reconciliation, but, in the end, admitted that "they could not do it."[57] Beecher returned to the empty halls at Lane. The rebels continued at Cummingsville, and it was there that John Jay Shipherd, agent for the tottering, debt-ridden Oberlin Collegiate Institute, found them.

Shipherd seized the opportunity of "linking men & money" and pressed the choice of Oberlin upon the pilgrims. Still heady with the wine of victory, the agreeable rebels dictated their own terms: Asa Mahan must be president; John Morgan, their advocate on the Lane faculty, must come to teach; and Charles Finney, the revivalist who had plucked many of these brands from the burning, must be invited as professor of theology. Moreover, they must be guaranteed freedom of speech; and Negro students must be admitted to the school. (Ironically, the last condition threw "Officers, Students & Colonists" into "General panic & despair," for they feared an influx of "hundreds of Negroes."[58] Some of the women at Oberlin vowed to "wade Lake Erie"[59] if necessary to escape an institution that would house colored men.) Yet though by the narrowest of margins, even this demand was met, and Lane's avengers became the angels of Oberlin.[60]

Publication and counterpublication by all concerned had stated and restated the facts and alleged facts to the point of unspeakable tedium. The rebels had protested that they left not because administration claimed "the right to exercise a supervision," not for difference of opinion regarding slavery, but because by imposing "their own arbitrary wills" upon the students, trustees and faculty left them no other choice. [61] Faculty likewise disavowed any relation between official action and disagreement with students. Rather they deplored "the spirit and manner" in which "reckless of the consequences" students acted "against the advice of the faculty."[62]

Beecher, admitting the "bitter sarcasm and over-bearing contemptuous denunciation,"[63] was both honest and accurate in assigning a key role in the drama to Weld.

> [I]n our opinion [he wrote], all our difficulties were origi-
> nated and continued by the instrumentality of an influential
> member of the Abolition Society, with the express design of
> making the institution subservient to the cause of aboli-
> tion . . . this [goal] . . . render[ed] it not only lawful, but a mat-
> ter of duty, to sacrifice whatever might obstruct . . . even . . . the
> prosperity of the seminary itself.[64]

"We regard it as an eminent instance of . . . monomania."[65]

It is a mark of an essentially gracious character that, with Lane all but destroyed and his dreams shattered, Beecher paid willing, if melancholy, homage to Weld's "talents, and piety, and moral courage, and energy,"[66] and acknowledged that, in spite of their differences, he and Weld "never quarrelled."[67] But as it was finally beyond Lyman's power to dissemble, it was equally characteristic of him that before long, with constitutional good humor and salty idiom, he called the rebels "he-goat men, who think they do God service by butting every thing in the line of their march, which does not fall in or get out of the way."[68]

Even if he had borne grudges, Beecher would have had no more time than inclination for them in the year 1835. For it was then that Joshua Wilson's self-righteous rage, which had long smouldered, burst forth in such accusations against Lyman that the ordeal of a heresy trial was unavoidable.

Notes to Chapter XI

1. *Autobiography*, II, 309.
2. Robert Samuel Fletcher, *A History of Oberlin College, From Its Foundation Through the Civil War*, 2 vols. (Oberlin, 1943), I, 162.
3. Gilbert H. Barnes, *The Antislavery Impulse 1830-1844* (New York and Chicago, 1933), p. 230.
4. *A Statement of the Reasons Which Induced the Students of Lane Seminary to Dissolve Their Connection with That Institution* (Cincinnati, 1834), p. 27.
5. William C. Beecher and Samuel Scoville, *Henry Ward Beecher*, p. 153.
6. An open "Communication," signed "Many Colored People," *Cincinnati Journal*, April 7, 1829.
7. William C. Beecher and Samuel Scoville, *Henry Ward Beecher*, p. 153.
8. *Statement of Reasons*, p. 26.
9. *Autobiography*, II, 324.
10. *Ibid.*, p. 221.
11. Calvin E. Stowe, "Sketches and Recollections," p. 233.
12. A. T. Rankin, "Recollections of Lane." Beecher's paternalistic attitude was not entirely different from that of his daughter Harriet. See Harriet Beecher Stowe, "Sojourner Truth, the Libyan Sibyl," in *Dred: A Tale of the Great Dismal Swamp, together with Anti-slavery Tales and Papers, and Life in Florida after the War*, 2 vols. (Boston and New York, 1896), pp. 312-314, for the account of the reception of the woman evangelist by the Beechers.
13. *Autobiography*, II, 322.
14. Theodore Weld, [Rochester, N.Y., March 9, 1836], to Lewis Tappan in Gilbert H. Barnes and Dwight Dumond, *Weld-Grimké Letters*, I, 273.
15. Theodore Weld, [New York, March 12, 1838], to Angelina Grimké, *ibid.*, II, 59.
16. H. Lyman, "Lane Seminary Rebels," in W. G. Ballantine, ed., *Oberlin Jubilee 1833-1883* (Oberlin, 1883), p. 63. Gilbert H. Barnes, *Antislavery Impulse*, pp. 65 ff.
17. H. Lyman, "Lane Seminary Rebels," pp. 61-62.
18. *Ibid.*, p. 62.
19. The unfortunate phrase occasioned much misunderstanding among and between various groups endeavoring to find solution for the problem.

20. *Autobiography*, II, 324.
21. H. Lyman, "Lane Seminary Rebels," p. 61.
22. Theodore Weld, [Cincinnati], March 18, 1834, to Lewis Tappan, in Gilbert H. Barnes and Dwight Dumond, *Weld-Grimké Letters*, I, 132.
23. *Ibid.*, p. 133.
24. *Ibid.*, p. 135.
25. *Autobiography*, II, 325.
26. Asa Mahan, *Autobiography, Intellectual, Moral, and Spiritual* (London, 1882), p. 175.
27. W. T. Allan, "Statement of the Faculty, Concerning the late Difficulties in the Lane Seminary," *The Liberator*, January 17, 1835.
28. Lyman Beecher, "Report," *ibid.*
29. Gilbert H. Barnes, *Antislavery Impulse*, p. 226.
30. *Statement of Reasons*, p. 25.
31. John Morgan, Clinton, [N.Y.], January 13, 1835, to Theodore Weld, in Gilbert H. Barnes and Dwight Dumond, *Weld-Grimké Letters*, I, 199.
32. *Autobiography*, II, 324.
33. *The Liberator*, October 4, 1834.
34. *Ibid.*
35. "Minute Book," MS document, Lane Collection, Cincinnati Historical Society, pp. 216-221. See also *The Liberator*, October 4, 1834.
36. Theodore Weld, [Cincinnati, c. May 20, 1834], to James Hall, in Gilbert H. Barnes and Dwight Dumond, *Weld-Grimké Letters*, I, 146.
37. *Autobiography*, II, 328.
38. Charles Stuart, Apulia, [N.Y.], August 5, 1834, to Theodore Weld, in Gilbert H. Barnes and Dwight Dumond, *Weld-Grimké Letters*, I, 165.
39. *Autobiography*, II, 323.
40. "Union of Colonizationists and Abolitionists," *Spirit of the Pilgrims*, VI (July, 1833), 396.
41. *Ibid.*, pp. 396-400.
42. Asa Mahan, *Autobiography*, p. 177.
43. *Ibid.*, p. 178.
44. Lyman Beecher, Frederic[k, Maryland], October 8, 1834, to Theodore Weld, in Gilbert H. Barnes and Dwight Dumond, *Weld-Grimké Letters*, I, 171.
45. *Ibid.*, p. 172.
46. *Ibid.*
47. *Ibid.* Henry B. Stanton, one of the Lane rebels, wrote to James A. Thome, another, on September 11, 1834, regarding Beecher's compliments: "Dr. Beecher is bragging all over N. England what glorious fellows we are—never has seen such a set of students—is proud to be at the head of them—they will do immense good at the west &c. &c. Let

him go on—we are so identified with A - - - - - - - n, that bragging in such
a character he will help that cause greatly,—& his recommendation too,
will be a kind of endorsement for the correctness of our future course,
whatever that may be." ALS, Thome MSS, Oberlin College Library.
  48. Lyman Beecher to Theodore Weld (*supra*). Henry B. Stanton
had assured Thome, "We shall spread the whole matter before the
public, & I trust tell a story that will make some ears tingle," Henry B.
Stanton to James A. Thome (*supra*). His promise underscored the faith
of Huntingdon Lyman, expressed in an August 17 letter to Thome, that
"God will never let this work go back till all Israel has come up out of
Egypt," ALS, Thome MSS, Oberlin College Library.
  49. *Autobiography*, II, 329.
  50. Henry B. Stanton to James A. Thome (*supra*).
  51. Huntingdon Lyman to James A. Thome (*supra*). Later, on
October 4, 1834, Lyman wrote again to Thome of the same matter:
"There are several new students upon the ground some of whom will
not enter under the gag law, and concerning others it is doubtful.
Several who expected to have been here have been struck as with a
palsy on perusing the proposed laws." ALS, Thome MSS, Oberlin
College Library.
  52. *Cincinnati Gazette*, October 22, 1834; Benjamin P. Thomas,
Theodore Weld, p. 84.
  53. Asa Mahan, *Autobiography*, pp. 182-183.
  54. H. Lyman, "Lane Seminary Rebels," p. 66; Asa Mahan, *Autobiography*, p. 183.
  55. Lewis Tappan, *Arthur Tappan*, p. 236.
  56. Asa Mahan, *Autobiography*, pp. 183-184.
  57. *Autobiography*, II, 329-330.
  58. Robert Samuel Fletcher, *History of Oberlin*, I, 170.
  59. James H. Fairchild, *Oberlin: The Colony and the College* (Oberlin, 1883), p. 56.
  60. Fairchild points out that the school was already operating
before the arrival of the Lane rebels: "Thus Oberlin was first established and then enlarged, and the enlargement was so conspicuous a fact
that it has sometimes been mistaken for its origin . . . the men from
Lane joined a school already in existence, and numbering more than a
hundred pupils." *Ibid.*. p. 77.
  61. *Statement of Reasons*, pp. 26-27.
  62. *The Liberator*, January 17, 1835.
  63. *Ibid.*
  64. *Ibid.* On June 3, 1835, Weld wrote from Lane Seminary to Mrs.
Child, c/o David L. Child, Esq.: "[O]ur cause is onward in this
region—tho every step of its progress is controverted by a blind,
unreasoning, bitterly prejudiced and ferocious opposition breathing out
threatenings and proscriptions—The students of this Institution—(with

the exception of three or four—and those decidedly under the *mediocrity* of talent)—are decided Abolitionists and Anti-Colonizationists." ALS, Weld Correspondence, Boston Public Library.

65. *The Liberator,* January 17, 1835.
66. *Ibid.; Fifth Annual Report,* appendix, pp. 31, 39, 41, 47.
67. *Autobiography,* II, 321.
68. *Ibid.,* p. 345.

Chapter XII

Heresy Trial:
An Attempt to Liberalize Calvin – 1835

Freedom of religious expression in America, which guaranteed toleration for new sects, made controversy and schism almost inevitable within the older communions. Having cooperated with Congregationalists in 1801 in a Plan of Union for the sake of evangelizing the frontier, Presbyterians, never completely tranquil with the arrangement, were soon apprehensive at the western invasion of the Congregational, New Haven theology. As liberal views were adopted by Presbyterians in growing numbers, traditionalists of the church endeavored to check the trend. In 1826 Ashbel Green, Philadelphia editor of the Christian Advocate, *attacked Eleazer Fitch, Taylorite professor of divinity at Yale. Albert Barnes, liberal minister, was tried for heresy in 1831 (provisionally censured), and again in 1835-1836 (acquitted). In 1836 the faculty of Princeton, alarmed, shifted from a moderate to a conservative theological position. The trial of the president of Lane Seminary for heresy bespoke the mounting anxiety of conservative Presbyterians, and added to the evidence that liberal thought within their body was too virile and too widespread to yield to discipline or be expunged by contradiction.*

Lane Seminary Faculty 1840-1850
(Cincinnati Historical Society)
Calvin E. Stowe   Lyman Beecher   D. H. Allen

Joshua Lacy Wilson, the inquisitor who brought Lyman to trial for heresy, was a frontier man, tender of his honor and quick for combat. In his youth he had attended horse races and shooting matches for amusement; danced, gambled, and sworn for pleasure; and contended with Indians and wild beasts, presumably out of necessity. (Whiskey he did not drink, but only because he disliked the taste of it.[1]) When (after several unsuccessful attempts) he became a thorough Calvinist, however, there was no stauncher "Pioneer of the Church" in all the West. "His ripe manhood unobscured by scandal," and "his old age preserved from the utterance of blasphemies,"[2] he was until his death in his seventy-second year a stalwart guardian of the symbols of Old School Presbyterianism. Wilson, strikingly similar to General Andrew Jackson in appearance, had that warrior's same "headlong vigor and sincere, unflinching constancy,"[3] being constitutionally unable to understand or to tolerate deviation. In the arbitrary imposition of his own ideas upon others he acted rather like Constantine, commanding a whole synod to agree before the sun went down.[4]

Wilson, who arrived in Cincinnati in 1808 when there were scarcely four hundred dwellings there,[5] became minister of the First Presbyterian Church, which was housed in a building constructed sixteen years earlier by James Kemper's flock.[6] By the 1830's, when Lyman made his appearance, Wilson, who had grown up with the town, was an acknowledged mentor of rectitude in faith and puritanical practice. He excoriated the profligate life so continually that local players satirized him in a production of The Hypocrite,[7] and devotees of the stage paid him unwitting compliment in toasting the first theater building of Cincinnati with the hope that it might "not like the walls of Jericho, fall at the sound of Joshua's horn."[8] Even more austere than Wilson's criterion for society was his inflexible standard for orthodoxy. He was, therefore, a natural and wrathful enemy of Yankee

heresy, of which Dr. Beecher in time became for him a
distressing exponent. Some forty years after Lyman's trial
Henry Ward Beecher, remembering that Dr. Wilson had been
as "stiff [and] . . . pugnacious as two Calvins rolled into
one,"[9] represented so convincingly the "abyss of whirling
controversies" that resulted from Dr. Wilson "contending
against" his father, as to call forth angry rebuke from Wilson's son.[10]

The rift between Beecher and Wilson did not develop until
after Lyman first heard that he might be called to Lane as
president. Wilson had sat with the Lane board when Beecher's name was suggested, and voted for the resolution, which
passed with "reverential silence . . . not a word . . . spoken
but 'Aye.' "[11] Now, it was not Wilson's nature to stand mute
when he disapproved of procedure; and any possibility that
his silence withheld endorsement is dissolved by testimony of
the Pandect, a periodical Wilson himself began in 1828, for
the purpose of "setting forth Calvinistic doctrines."[12] Before
Lyman reached Ohio, Wilson had not only published in this
journal glowing accounts of Beecher's revival activity in
Boston as a "work of grace,"[13] but he had also reprinted
from Beecher's sermon on the *Gospel According to Paul*[14] a
long passage which, lacking any editorial dissent, most certainly enjoyed Wilson's approval. Such unqualified recognition was high in a periodical often held in "contempt and
ridicule"[15] by religious sophisticates precisely because it
was directed to a public inclined to "dispute fiercely, for the
slightest shade of difference of religious opinion."[16] Moreover, when Wilson heard that Beecher would surely come to
the West, he had danced about happily, crying "Glory to
God, Glory to God."[17] Yet by the time Lyman and Catherine arrived to scout the area, Wilson had done an about-
face, and chill winds of suspicion already blew from the
fortress of his orthodoxy. "Everybody gives a welcome except Dr. Wilson's folks," Catherine wrote sister Harriet, and,
as it developed, attaching too little importance to such opposition, she added, "Father is determined to get acquainted
with Dr. Wilson, and to be *friendly* with him, and I think he
will succeed."[18]

It is, of course, possible that Wilson nursed unrecognized hostility toward Beecher. The invitation to the presidency of the seminary was coupled with a call to the pastorate of Cincinnati's Second Presbyterian Church, a splinter group that had broken away from Wilson's congregation only after repeated and flinty exchange, and over Wilson's almost successful opposition. Thereafter, the church orphans had limped along with little hope of doing more, until Providence summoned them to march to the generalship of Dr. Lyman Beecher.[19] (It is a matter of history that the Second Church eventually eclipsed the First.[20]) Or it may have been that Wilson was not ready to have an interloper appropriate sponsorship of a seminary for which he had contended more than a decade. As early as September, 1822, Wilson had circularized the brethren, urging a "School of the Prophets" as a "great desideratum in the western section."[21]

Although in the employ of heaven, Lyman, characteristically, evaluated the matter from human perspective. Princeton folk, he felt, had not "swallowed it comfortably" that the school at Cincinnati (which they had by-passed as a site for their own outpost Western seminary) might now overshadow or even displace their effort to dominate religious affairs on the frontier. Through a "flattering letter," therefore, Old School Easterners, realizing what was afoot, enlisted Wilson's help in frustrating Lyman's acceptance in Ohio. Beecher subsequently "had it from Wilson's mouth" that the Princetonians desired father Joshua to "take back his invitation." The "scampy concern" even provided Wilson an Assembly moderatorship. Consequently, said Lyman, "Wilson turned square around," prodded local churchmen to obstruct Lyman, and himself "fired off a forty-four pounder in the New York papers." Peace might still have come from the actual encounter of the titans (for Wilson melted under the numinous effect of Lyman's public prayers) had not "the devil in a good man jumped up" and prompted the bystander to make so snide a remark about Dr. Wilson that, as Lyman said, thereafter the "fat was in the fire" and there could only be a "pitched battle."[22]

According to the transcript of the trial, probably the

chief—certainly the immediate—cause of Wilson's attack was his belated conviction that Beecher was no proper Presbyterian. This, at least, is the face that Wilson put upon it. He resigned "as President and as member of the Board of Trustees" of the seminary, and warned the churches against supporting Lane, charging that there was an effort, if not a conspiracy, "to render the Institution subservient to the New School Theology." He predicted that Dr. Beecher's appointment would forfeit the charter of the seminary, because he was not a Presbyterian, and could "not become so without a great change in his Theological" views.[23] Whether Wilson's verdict was just is a matter of opinion; but the peculiar structure of Presbyterian government enabled Wilson to do more than voice his prejudice.

Presbyterians are bound together (when they are) by polity and not by theology. Control lies within presbyteries, church courts that in the eyes of non-Presbyterians appear as divisions of the parent body, comprising in membership ministers and laymen from small districts. A clergyman moving any distance at all to another parish is likely to change presbyteries. Each presbytery determines by examination whether a new arrival is orthodox, and may bar him from membership if he does not own the covenant to the satisfaction of the brethren. Thus a man considered in one presbytery as acceptable as John Knox may very well be anathema in another. This particular circumstance both complicated and explained the confusing history of Lyman's relationship with the Presbyterian church in Cincinnati.

In Lyman's day, as in any, churchmen numbered the usual disputants who—if salvation were reduced to the single necessity of jumping from a church steeple—would still create factions by long and learned speculation regarding the height of the steeple and the direction of the plunge. Of broadly opposing Presbyterian camps, however, there were but two, denominated Old School and New School. A presbytery with a clear majority of New or Old School men bore a recognizable profile, and understandably, if not charitably, extended only grudging hospitality to visitors with variant views. But where there was no clearly dominant party, in a presbytery with the delicate equilibrium constantly changing as men moved away or died and were replaced by others, or where men changed or could not make up their minds at all about the proper face truth should wear, theological chaos resulted. It was, therefore, no tolerable thing, in Wilson's opinion, that a liberal of New School persuasion should be admitted to the Presbytery of Cincinnati, and allowed further to jeopardize an already hazardous balance as well. Accepting Lyman, Wilson came to see, could only breed mischief and unavoidably cast him in the role of natural marplot.

When Lyman was called to Cincinnati he was not a Presbyterian, but a Congregationalist, and a prominent one at that. No one, however, least of all Lyman, foresaw the affiliation as a hindrance, assuming that the Plan of Union[24] that had enabled Beecher to come from the Presbyterian parish of East Hampton into a Congregational parsonage of Litchfield would also provide for his transfer from Massachusetts to Ohio and assist his metamorphosis in passage. F. Y. Vail, more confident than clairvoyant, said firmly that there would be "no difficulty in having the Dr. Presbyterianized."[25] He was wrong. On July 9, 1832, Beecher was dismissed from the Suffolk Association of Massachusetts (Congregational) to the Third Presbytery of New York, for it seemed no more than commonly courteous to arrive at the new post already enrolled with the elect. Two months later, by "his own request," as their records show, the Third Presbytery "very affectionately recommended [Lyman] to the communion & esteem of the Presbytery of Cincinnati," acknowledging him in the same document as a "member in good and regular standing."[26]

Unfortunately for Beecher, that endorsement was a questionable distinction in the eyes of the intransigent Old School Presbyterians of Cincinnati. They held that the Third Presbytery of New York had been organized with uncertain propriety, and they regarded it as "a most active and powerful instrument for corrupting the Church,"[27] because of the insidious practice of "flooding the Presbyteries of the West" with freshly ordained New School missionaries.[28] It distressed conservatives of Cincinnati that Ohio seemed a special object of conquest for New England liberals. When the "venerable Wilson awoke from his sleep," a contemporary related, he found "himself betrayed and bound."[29] The Western Samson may well have been in such sorry estate, but he was not muzzled, and immediately roared an anguished objection. It was one thing to hear that Beecher, the great gun of Calvinism who had blasted Boston Unitarians, was coming now to the West, and quite another to realize that he fought under the banner of New School Presbyterians, who were at the very moment laying siege to the citadels of truth.

Old School Presbyterians embraced the Westminster Confession of Faith without alloy. They loved the document, covers and all. Too late, Dr. Wilson decided that Beecher was untrustworthy at the point of his loyalty to the symbol. Any person might, of course, knock at the gate of Presbyterianism: the doorway was not more exclusive of access than that to the kingdom of heaven, only more tortuous of passage, for it was necessary for Presbyterians to affirm the standards in a certain way and with a particular voice, a challenge some never met. Conservatives deplored what they took for casual, even irresponsible, compromise of pure doctrine by liberal and alleged Presbyterians. And most of all, Old School churchmen rejected the nascent, cankering insistence upon man's ability and freedom that threatened the sovereignty of their God, who, for his own good pleasure, out of all eternity had foreordained whatsoever comes to pass. As Dr. Wilson considered the matter, he judged it unlikely that Beecher could qualify as untinctured Presbyterian.

Already the Rev. Mr. James Weatherby, Old School, of Mississippi, had been scandalized when on a visit to the East he had inquired if Beecher could "sincerely receive and adopt the Confession . . . as containing the system of doctrine taught in the Holy Scriptures." Lyman had parried with a "Yes, but I will not say how much more it contains." Mr. Weatherby retorted that "no such Yankee answer would do." Whereupon Lyman, after several attempts, gave a simple, affirmative response. This incident alone (which Weatherby was quick to report) was sufficient to arouse doubt in Wilson's mind. So uncertain a sound as Beecher's would have satisfied no Old School man as a fitting voice for a Presbyterian prophet.[30] The intelligence set Wilson wild, and he was already distracted by engagement with Eastern liberals, one of whom at least had held the Confession in his hand and boasted, "In a few years we will . . . alter this book as we please."[31]

The information brings into review the accusation by a New School partisan that Wilson joined with trustees in calling Beecher only in the belief that he would not accept, but, chagrined to hear that Lyman was actually on his way to Ohio, "resigned [from] . . . the board, and . . . prepared to oppose his being received by the presbytery of Cincinnati."[32] It also sheds light on Wilson's obvious embarrassment at the trial when faced with the evidence that he had plainly concurred in the invitation to Lyman. "The question," Wilson raged, "is not what the man once was; but what he has since said and done."[33] Still it is strange that Wilson came so tardily to the understanding of Lyman's New School position. Beecher's fondness and admiration for Nathaniel Taylor were famously known. Moreover, Beecher's published sermons, early available, were little short of romantic in their estimate of man's ability—the precise point at which Lyman seemed least in accord with the standard of the Westminster Confession.

Pharisee, Wilson undoubtedly was. That he was a hypocrite is not completely clear. He did not blanch, though, at leveling the charge of duplicity against another, and formally accused Lyman of heresy, slander, and hypocrisy.[34] His managing to have the indictment even considered was a minor victory. Only after repeatedly unsuccessful attempts to secure condemnation on the basis of "common fame charging the Doctor with doctrinal error," did Wilson at length, in November 1834, present "himself at the bar of presbytery," and table charges against Beecher.[35]

Later, in the opening session of the trial, Wilson forthrightly admitted that he had indeed looked for Lyman to decline the presidency of Lane, but only, he pleaded, because he had no expectation that the New Englander could sufficiently alter his theology to make the necessary transition to Presbyterianism. Commissioners to the church court sitting on Lyman's case most likely responded to this statement as their relation to Wilson dictated; but no perceptive witness of the litigation doubted that the ideological crux of the conflict was the doctrine of man's ability (or lack of it) to help in the salvation of his own soul.[36]

For whatever reason Wilson had delayed or neglected careful examination of Lyman's views, when he came to press charges he was relentless. As for Lyman, neither risk of being shut out of heaven forever (the awful price of the heretic's folly) nor possible professional disgrace could long repress his spirit, or relieve him of the slightly absurd appearance that was forever breaking through his imperfectly maintained decorum. Henry Ward Beecher had, as a child, appreciated his father's drollery, and used to reduce his playmates in the haymow to helpless laughter by mimicking his celebrated parent. Donning immense blue goggles, he would preach behind an improvised pulpit, with a "jargon of word-sounds" wonderfully like those of Lyman, and then roll down the loft into their hysterical midst.[37] Henry never lost, or, perhaps, never went beyond his penchant for laughing at his father's superficial characteristics. He has left a description as wistful as it is amusing of his father's departure for one of the tedious sessions of the various church courts in which he had to prove his orthodoxy. The familiar and—it is true—sometimes ridiculous shape of the event has partially obscured the essence of the defendant, and the solemn indictment of American Christianity implied in the heresy trial. Horror lies often, but poignancy always, at the heart of humor.

On that morning, Beecher's son reported, "the doctor was standing in his study doorway, a book under each arm, with a third in his hands, . . . searching for quotations." The boat was to leave in an hour and a half, and Lyman was almost totally disorganized. "Where did I put that paper of extracts? Can't you make out another? Where did I lay my opening notes? . . . put this book in the carriage. Stop! give it to me. . . . run upstairs for my Register. No, No! I've brought it down." With no margin left, Lyman raced from the house, papers, books, clothes crammed into a gaping carpet bag, the handles tied together because the key was lost, the contents threatening to spill out in a moment. Wildly gesticulating to students and friends, holding the lines of harness as best he could with an apple in each hand, and "raising and lowering the reins like the threads of a loom" as he bit first one piece of fruit and then the other, Beecher drove out of the seminary grounds at "full canter down the long hill, . . . bouncing and bounding over the stones, alternately telling Tom how to get the harness mended, and showing" Henry Ward "the true doctrine of original sin." He thundered "alongside the boat just in time."[38] In a world of self-important conventionalists, a forthright man like Lyman never appears completely sane or wholly serious.

Had Lyman departed, or arrived, otherwise, friends might have suspected an impostor. Always his own man, he could be no other in the face of ordeal. When it became apparent that he must testify, he called for assistance from the erudite Calvin E. Stowe, professor of Biblical literature at Lane.[39] Stowe was marvelously eccentric himself, one of the less outré evidences of his individuality being an unwillingness ever to be without (in some pocket of his jacket) a copy of the Greek New Testament and of Dante's *Divina Comedia*.[40] The forgivable conceit is indicative of Stowe's spontaneous scholarship. Beecher's future son-in-law went painstakingly about the business of arming Lyman against the foe. "I loaded myself with the proper books," he recalled, "went to his study and began to read, now from one author and then from another, while he wrote. We had not continued long in this employment before he began to grow cloudy, bewildered, and perplexed; and at length exclaimed, with an impatience that was laughably pettish, 'Pish! Pshaw! take your books away, Stowe; they plague me,' " and proceeded in his own way.[41] "He had his work to do," added Stowe, "and he did it; but it was not investigation among words and books; it was striking at living men with a living truth of the present hour."[42]

For Lyman, no truth was more significant for men to learn than the fact of their freedom. If confidence in liberty was more obvious in Lyman than in others, it was only proof of

his intense nature, not a sign of radical difference from his
generation. Beecher, born in 1775, had come of age in the
self-reliant atmosphere of risk and revolution. People who
had but lately wrenched security from the wilderness, killed
off the Indians, and successfully rebelled against England
were not emotionally prepared to hear that human freedom
was any more bound in the matter of salvation than in that
of government. Stalwartly outwitting the insolence of time,
they were ready to look full face toward eternity. The
Apostle had preached as dying man to dying men. Lyman
spoke as an unfettered Adam to free souls. His optimism
reassured those whom traditional orthodoxy would have
counseled to repent, even of their holiest deeds.

Laymen of Lyman's times, however, if they were religious
(as all by no means were) did not find it easy to turn their
backs upon their fathers in Israel. Never doubting the existence of a hell of brimstone, describable by degrees Fahren-
heit, nor yet denying their own moral responsibility, which,
dishonored, might well bring them to everlasting residence in
such a place, they still demanded more freedom than their
New England forebears allowed, preferring, as it were, to go
to perdition, when they did so, by their own choice. Puritan
divines had said in more ways than words that, although mortals might and must throw themselves in the way of God,
they were finally unable to affect his attitude toward them.
Such doctrine frustrated and offended post-Revolution New
Englanders, although they did not always recognize the fact.
Theologically they were children not so much of Calvin, and
certainly not of St. Paul, as of Jonathan Edwards; but for all
their elaborate lip-service, they had departed from his teach-
ings by some distance: they were more concerned to reclaim
Eden by their industry than to glorify God through their
dependence.

Many in the mid-nineteenth century advanced to storm the
gates of heaven through a breach in the wall made by Beecher's bosom friend, Nathaniel Taylor, who in effect explained
to his generation that what Edwards intended was what they
wanted him to have said.[43] Great numbers of those who had
rejected the restrictive bonds of Calvinism for a newly proved

freedom marched toward Zion by way of the West. Between the end of the Revolution and the beginning of the century, New Englanders moved to the western country in throngs. In the winter of 1795, inhabitants of Albany, New York, situated on the principal avenue to the frontier, regarded the tide of pioneers passing through their city, with dumb astonishment at the great number of sleighs and ox-sleds, loaded with men, women, children, and furniture. "On the 28th of February, five hundred [sleighs] were counted . . . between sunrise and sunset."[44] Emigration followed the century, and the missionaries blazed their own trails when they could not trace the way by which the settlers came. Bringing memory as naturally as they brought themselves, New Englanders transplanted Yankee ideas and attitudes, especially in Ohio.[45] The concepts of liberty the Revolution had secured flourished in the natural environment of the frontier.

Thus, much of Lyman's appeal to these optimistic and confident Americans lay in the similarity of the perspective that informed their philosophy and that which determined his theology. He proclaimed a gospel that—in essence—supported their claim to freedom. His words were the words of a theologian, but his meaning was the insight of a pioneer. And in all this, Beecher gave popular statement to the faith of Nathaniel Taylor, who taught that men, inevitable sinners, nevertheless had "power to the contrary."[46] Also, in any case, the resourcefulness and character Americans had demonstrated in the conflict with troops and wilderness could be equally effective in the struggle for the soul.

The analysis seemed at once to stay with tradition (which called man totally depraved) but to guarantee that at a practical level the situation was not hopeless. God's honor was saved, even if man's plight was still wretched. Such alleged Calvinism appalled Joshua Wilson. Derelict of orthodoxy at numerous points, Beecher was culpable in the extreme by reason of his doctrine of man; and Wilson rightly saw that Lyman had consistently argued for self-determination of man's fate.

In all fairness it must be admitted that Lyman was innocent of conscious departure from Calvin. From his youth he had shown a becoming grace in accommodating to the universe as it is. During his Yale days he had kept the buttery and easily bartered a traffic in lemons and shoe black, corkscrews and soap balls for an education.[47] Now trading old language for new was small price to pay if by clothing fundamentals in acceptable idiom he might give citizens of a new nation suffrage in the kingdom of God. Preaching at Lyman's funeral, Leonard Bacon pointed out that a "critical eye" could have discovered in the man's early sermons "the identical body of thought" for which he was later charged with heresy.[48] And indeed, Lyman was given to speaking of man as "entirely free,"[49] and "the voluntary cause of his own destruction."[50] It was his insistence "that men are free agents, in possession of such faculties, and placed in such circumstances, as render it practicable for them to do whatever God required"[51] that, by Wilson's interpretation, put him hopelessly at odds with the Calvinistic system.

Controversy over forgotten shibboleths excites little save apathy, but the actual trial was lively. More than two years earlier Wilson, in formal, if regretful, fashion, had shut out of heaven anyone infected with Beecher theology. When Lyman's son George stood before the presbytery, seeking membership, Wilson, horrified at how loosely the Beecher tribe dared sit to creedal obligation, had opined that they "would never see the gates of eternal bliss."[52] Less decorous, even scornful now, he concluded his accusation of Lyman by saying that the culprit might expect acquittal "when his powerful intellect [should] . . . have demonstrated that white is black and that two and two do not make four."[53]

It was Tuesday, June 9, 1835, when Wilson read the charges. Beecher, with great dignity, rejected them, disclaiming all guilt of slander or hypocrisy. As for his view of man, he confessed: "I do not say that I have not taught the doctrines . . . but I deny their being false."[54] Not until Friday afternoon did Beecher begin his defense, but when he did, what happened did not greatly differ from his own description of the powerful effect of Daniel Webster's oratory—"like a cannon ball rolling through eggshells."[55] Had Wilson been forthright, Lyman insisted, he would have gone to him and "wept upon his bosom," and presumably made peace. But, wailed Lyman, "he never did."[56] Disadvantaged by his seeming duplicity, Wilson retreated in avowal that he had not seen Lyman's allegedly heretical sermon, "The Native Character of Man," when he wrote to the Hanover congregation in Boston urging them to release Beecher so that he might save the West. And Beecher rejoined that the document would have given Wilson no intelligence he did not already have.[57]

There was, of course, a radical difference between the principals. Wilson was obsessed with Lyman's (or anybody's) departure from the Westminster Confession, and the cavalier way in which Beecher defined doctrine, "contrary to the word of God and the standards of the Presbyterian church,"[58] because Wilson sought always to safeguard jot and tittle of the historical symbols. Lyman, on the other hand, while maintaining that if the Presbytery rejected him they would have to reject Calvin ("Calvin was as bad as I am," he said. "The doctrine for which I am to be turned out . . . is not new divinity, but old Calvinism"[59]), nevertheless was primarily concerned to show man's true relation to God. If this necessitated reinterpreting ecclesiastical symbols, and Lyman saw no other way, he was ready to do so. "The language never stands still," said Lyman, and suggested that there was no more compatibility between Wilson's slavish repetitions and the true meaning of the Westminster Confession than between Queen Elizabeth's speech and Webster's dictionary.[60]

The trial lasted for a week. As the days wore on, Beecher was repeatedly accused of holding and teaching unorthodox views regarding man's freedom and accountability, original sin and total depravity, and regeneration. Moreover, he was called hypocrite, on the assumption that he knew his views to be Pelagian and Arminian, yet deliberately and deviously represented them as Calvinistic for the sake of securing popular acceptance. In the face of the indictment Beecher continued to argue that "there was nothing in the fall to destroy free agency,"[61] and that man was "fully adequate" to perform anything God required of him, though, shamefully, he always failed to do so. "If I ever preached any truth to dying men," he said, it was "man's total depravity."[62] Inevitably the contest became acerbic, with interruption and covert invective.[63] But Beecher won.

Late in the afternoon of the last day, the following minute was recorded: "Resolved, That in the opinion of this Presbytery the charges of J. L. Wilson, D.D. against Lyman Beecher, D.D., are not sustained. . . . "[64] The vote was strongly, though not overwhelmingly, in Lyman's favor. Presbytery did not presume to censure Wilson for having wrongly accused his brother of heresy, but referred that responsibility to the Synod.[65] Wilson was hobbled, but not stopped. Nor was he contrite. He gave notice of appeal though he was destined never to secure Beecher's conviction.[66] But Presbytery adjourned, and all went home, Wilson to his thoughts, and Beecher to the bedside of Harriet Porter, his wife, who was dying of consumption. She did not last through the summer.

Notes to Chapter XII

1. Raymond L. Hightower, "Joshua L. Wilson, Frontier Controversialist," *Church History*, III (December, 1934), p. 302.

2. Samuel R. Wilson, *Beecher's Slander against Dr. Wilson Repelled* (Cincinnati, n.d.), unpaginated pamphlet, Beecher Collection, Cincinnati Historical Society.

3. Harriet Beecher Stowe, *Men of Our Times*, p. 534.

4. *Ibid.*

5. Henry Howe, *Historical Collections*, I, 754.

6. *Ibid.*, p. 753.

7. *Cincinnati Journal*, July 6, 1830.

8. Henry A. Ford and Kate B. Ford, *History of Cincinnati, Ohio* (Cleveland, 1881), p. 369.

9. Lyman Abbott and S. B. Halliday, *Henry Ward Beecher: A Sketch of His Career* (Hartford, 1887), p. 607, reporting a speech of Henry Ward to the board of London Congregational ministers and their wives.

10. *Ibid.*

11. *History of the Foundation and Endowment of the Lane Theological Seminary* (Cincinnati, 1848), p. 12. See also E. H. Gillett, *History of the Presbyterian Church*, II, 463n.

12. Raymond L. Hightower, "Joshua L. Wilson," p. 311.

13. *Cincinnati Journal*, April 21, 1829. *The Pandect* became the

Cincinnati Journal, and Wilson subsequently established the *Standard* as an Old School organ. He was, however, editor of the *Journal* in 1829.

14. *Ibid.,* June 16, 1829.

15. *Ibid.,* June 9, 1829.

16. Timothy Flint, *Recollections,* p. 45.

17. ALS, G. W. Perkins, Walnut Hills, August 17, 1838, to his wife, Beecher Collection, Stowe-Day Foundation. *Autobiography,* II, 282.

18. *Ibid.,* p. 201.

19. Raymond L. Hightower, "Joshua L. Wilson," p. 308.

20. *History of Cincinnati and Hamilton County, Ohio; Their Past and Present* (Cincinnati, 1894), p. 198.

21. William Warren Sweet, *Religion on the American Frontier,* II, *The Presbyterians* (New York and London, 1936), 591.

22. *Autobiography,* II, 282-284.

23. *History of the Foundation and Endowment of Lane,* pp. 13-14.

24. *Supra,* p. 55.

25. Robert Samuel Fletcher, *History of Oberlin,* I, 51.

26. "Document of Dismission," September 11, 1832, Reuben T. Durrett Collection, University of Chicago Library.

27. Samuel J. Baird, *History of the New School,* p. 403.

28. *Ibid.*

29. *Ibid.,* p. 337.

30. *Ibid.,* pp. 457-458; ALS, W. D. Snodgrass, New York, October 9, 1832, to Joshua Wilson, Reuben T. Durrett Collection, University of Chicago Library; ALS, James Blythe, December 1, 1832, to Joshua L. Wilson, *ibid.,* in which he says that Beecher will have to write in "less ambiguous terms" before he will be acceptable as a Presbyterian.

31. Samuel J. Baird, *History of the New School,* p. 340.

32. Zebulon Crocker, *The Catastrophe of the Presbyterian Church in 1837,* p. 105.

33. *Trial and Acquittal of Lyman Beecher,* p. 83.

34. *Ibid.,* pp. 3-6.

35. Samuel J. Baird, *History of the New School,* p. 470.

36. Lyman Beecher, *Views in Theology,* p. 15: "I COMMENCE with the subject of Free Agency, or the Natural Ability of man, . . . because it is, as Dr. Wilson has said, 'the hinge of the whole controversy.'"

37. Alain C. White, *History of Litchfield,* pp. 34-35.

38. *Autobiography,* II, 354-355.

39. When the Beechers came to Cincinnati, Calvin Stowe was married to Eliza, daughter of Bennet Tyler. She was a particular favorite of Mrs. Harriet Porter Beecher.

40. Edward Dwight Eaton, "Calvin Ellis Stowe," *Dictionary of American Biography.*

41. Calvin E. Stowe, "Sketches and Recollections," p. 229.

42. *Ibid.*

43. George Park Fisher, "The System of Dr. N. W. Taylor in Its Connection with Prior New England Theology," *Discussions in History and Theology* (New York, 1880), pp. 285-354.

44. E. H. Gillett, *History of the Presbyterian Church*, I, 395.

45. William Warren Sweet, *Religion on the American Frontier*, II, 47.

46. Frank Hugh Foster, *A Genetic History of the New England Theology* (Chicago, 1907), p. 247.

47. Franklin Bowditch Dexter, "Reminiscences of the Officers of Yale College in 1857," in *A Selection from the Miscellaneous Historical Papers of Fifty Years*, p. 384.

48. Leonard Bacon, *Sermon at the Funeral*, p. 12. See also, Lyman Beecher, "The Government of God Desirable," *Sermons Delivered on Various Occasions*, pp. 21-22.

49. *Ibid.*, p. 10.

50. *Ibid.*, p. 25.

51. "The Faith Once Delivered to the Saints," *ibid.*, p. 218.

52. *Autobiography*, II, 293-294.

53. *Trial and Acquittal of Lyman Beecher*, p. 32.

54. *Ibid.*, p. 6.

55. H. P. Hedges, "Anecdotes."

56. *Trial and Acquittal of Lyman Beecher*, p. 36.

57. *Ibid.*, p. 35.

58. *Ibid.*, p. 3.

59. *Ibid.*, p. 51.

60. *Ibid.*, p. 40.

61. *Ibid.*, p. 46.

62. *Ibid.*, p. 62.

63. *Ibid.*, pp. 87, 92.

64. *Ibid.*, p. 106.

65. *Ibid.*, p. 107: "Presbytery then resolved that they do not decide the amount of censure due to Dr. Wilson, but refer the subject to the Synod for their final adjudication."

66. E. H. Gillett, *History of the Presbyterian Church*, II, 465: "Dr. Wilson appealed to Synod . . . and again he was defeated. . . . he appealed to the Assembly of 1836, but, on learning the facts in regard to another case which was to come before that body, in which the same principles were involved, he asked and obtained leave to withdraw his appeal."

Chapter XIII

Divided Company: Schism of Old and New School Presbyterians – 1835-1846

Distinction between Old and New School Presbyterians, which arose in reaction to the Great Awakening, crystallized as the Old School espoused conservative and traditional standards, while the New School exercised latitude in polity and doctrine. Disagreement long preceded open rupture. The Old School deplored churches organized under the Congregational-Presbyterian Plan of Union as not truly Presbyterian, and regretted a lack of means to discipline, or strict denominational boards to guide, local churches. The Old School spurned the New Haven theology as heretical, and in 1835 through an "Act and Testimony" alerted churches to present danger of false doctrine. The 1837 Presbyterian General Assembly abrogated the Plan of Union, and excised the synods constituted by it. The New School, thus ousted, organized separately in 1838. The resultant divisions were designated Old School and New School Presbyterian Churches. In 1857 New School Southerners withdrew to form the United Synod; in 1861 Old School Southerners separated to form a church in the Confederacy; Old and New School Presbyterian bodies of the South joined in 1864 to comprise one Church that, after 1865, was, officially, the Presbyterian Church in the United States. Northerners of both Old and New School persuasion reunited as the Presbyterian Church in the United States of America in 1869. Thereafter the divisions were popularly styled Northern and Southern Presbyterian Churches.

Beecher Home at Walnut Hills (Cincinnati Historical Society)

Harriet Porter had not wished to live in Cincinnati, nor to leave the East at all, but she had acquiesced to Lyman's decision, and graciously, because she believed her husband to be led by God,[1] to remove to the West. It was a willing, external, though indeed minor concession to the Beecher way of life, the essence of which she accepted, while continually attempting (and with some success) to change the outward shape of it. For that matter, Harriet just possibly had not wanted to marry Lyman (or anyone else). Well born and beautiful, she was already twenty-seven years old when Lyman, wifeless scarcely a year, began an impassioned suit, and wooed with such ardor that her reticence melted, in spite of parental reservation and her private ambivalence about the whole affair.

Harriet was frightened of marriage, and Lyman knew it. The intelligence moved him only to change his tactic, not to relax his pressure. "I have sometimes feared," he wrote, "that my ardent spirit may have poured out a stream of affection too copious & rapid in its course, creating in you the alarm of inundation. But the fountain was full & would overflow." Lyman, therefore, reassured Harriet regarding his devotion. "It shall come to you hereafter," he vowed, "in a thousand little channels half covered by a thousand equivocal meanderings all still finding their way to you." Without denying his fervor, he promised control of a love so intense that it would "flow" in "no other direction" than "up hill."[2] Somewhat tranquillized, Harriet confessed in aquatic metaphor of her own that she "saw only the waves & they were nigh to overwhelming" her until, in good sense, "recollecting the sermons" of her lover, she "flew to them."[3] It was enough for Lyman, who, though he continued to think of her love as "gold shut up in a box," yet, because he knew it to be "a box of perfumes," rejoiced that for trust in him she had "broken the box & poured it out."[4] Lyman subsequently, in his cicisbeo-theologian role, obliged the situation by sprinkling scriptural quotations throughout his letters, and including outlines of sermons for Harriet's edification and peace of mind, or, perhaps, to insure his case by reminding her that whatever she might think of him, he was, after all, and before all, a man of God.

They were citizens of different worlds, these two, Lyman of the world of the West, and Harriet of the New England world of her father, that small, elegant man "always dressed with scrupulous neatness, silver buckles" and "black silk stockings." Outwardly she rather resembled him, appearing herself to be "all in the antique style."[5] Inwardly Harriet was her mother's child, akin to the spirit of that neurotic woman, who "endured great disease, bodily suffering & discouragement."[6] The disparity between Lyman and his second wife was wide. Whatever the reasons, the fact is that he (though mindful of eternity) belonged to this world and to the evolving future of it, and she to that next, and other-worldly, existence. Thus underscored by the Cincinnati episode, Harriet's uneasy truce with finitude—especially in contrast with Lyman's natural adjustment to the West (quite apart from his failures there)—makes clear far more than the difference between the man and his wife. It puts in bold outline the character of Beecher, who sometimes gazed through the spectacles of supposed orthodoxy toward so distant a horizon that he could not focus sharply upon the immediate. At these times he seemed to his peers to stumble, in disregard of the world about him, when the pertinent datum was that he looked over their heads. His purpose in such circumstances was only to be certain of the model by which he was endeavoring to rebuild this world in the likeness of the heavenly city upon the hill. He lived in the present.

Harriet Porter was sensible of Litchfield elegance and Boston refinement, and no stranger to prestige: one of her uncles had been governor of the state of Maine, and another ambassador to England.[7] Her empathy for the life of privilege, however, indicated no predilection for status, but rather the perception that obstreperous people could be polished and shaped by rituals of the past, which cultivate excellence through mandatory conformity to heritage. In the raw setting of the expanding West, it was plain to her that the residual virtue of looking to the past lay in a subsequent orientation to the sustaining foundation of all life—that is, to God himself. Trapped in a generation that, through eagerness to multiply the world of tangibles, was by turns ignorant and disdainful of its origin, she therefore turned her face more and more toward eternity, counting it a little thing to bid the earth good-bye.

The point at which Lyman Beecher's second wife first knew herself a stranger in a foreign land is by no means clear. Perhaps it was when her little Frederick, the angelic child whose eyes Lyman never forgot,[8] whose potential Aunt Esther unerringly intuited,[9] died of scarlet fever.[10] Perhaps Harriet was never anything but a sojourner; but certainly she was only such after her arrival at Cincinnati—and probably for some time before.

In the Litchfield days, when Henry Ward was still "a little fellow, whose feet could not touch the bottom of the old family chaise," he was driving with his stepmother on an errand once when he heard the "bell tolled for death, as was then the custom in rural places. 'Henry, what do you think of when you hear a bell tolling like that?' she asked. Astonished and awe-struck, . . . the child only flushed" and "looked abashed, and she went on as in a quiet soliloquy, 'I think was that soul prepared? It has gone into eternity!' " Her reflection brought down upon the lad a "shiver of dread."[11] No sooner had Mrs. Beecher seen the "retired and beautiful graveyard" in the compound of Lane Seminary than it was for her "an object of peculiar interest and pleasure. She often spoke of it with delight, and seemed to feel that it was speedily to be her resting place."[12] Harriet Porter had been briefly distracted by an intense friendship with the first wife of Professor Calvin Stowe, the distinguished Biblical scholar of Lane, and subsequent husband to Lyman's longest remembered child. But her lovely friend died untimely soon after the Beechers reached Ohio, and the cemetery was thereafter "still more pleasant."[13] The spot where Eliza Stowe's body lay, set about "with weeping willows & shrubs" and enclosed by "a white fence," became for Harriet Porter Beecher a place of special pilgrimage where often in the evening there were as many as "five or six humming birds" hovering at the "honeysuckle . . . trained . . . over her grave."[14]

Willingly, and as easily as the stubborn forces of nature would allow, Harriet died of consumption while her husband was in the vortex of the heresy trial. Although at the time of her death she had no longer desired to grasp at life, Lyman was by no means ready to release his hold upon it. Undone, and genuinely saddened by loss of Harriet, Lyman was, after the catharsis of his grief, soon busy with arrangements for his third wedding. His children at first were charmed, and rather amused by his attachment to the no-nonsense Lydia Jackson, a downright widow who took the good doctor over with the same efficiency by which she successfully ran her Boston boarding house—where, indeed, Lyman had sought her out and prayed her into matrimony.[15]

Before and during this domestic transition, in which familiar actors assumed new roles in Lyman's private world, a drama was being played out in Presbyterian-Congregational affairs, in a manner more public than was comfortable for the principals. Riven by disputes over theology and property, the Old and New Schools of Presbyterians split asunder in 1837 and did not reunite until 1869, and not completely then. By that time Southern Presbyterians were organized as such, and though sympathetic generally to Old School thought, far from joining churchmen with immediate past histories of federal and abolitionist persuasion. The struggle had begun previous to Beecher's entrance onto the stage, and was not finished in his lifetime. His trial, however, focused the major energies, at least temporarily, so that the contest between him and Wilson was a key scene of the piece, and Beecher himself was exhibited as a pivotal figure. The production was little short of melodrama, as two divisions of the Presbyterian church contended each with the other for control of the whole body. Beecher spoke some of the best lines, wrote part of the script, and directed as much of the action as his peers would allow. Of his personal and ubiquitous influence, one observer remarked that in the conglomerate of unbelievably diverse people and enthusiasms, within the New School camp "the ambiguities and versatility of Dr. Beecher, his catholic affinities and schemes of comprehension, presented a solvent, to fuse and cement in one the entire mass."[16] Lyman's personal situation is typical of a larger one of which he was exponent, because he had first been catalyst. Without bothering too much about the niceties of theology, Beecher was popularizing the notion of man's ability, intoxicating a generation with the new wine appropriate for a nation coming of age. Yet Lyman discovered that men—heady on the distillation he had fired, and even seeing theological matters at a practical level through the roseate glow of self-confidence which that brew induced within them—were still reluctant to accept the cup directly from the pulpit. The drama in progress and Lyman's role in it illustrate not only what was happening to his generation in the realm of ideas, but, in spite of his effort, what would never during his lifetime happen within the religious community, a formal statement of restructured creed.

The origin of the squabble is shrouded in the imponderable events by which the Presbyterians in the West separated into opposing companies. Disagreement, probably inevitable, had followed much too soon upon the Plan of Union that blurred denominational distinction and thus provided for, if not invited, the arrangement by which a Beecher could with impunity transfer from the Congregationalism of Massachusetts to the Presbyterianism of Ohio and, moreover, bring the new divinity of Nathaniel Taylor with him into the West.[17]

As the time for the 1837 General Assembly of the Presbyterian Church approached, dormant anxieties were aroused. The heresy trials of Albert Barnes and Lyman Beecher (for much the same offenses) had "awakened new alarm in the ranks of the Old School party,"[18] who were adamant in their avowal to reclaim the church for the true faith. Moreover, they acknowledged the urgency of swift and decisive action. It was apparent to all—or it should have been—that New School men, jealous of their strengthening proprietary status, and agile in their effort to maintain it, were not likely to be snagged on so obvious a lure as doctrinal misstatement. Beecher was quite realistic about the matter. Recalling his trial, he confessed that from the first he had "laughed in [his] . . . sleeve" and had never during the skirmish "got into a corner," although Wilson "never got out."[19] But then, Beecher had ever been cautious as he nourished men on new ideas. His sensitivity to theological allergies dictated his care in advising those endeavoring, as he was, to lead into a promised land men who, like Lot's wife, seemed forever to walk with their longing and their eyes turned toward the past. Because such people accept new thoughts more easily when they believe themselves to have conceived them, Lyman always introduced his case at the propitious moment and in familiar language, so that those whom he addressed might comfortably—even unconsciously—move toward conclusions that, in his opinion, the gospel not only admitted, but demanded. When his New Haven idol, Nathaniel Taylor, had once spoken too brashly about man's ability, Beecher, said an enemy, had sent such an effective warning "to Dr. Ta. calling on him to hold! hold!" because congregations were not yet "prepared for such disclosures" that the professor "had replied in a long letter of 2 sheets."[20]

Beecher customarily busied himself with matters weightier than mint, anise, and cumin. In the clash between men of Old and New School, therefore, he was sensible of what was at stake. Old School partisans had concluded to turn the New School heretics out-of-doors. Beecher, on the other hand, was concerned to move toward a millennium. What mattered was not who would win, but what might be lost. For him the question could never be "whether one side or the other [should] . . . be expelled from the church, as hypocrites and heretics." The only question was whether they would "dissolve partnership; or attempt its continuance upon the new conditions of exact agreement in speculation and language on every subject, as well as on fundamental doctrine. Whether . . . the *imprimatur* of the church should be given to the doctrine that man possesses no ability of any kind to obey the gospel."[21] So Beecher, for the sake of a world community in which the gospel influence should redeem not some group's pride in creedal statement, but all the waste places— "the wastes of paganism—the wastes of Mohametanism—the

wastes of popery—the wastes of atheism and heresy"[22] —
strove to slip through the snares of the enemy, thinking it
foolish to divide the forces of righteousness over picayunes.
When Wilson through appeal of the Presbytery case had
brought Lyman in confrontation before the Synod, that
body admitted that Beecher "satisfied the majority," but at
the same time the Synod still deplored the doctor's "disposition to philosophise, instead of exhibiting" his creed "in
simplicity and plainness." They admonished him to be "more
guarded in the future,"[23] and requested a clear and succinct
summary of just what he did believe. Instead, said an unsympathetic critic, he produced "not a concise pamphlet statement, as recommended, but a volume," although the detrac-
tor did grudgingly concede that the work was "comparatively
orthodox."[24] Yet Lyman with all his care and effort could
not stay the split of the Presbyterian body into formal Old
and New School churches, a severance that—though later
repaired after a fashion—continued to exhibit the scars of
combat.

Enjoying a majority at the 1837 Assembly, representatives
of the Old School were quick to push through that body a
resolution declaring the 1801 Plan of Union with the Congregational Church—together with all that had been done under
that Plan—a "nullity." The action lopped off, root and
branch, four entire synods of the West that had been thus
organized, and divided the church into two parts. In the
following year, 1838, New Schoolers made a desperate attempt
to outflank the conservative elements and thus recapture a
foothold in the compound. Their leaders arrived promptly
for the opening session of the Assembly, which was to be
held at the Seventh Church of Philadelphia, located at Ran-
stead Court.[25] They found Old School men already there,
entrenched in the prominent and strategic seats of the hall. It
was an omen. Although Nathaniel Taylor had come down
from New Haven, ready "at a moment to stimulate" any New
School man weakened by "failing courage," and though he
and Beecher, sitting close together, from time to time urged
their men in "earnest tones . . . 'Go on! Go on!' " it was of
no use.[26] The reply of the Assembly to a spokesman of the

alleged heretics of the New School was, "We do not know
you, sir."[27] Courtesy was strained and the pitch raised. In
the bedlamite confusion, members of the "New School
marched down the aisle,"[28] advised by Lyman's son Edward,
who shouted over the hubbub that they would find sanctuary in the First Presbyterian Church. They took refuge in the
available shelter and organized themselves with whatever
grace and dignity they had managed to salvage.[29]

Philadelphia might have noted the affair more closely had
it not been for another disturbance in the city. Hardly had
the echoes of these theological disputants subsided when the
"flames of Abolition or Liberty Hall in Sixth Street" lighted
up the faces of angry rioters who had set fire to the building
where Abolitionists had had the brass to go, black and white
together. Angelina Grimké Weld, bride of Theodore by only
several days, had spoken there in the very afternoon. The
crowd was content to shout insults and break windows until
they actually saw "a huge Negro darken the door arm in arm
with a fair Quaker girl." The mob "screamed and swore
vengeance," and the blaze was soon lit.[30]

Strife set thus in confusion (with neither defeat nor tri-
umph unalloyed) approximated a relatively normal state for
Beecher. After the heresy trial friends had buzzed about him
like bees, and he was almost giddy with success; but such
victory was exceptional. In his effort to free men from the
chrysalis of convention so that they might soar in freedom,
he strove too often against their leaden wills. Envisioning a
community released through the magnitude of its goals,
Lyman battled opponents anchored to the past. Old School
men equated truth with propositional statement and found
authority in the alembic of creed. Although legalists would
never have accepted Lyman without qualification, their dis-
taste for him had multiplied as his prominence had increased.
Perceptive ministers understood that Beecher invited people
not to repeat a creed, but to discover a way of life. Where the
challenge was met, conformity was threatened.

Lyman had not yet left Boston when sharp-eyed heresy
hunters began to ask slyly if he were not "the ringleader of
the sect" attempting to baptize "anything or everything

which" might be called "religion of any place or people."[31] Among the guardians of the tradition, even the amiable had now and again looked askance at Lyman as at one who appeared to be too much "aiming at popular effect,"[32] and the mean-spirited openly charged the minister of Bowdoin Street with dismissing disputations of their solemn assemblies as bickering over "shades of difference" that were of only doubtful "importance," when ironically, they pointed out, "little occasion to use pen or . . . tongue" in defense of Calvinism would have arisen, had Lyman Beecher preached (as he protested that he did) "the Edwardean theology" of the orthodox.[33]

Regardless of how exactly Lyman's professed or published statements comported with theological symbols, his enemies were never quite certain about the man's personal creed. Unable to prove him a heretic, they held him up to scorn. Following the appearance of his *Views in Theology,* the editors of the *Biblical Repertory,* in a captious review, tediously documented Lyman's alleged error and inconsistency, though at the same time disdainfully confessing themselves unaware "that Dr. Beecher . . . ever enjoyed the reputation of possessing views of theological truth that were profound, well-defined, and carefully adjusted to the standards of Presbyterian orthodoxy."[34] To the charge of ineptitude Lyman's critics added that of duplicity,[35] and though inadvertently recognizing the man's genius in an admission of a character in his work that was "altogether peculiar to himself,"[36] they cruelly suggested that Beecher's feeling of persecution was no more than a phantom, although surely no less painful for him "than if the apprehended danger were real."[37] In this kind of engagement Lyman, who was often sharp but never snide, came closer to sustained bitterness than ever before or since. As the contest had worn on, old loyalties were forgotten and men like Asahel Nettleton and Bennet Tyler, former friends and fellow soldiers for Christ, had assailed him with "the vilest misrepresentations." The strife grew sordid, with whisperings and rumor. "When a man comes out openly & opposes me, I am glad of it. I like an honorable enemy," said Lyman; and so much was true. But, he continued, "I despise" him "when he comes up in the guise of friendship, smears me over with molasses, & then stabs me."[38] Lyman Beecher noted little that was admirable in his Old School adversaries: "They took burning arrows dipped in gall, and shot them over into the Presbyterian camp." Worst of all, "[t]hey rifled the graves of my dead friends, out of their ashes to evoke spectral accusations against me."[39]

How certainly these attacks drew blood and how long Lyman remembered and smarted under them is evidenced in the notation by Charles in the *Autobiography* that the "last effort at composition in which the mind of Dr. Beecher was efficiently engaged"[40] was in reworking for the 1853 edition of his formal statement of theology an essay in answer to the Princeton accusations he still considered an unfair and inaccurate criticism intermixed with "personal assaults on [his] . . . moral integrity, . . . [his] capacities as a metaphysician, and . . . [his] trustworthiness as an expositor of Scripture."[41]

Beecher had been badly used, but he was not one to sit in his tent and lick his wounds. There was work to be done. The Cincinnati years following the heresy trial, and the Presbyterian civil war of which it was a part, were lean ones for Lyman. They were half-loaf times; for though he maintained enthusiasm and energy, problems continued and multiplied. It was a period when "except for two or three" there was "not a newspaper or Review in the Presbyterian Church that [was] . . . not firing off something" against him.[42] Also, the seminary suffered undeservedly from the stigma of being anti-Negro, with the result that—regardless of whether their reasons were eccentric or valid—prospective students rejected Lane as a choice for theological training. Yet as late as 1868, Cincinnati still dubbed Lane "that d----d abolition hole," [43] and, ironically, it had remained, and not just in myth, a haven for Negroes even when it was dangerous to offer such shelter. One liberated slave, when he knew he was finally free, had headed straight to Lane, "because he knew he would find friends there."[44] The vigilance in Walnut Hills was that which searched for ways by which to combat the distorted image of Beecher as the alleged apostle of charity who did not really love his black brother. The sympathetic *Cincinnati Journal,* while insisting that Lane was "never more flourishing," observed icily that this was true despite "the most strenuous efforts" of "those who seceded" and the "Editors of most of the leading Abolition papers . . . to prostrate the institution."[45] In substantiation, the *Journal* published, as typical of such persecution, the *New York Evangelist* report that Lane had "seen its best days" and was only a "dry and withered trunk," with the "leaves . . . stript off."[46]

Throughout this season of harassment, Lyman continued, for the most part, to train his sights above provincial goals, and refused to equate the gospel with a narrow or specific application of it. Nevertheless, he offered, as he always had, an openness to blacks and an affection for them that was no more patronizing than his attitude to anyone else who had not enjoyed the good fortune to be born a Beecher.

In 1841 a riot between Irish and Negroes disturbed Cincinnati with violence and fire and death.[47] After several days of lawlessness, street fights, and vandalism, the whites, nourished by new insult and old Bourbon, easily accepted a report "that a number of the Negroes had fled to Walnut Hills, and were concealed at Lane Seminary."[48] Certainly many of the blacks had deserted their customary residences. A band of rowdies, breathing threats, vowed to ferret out the blacks and have satisfaction. The Lane students discovered what was afoot, and immediately began to organize. "The Seminary was some three miles distant" from the heart of the city, and the only access to it was by a road that was most of the way uphill, and all the way "ankle-deep in clayey sticky mud, through which the mob must flounder," a circumstance that would have frustrated even the sober. Lyman recounted the story with great zest. "I told the boys," he chortled, "that they had the right of self-defense, that they could arm themselves and if the mob came they could shoot." Then, with a conspiratorial, but characteristically comic whisper, he added, "but I told them not to kill 'em," just to "aim low" and "hit 'em in the legs! hit 'em in the legs!"[49] Lyman's public attempt to speak moderation, however, continued to be suspect by those who, like the Lane rebels, persisted in

hearing both more and less than the president of the seminary said. "Our trustees and faculty are not abolitionists,"
Lyman insisted, "and our students are conservative [a good
word for him] rather than ultra." But, he continued, "young
men from the South will not be annoyed here or disqualified
for usefulness at home."[50] Lyman seemed obligated to pro-
test the validity of the school, and he did so. In the 1840
catalogue he boasted more students for that year than for the
last, and announced that there was good reason "to anticipate a great number for the year to come."[51] Yet the
seasoned reflection in his *Autobiography* is that from 1836
to 1840 classes averaged only five.[52] Pressed by such circumstance, the only one of the administration who did not lose
hope was Beecher himself. Long afterward, Calvin E. Stowe
remembered Lyman's buoyancy during the "dry time" of
1845 when the land suffered from drought as never before,
and the seminary, as if in empathy, almost succumbed for
other reasons. It was possible to wade across the river bed.[53]
Most green things died, and grasshoppers "destroyed every . . . thing the drought had spared, even to the thistles and
elder-tops by the roadside."[54] Lane was equally distressed,
for no one had registered for the coming term. Stowe took to
his bed, surely sick at heart, whatever his physical condition,
and Lyman took to the provinces, searching for students. On
his return, the president of the school heard his son-in-law
and colleague without waiting to have a report, groan that
" 'twas all over . . . of no use . . . might just as well leave, and
go back East." And then Lyman, like a prophet emerging out
of the wilderness, shouted to Stowe, "You've got no
faith. . . . Get up and wash, and eat bread, and prepare to
have a good class." Lyman had brought the promise of twelve
students. Another was added before the term opened, and
the next year there were thirty-five. "I've got nothing but
faith," Lyman declared. His confidence that the seminary
would grow was justified, but slowly, slowly.[55]

Lane Seminary buildings graced the hills on which they
stood. The completed chapel was "in the style of a Grecian
temple," with Doric columns and impressive plaster and
woodwork—much of it executed by students.[56] Calvin Stowe

was bringing distinction to the library. Sent to Europe by the state of Ohio to study educational methods in use there, he utilized the occasion to buy books for Lane. The project required money, but that was Lyman's responsibility. Calvin merely selected the volumes, though he did so with stunning taste. Presently Lane boasted a "fine collection of the Fathers," more complete, said a visitor, "than any other in the states," except possibly that at Harvard; certainly "Andover had nothing to be compared to it."[57] By 1848 Lane had 10,000 volumes in her library.[58] Nor was the collection narrow, for, with the Patristics, Stowe bought also the Reformers, and Gibbon, and Dr. Johnson and Stillingfleet, and Kant.[59]

Partly to maintain his family (for there was always more confidence than currency at Lane), Lyman served the Second Presbyterian Church as pastor for almost eleven years, so vigorously, incidentally, that he added to the roll five hundred forty new members, two hundred forty of them by profession of faith.[60] Little wonder that in those days he would retreat to his home, as to his castle, exhausted and in need of encouragement and more, and marvelously appropriate that he could find a Lydia Jackson waiting for him there. The response her intuition dictated for his need is clear in a vignette of Beecher returning to the manse after three preaching services in a single day, weary, and "inclined to have something good." The resourceful woman produced exactly the right thing, "a huge watermelon," which, according to the word of a guest who was there, the doctor at once "commenced [to] . . . attack."[61]

No intellectual Roxana, nor quasi-mystical Harriet Porter, Lydia was a fitting helpmeet and a possible argument that a wise and gracious Providence had not forsaken his servant Lyman. Either by instinct or information, Lyman had known this, too, and for that reason was set to marry her before she had dreamed of the honor. She had been a member of his Bowdoin Street Church in Boston; and after his wife, Harriet Porter, died "he soon made his way" to her and "asked of her a private conversation, in which he proposed marriage with almost desperate earnestness, and with not a little bluntness." Mrs. Jackson was "pre-eminently a practical business woman, and no less a Christian lady. But now she was taken by surprise, and could only reply, 'Doctor, this is wholly unexpected. I can give you no answer at present. It is a very serious question. I will think of it, and make it a subject of prayer, and—,'Yes, yes, all right,' said Doctor Beecher. 'It ought to be made a subject of prayer. Let us pray over it now.' So down went the Doctor on his knees before the good Father in heaven, and pleaded his own cause as few could plead in prayer; and he pleaded not in vain."[62]

Lydia Beecher assumed supervision not only of Lyman and his household, but, in her own way, over the entire seminary community. She did well, even succeeding where others had miserably failed in making Lyman a bit neater. "I think . . . that father & mother are the youngest & briskest married pair in these parts," wrote Catherine in 1837. "Our only fear is that father may yet turn out a dandy. Mother keeps his boots & shoes so bright & his coat so well brushed and his cravat tied so genteely & his hair & beard in such first rate order that it is quite amusing to see how spruce he looks. And she is such a fine looking woman herself that both together make folks turn around to see if that *can be* Dr. Beecher."[63]

That Beecher should have drawn attention only by presenting a marked contrast to his customary harum-scarum appearance is poignant, indeed. If perhaps he had ever been, he was certainly no longer a celebrity of intrinsic interest. Though the decline was gradual, his star had begun to set. A faithful friend admitted that the "West never knew Lyman Beecher in the fullness of his pulpit power," because in Cincinnati he was never "entirely at home. Like a mighty locomotive engine, he had leaped his track in coming West."[64] When the London *Times* in 1846 reported the "grand muster of teetotalers" who had arrived in England to attend a World Temperance Convention,[65] complete with a soirée in Freemason's hall and a "large demonstration in Covent Garden Theatre," Beecher's name was simply listed along with the others, and it was Elihu Burritt, "the learned blacksmith" (not the author of sermons against drink that had been translated even into Greek), who was singled out for special notice.[66]

Lyman was delighted with Liverpool, "a great city of brick and mortar strung along the banks of the Mersey, bordered with . . . acres of docks, and a swamp of masts, and great, high, clumsy warehouses, the streets, like Boston, of all widths, and angles, and wedges."[67] Mrs. Beecher pictured Lyman in England, not only enthusiastic, but youthfully vigorous, scrambling to the very top of the dome of St. Paul's ("much to the astonishment of the guide"), preaching in a chapel "never before so well filled," and the people afterward charging her to "take care of that blessed man," because there were no more like him.[68] The *Times,* however, reported factually that when Beecher addressed the mass meeting he was interrupted with cries of "Hear, Hear," a courtesy extended to all who spoke, but that others had enjoyed applause and cheers as well. Lyman assured the convention that after watching the movement for thirty-six years he had happily "lived to see the beginning of the end,"[69] by which presumably he meant that the victory of temperance was in sight. The end that was beginning was Lyman's own, a *finis* not necessarily synonymous with the *telos* of his dreams. Twilight was not yet. It approached, but Lyman could still rise to the occasion, as he very shortly did, and upon the high seas at that.

In mid-Atlantic, on the return voyage, a hurricane overtook the *Great Western,* on which the Beechers had booked passage, with a "fury and power unknown . . . to the most experienced navigators on board."[70] At the height of the storm, there were only terror and darkness. The captain had been struck senseless, and passengers were variously attempting to unite in prayer or receive the sacrament under conditions that would have equally daunted acrobat or saint. Lyman remained resolute and steadfast. When the wind had passed there was a service of worship, and he delivered "God in the Storm," an evangelical exhortation to thanksgiving and renewal of faith. Ever the revivalist, he concluded with the hope that by the ordeal all might be made "more spiritual,

more prayerful, more faithful."[71] Though lacking the old fire,
the sermon speaks the fidelity that was at the core of the man;
for he had indeed seen God in the storm at the very moment
when he believed his own death imminent. "I prayed . . . to
be spared, to do a few more things, which I had projected,
for his service and glory. And I go home, resolved to postpone the work no longer, but with double diligence to
attempt its completion." Yet Lyman, as he himself surely
knew, stood at that point at which opportunity to start
afresh is hardly a viable option. The time had come when it
was necessary, perhaps even possible, to identify those sweep-
ing currents that had moved the stream of his years toward
their appointed end.

After East Hampton there had been Litchfield, and then
Boston, and Cincinnati—each offering new challenge, and
each creating new frustrations. Every succeeding pastorate
began with promise, and ended without allowing him to
achieve all that he dared. Extraneous forces forever inhibited
his effort to prod the world closer to model existence under
the moral government of God. It was not different in his
seventy-first year. The journey to England had appealed to
him not solely for the sake of the temperance rally, but also
for the foregathering of the Christian Alliance, an organization dedicated to effective counter-move against the threat of
world domination by the papacy.[72] That dream had foun-
dered on a resolution regarding slavery concerning which the
Alliance could not agree. In the instance it was well enough
that one prejudice had thwarted another; but the pattern
indicates the deceptive character of surface events in Lyman's
life. The unavoidable relation to enthusiasms of his own
generation makes it easy to misjudge Beecher as a man of
more turbulence than depth. The fact was more nearly the
other way around. Increasingly as his years flowed on, Beecher appeared as a man of faith, and never more so than when
action and participation were denied him. He had come back
from England with fewer days and less energy than he had
already spent. Customarily his sermons had been exhortations to others; "God in the Storm" was a confession of his
own faith. It was faith that sustained him in the dusky

interval that separated his last days in Ohio and the final stilling of his oaken heart. In this support Lyman was fortunate: hardly had he returned to Cincinnati before he was embroiled in litigation as, once again, his integrity and his relation to Lane were put in jeopardy.

Notes to Chapter XIII

1. Obituary for Harriet Porter Beecher, *Cincinnati Journal*, July 24, 1835.
2. ALS, Lyman Beecher, Litchfield, September 24, 1817, to Harriet Porter, Beecher Collection, Stowe-Day Foundation.
3. ALS, Harriet Porter, Boston, September 11, 1817, to Lyman, Beecher Collection, Stowe-Day Foundation.
4. ALS, Lyman Beecher, Litchfield, September 25, 1817, to Harriet Porter, Beecher Collection, Stowe-Day Foundation.
5. Calvin E. Stowe, "Sketches and Recollections," p. 221.
6. ALS, Harriet Porter, Boston, September 22, 1817, to Lyman, Beecher Collection, Stowe-Day Foundation.
7. Catherine E. Beecher, *Educational Reminiscences*, p. 23.
8. *Autobiography*, I, 20.
9. *Ibid.*, p. 412.
10. ALS, Lyman Beecher, Litchfield, July 31, 1820, to Edward, Beecher Collection, Stowe-Day Foundation. Also see *Autobiography*, I, 430.
11. Harriet Beecher Stowe, *Men of Our Times*, p. 511.
12. *Cincinnati Journal*, July 24, 1835.
13. *Ibid.*
14. ALS, Catherine Beecher, Walnut Hills, May 29, 1837, to Mary Cogswell, Beecher-Stowe Collection, Schlesinger Library, Radcliffe College.
15. ALS, Henry Ward Beecher, Walnut Hills, October 4, 1836, to William, Beecher-Stowe Collection, Schlesinger Library, Radcliffe College.
16. Samuel J. Baird, *History of the New School*, p. 546.
17. *Ibid.*, p. 472: "That Dr. Beecher had held and taught the leading points of New England theology, is unquestionable. . . . About the time of Dr. Beecher's removal to Ohio, there existed in Yale Seminary an association of young men whose attention was turned to the West, with a view to the same object which brought him to Cincinnati. . . . Dr. Taylor and the other divines of New Haven were the counselors of the enterprise."
18. Zebulon Crocker, *The Catastrophe of the Presbyterian Church in 1837*, p. 108.

19. *Autobiography*, II, 351.

20. ALS, Asahel Nettleton, East Windsor, July 27, 1835, to Leonard Woods, Nettleton Correspondence, Hartford Seminary Foundation.

21. Lyman Beecher, *Views in Theology*, pp. 236-237.

22. Lyman Beecher, *A Sermon, Delivered at the Installation of the Rev. John Keys*, p. 3. The sermon is elsewhere designated "Building of Waste Places." See *Autobiography*, I, 268-275.

23. *Autobiography*, II, 359n. The reference is to an extract from the minutes of the meeting.

24. Samuel J. Baird, *History of the New School*, p. 471.

25. *Ibid.*, p. 545.

26. *Ibid.*, p. 550.

27. *Ibid.*, p. 549.

28. *Autobiography*, II, 430.

29. Samuel J. Baird, *History of the New School*, p. 553.

30. *Autobiography*, II, 430-431.

31. Walter Balfour, *A Letter to the Rev. Dr. Beecher*, pp. 19-20.

32. *Autobiography*, II, 375.

33. [Asa Rand], *Letter to the Rev. Dr. Beecher on the Influence of His Ministry in Boston* (Lowell, 1833), p. 15.

34. "Beecher's Views in Theology," *Biblical Repertory* (April, 1837), p. 217.

35. *Ibid.*, p. 234.

36. "Beecher's Views in Theology" (a continuation), *ibid.* (July, 1837), p. 365.

37. *Ibid.*, p. 405.

38. ALS, G. W. Perkins, Walnut Hills, August 17, 1838, to his wife, Beecher Collection, Stowe-Day Foundation.

39. *Autobiography*, II, 402.

40. *Ibid.*, p. 546. The *Biblical Repertory* was superseded by the *Princeton Review*. The statement of Beecher's creed in his *Works* is entitled *Views of Theology*.

41. Lyman Beecher, *Works*, III, *Views of Theology; as Developed in Three Sermons, and on His Trials Before the Presbytery and Synod of Cincinnati, June, 1835. With Remarks on the Princeton Review* (Boston and Cleveland, 1853), 414-415.

42. ALS, Catherine Beecher, Walnut Hills, May 29, 1837, to Mary Cogswell, Beecher-Stowe Collection, Schlesinger Library, Radcliffe College.

43. Sydney Strong, "The Exodus of Students from Lane Seminary to Oberlin in 1834," in *Papers of the Ohio Church History Society*, Delavan L. Leonard, ed. (Oberlin, 1893), p. 12. See also Levi Coffin, *Reminiscences of Levi Coffin, the Reputed President of the Underground Railroad*, 2nd ed. (Cincinnati, 1880), p. 533.

44. Sydney Strong, "The Exodus of Students from Lane Seminary," p. 12.

45. September 29, 1836.
46. *Ibid.*
47. Henry Howe, *Historical Collections,* I, 762-763.
48. Levi Coffin, *Reminiscences,* p. 533.
49. Henry Howe, *Historical Collections,* I, 825.
50. ALS, Lyman Beecher, Lane Seminary, May 23, 1840, to Thomas Brainerd, Beecher Collection, Yale University.
51. *Catalogue of the Officers and Students of Lane Theological Seminary, Cincinnati, Ohio, 1839-1840* (Cincinnati, 1840), p. 14.
52. *Autobiography,* II, 407.
53. *Ibid.,* p. 408.
54. Henry Howe, *Historical Collections,* I, 683.
55. *Autobiography,* II, 409.
56. *Cincinnati Journal,* September 29, 1836.
57. ALS, G. W. Perkins, Walnut Hills, August 17, 1838, to his wife, Beecher Collection, Stowe-Day Foundation.
58. Noah Porter, *A Plea for Libraries. A Letter Addressed to a Friend in Behalf of the Society for the Promotion of Collegiate Theological Education at the West* (New York, 1848), p. 32.
59. Invoices, Lane Collection, McCormick Theological Seminary.
60. Henry A. Ford and Kate B. Ford, *History of Cincinnati,* p. 152.
61. ALS, G. W. Perkins, Walnut Hills, August 20, 1838, to his wife, Beecher Collection, Stowe-Day Foundation.
62. James C. White, *Personal Reminiscences,* p. 42.
63. ALS, Catherine Beecher, Walnut Hills, May 28, 1837, to Mary Cogswell, Beecher-Stowe Collection, Schlesinger Library, Radcliffe College.
64. James C. White, *Personal Reminiscences,* p. 16.
65. August 1, 1846.
66. *Ibid.*
67. *Autobiography,* II, 521.
68. *Ibid.,* pp. 521-522.
69. August 11, 1846.
70. Lyman Beecher, "God in the Storm," in the *American National Preacher,* XX (November, 1846), 255.
71. *Ibid.,* p. 262.
72. *Autobiography,* II, 522.

Chapter XIV

Quo Warranto:
A Search for Meaning — 1838-1863

Commitment to God as both author and end of history is an implication of the puritan belief in the divine sovereignty: the past is a memorial to God's activity. Though inscrutable, God is not capricious: he moves purposefully toward the consummation of history. Man, therefore, is not born by chance, but placed in finitude as an epistle to the world in his own and succeeding generations. As it is with men, so it is with all creation. No fragment of history is devoid of significance, and there is moral obligation to preserve the diverse forms of historical record, for all are potentially transparent to God's purpose, any event as germane as any other. It is an act of faith to search for the pattern in existence. The residual puritan mind of nineteenth-century America attempted to reconcile the chronicle of the past with God's lately rediscovered goodness and man's newly granted freedom, in such fashion that still allowed confident affirmation that God for his own good pleasure had foreordained whatsoever comes to pass. In the challenging endeavor the seeker merited puritan identity by refusal to admit defeat, even, and especially, when he failed to achieve victory.

Lyman Beecher, 1858 (Stowe-Day Foundation)

Religious commitment is no more easily relinquished than it is established. Some men for the sake of it have lost their heads, and in consideration of the controversy that too often attends it, many have puzzled over the true identity of the victor and the shape of the prize. So it was with the splintered companies of the Presbyterians after their division in 1838. Lyman reported that the Old School men who had "made arrangements to defeat" their brethren were so "taken by surprise" at the New School coup that they sat "amazed," and in a state of utter "paralasis" [sic],[1] but according to a partisan of the establishment, it was Lyman and his like who were "confounded and silenced"[2] and the traditionalists who, thankful "for a great deliverance" by the "retirement of the foreign elements from the Church," resumed "interrupted business" of the Assembly.[3] In any case, Beecher's enemies were relieved to have him out of the church. But they also wanted him out of the West—or at least separated from Lane. Their campaign to this end had begun before Lyman sailed for England. A writ had been served upon him in October, 1845, demanding that he prove by what right, *quo warranto,* as the initial words of the instrument began, he remained as president and professor at the seminary.[4] His accusers were awaiting him on his return.

The case of David Kemper (son of James and brother to Elnathan)[5] vs Lyman Beecher was argued in December, 1846.[6] Kemper, Old School man, charged that Lyman, New School outcast, and no longer a member in good standing of the Presbyterian Church, had "usurped," and, continued the complaint, "still doth usurp and intrude into the office of Professor of Theology in Lane Seminary, without any legal appointment or qualification, and without due warrant of law."[7] The accusation rested upon the assumption that only the Old School faction, by which Beecher and his associates had been ostracized, was truly Presbyterian. In the opinion of Lyman's enemies, therefore, only an Old School minister might legally hold official position in a Presbyterian school.

Lyman retained as counsel Salmon P. Chase, subsequently senator, and eventually Lincoln's Secretary of the Treasury. Chase defended Lyman with professional competence, for he privately lamented the occasion of the "many hard speeches" made against the liberal Presbyterians. He thought it wrong to "punish the New School" for the actions to which they were "almost, if not absolutely, constrained."[8] When the court agreed, the tenacious David Kemper continued his effort from the angle of chancery, attacking the Trustees of the seminary for dereliction of duty. The case came to nothing. "It was a vexatious suit," Lyman remembered, "but the fact is," he said, "we outwinded them."[9] Actually, it was Lyman's character that had prevailed. Having been born with one foot in the colony and one in the republic, he was related both to the new revolution and to the old covenant, but he was true child of neither. Mentors of Lyman's youth who inquired concerning life's goal received spontaneous and unequivocal answer—even from children—about the glorification and enjoyment of God. Folk who sang of bowing before "Jehovah's awful throne," and meant it, did not blanch at the reminder that the Creator of the ends of the earth was glorified in man's dependence upon him. By the time of Lyman's majority, however, there was also growing reflection upon the possibility that man's chief end might be to know himself and to be his own man, a course justified by right of membership within the human race. Beecher himself had little patience for those preachers who sat "all their lives on [the] goose eggs" of "imputation, inability, and limited atonement," until they "rotted under them."[10]

Simply by being himself, Lyman Beecher put the stamp of his own experience upon that which he passed along, so that the tradition he handed over to another generation still bore the indelible impress of his grasp. The question "by what right?" inherent in the human condition, and never more poignant than in its religious expression, had been continually asked of, and by, Lyman, since his days at Yale College. The Kemper suit was no more than a specific and pedestrian instance of how the question haunted Lyman for half a

century. By what right does God foreordain? By what
right does a man storm the gates of heaven? Foci shifted and
answers evolved, but the question endured. An older generation had demanded to know by what right Lyman had left
East Hampton, inquiring, if in no other way, by their stubborn silence and their unwillingness to grant him gracious
farewell. Even the sleeping dead whom he passed in the
graveyard on his journey toward Connecticut seemed to
indict him for leaving the place, which they never escaped,
nor—so far as anyone knew—ever wanted to. By what right
had he gone to Litchfield, and to Boston, and finally, to the
West? Lyman's whole career made answer: by right of being a
man, because such privilege was consistent not alone with his
own dignity and ability, but surely, with God's intentions.

Lyman honored, or at least understood, shibboleths.
Moreover, he knew that men listen uneasily to a prophet
who speaks in a foreign tongue. Thus, with serpent wisdom, though with burning heart, he nimbly placed the orthodox on the defense in asking, "By what right (and
with what logic) do you say that Edwards allows a man no
freedom?"

Perspective was steady, and existence of a piece for Lyman, and for him no wall separated sacred from profane, or,
if there were a boundary, it was no barrier. Lyman crossed
the line as easily and as naturally as he breathed, and just as
often. Once he rushed from mill pond to sanctuary, bounding
late into the pulpit with a freshly caught fish stuffed hastily
into his coat pocket, and then proclaimed the word with a
power that melted men's hearts.[11] Again, he wrote to Lydia
in high glee, ascribing his elation at once to the successful
treatment of a self-diagnosed and prescribed-for illness, and a
sensational theological discovery. His affliction had vanished,
he said, because for a season he had eaten "no meat or grease
& only crackers & tea & bread & butter & roast potatoes &
corn bread & butter & sugar—with coffee each morning," and
besides, he had been "interested, pleased & comforted" to
discover a writer who for the first time had "fairly & fully
stated Edwards" in such a way as to exclude fatalism and any
thwarting of free will. It was, said Beecher, such a work as

would pulverize the intransigent supralapsarians and bring both them and Edwards "to our side." Although exuberant, Lyman did not tarry to revel in doctrinal victory, but moved on to report meeting the thunder face to face in a storm "as exciting as a glass of brandy."[12]

It is not ultimately significant that Beecher either completely misunderstood what he read or incorrectly reported to his wife the book he had found.[13] In characteristic haste he had probably had time enough only to dip into the volume. The point is that Beecher had such faith in the universe finally becoming what he wanted it to be, that it was both consistent and necessary for him to believe that Edwards' voice and his own proclaimed essentially the same gospel—that any man, every man, was able without spurning his birthright or laughing at heaven, to control the circumstances of his own life.

How successfully Lyman communicated his optimistic ideas to others—especially to his children—is plain in a pitiful letter by his daughter Mary, pained in the discovery that, despite her father's positive analysis of the human condition, the implied advantages were restricted to one's own self, and did not necessarily affect one's children. Confronted with insubordination of a delinquent and irreligious son already involved in street brawls and arrests, Mary wailed to her sister Harriet, "I think I have acted all my life on mistaken views & hopes. I had true faith but I think I had no foundation for it. If I had been told, you must do the best you can for your children & perhaps they will be saved & perhaps not I should not now feel so bitterly disappointed—."[14] But this, of course, was exactly what she, nor anyone else, for that matter, would never have heard from Lyman, for he did not say it. As a matter of fact he said just the opposite, and "implanted the seeds of a younger and fresher type of Calvinism" in American soil, giving "currence" to a "broader view," first in New England, and then in the whole Presbyterian Church.[15] Mary's difficulty was that her personal creed accorded more nearly to her ancestors' than to the faith of her father.

Early and late Beecher preached optimism coupled with

concern for men's souls. Years before his trial he had announced that "human instrumentality is indispensable" in
the economy of salvation,[16] and long thereafter he insisted
that when the Confession says that man has "lost all ability
of will, it does not mean . . . that he is not able . . . to do that
which is right."[17] Accordingly, he not only cultivated his
own soul, frequently inspecting the roots to discover new
growth but, conscientiously and with confidence, prodded
toward salvation those committed to his care. "Oh, my dear
son," he wrote to Edward, "you *must* go to heaven; you
must not go to hell!"[18] Thus Lyman sponsored revivals that
were like autumn fires spreading in the leaves.[19] Edward,
happily, turned away from hell, nor did he do so as a solitary
pilgrim. Time and again Beecher fed the flames of zeal, as
true faith blazed in the hearts of his hearers.[20] It was God's
doing, of course, but, oh, man could help; and without sparks
thrown out from the agonizing struggle of the human soul,
there was no heat, nor any light.

Lyman endured, and more. He prevailed. As with his
critics of Long Island, and with his censors in New England,
so with his antagonists in the West, he outlasted them,
unyielding and unbested. His spirit was stronger than their
spirit, but unchallenged victory eluded the aging warrior, for
Lyman asserted his right more successfully than he secured it.
On surface he had vanquished none, nor conquered any.
Moreover, the rushing years brought new tests of his self-
sufficiency.

In 1843 the Second Church in Cincinnati had requested
Beecher's resignation, not because of his failing powers, but
because of disagreement over projected plans for prayer
meeting and Sabbath School.[21] His last years in the West were
not distinguished. When the presidential aspirant William
Henry Harrison barnstormed Ohio in a log-cabin campaign so
shamelessly emotional that one parade-wagon, purporting to
symbolize the hypocritical character of the Whigs, actually
displayed "a live wolf, enveloped in a sheep skin,"[22] Lyman
sat on the platform at the Cincinnati rally.[23] Beecher's
invitation to a place on the stage beside the Indian fighter
was prompted by political shrewdness and concession to

popular superstition. It was a blatant attempt to baptize the proceedings and exploit the benediction of an acknowledged religious figure. The doctor's political influence was, by that time, however, indifferent, and his endorsement of the Harrison-Tyler ticket of so little import that it did not preclude for him and Lydia a gracious reception by President Polk on their subsequent visit to Washington.[24]

What happened in Cincinnati had happened before—as at Litchfield, where, Beecher said, he "spent sixteen of the best years" of his life "at a dead lift in boosting" and thereafter could never "revert to the scene without shuddering."[25] And for their part, folk who were exposed to Beecher tended to remember the quips and cranks, not the impact upon their lives. Sometimes they did not acknowledge Lyman's influence at all. But whether he had been the agent of their transformation, it was undeniable that they had been altered, and he with them, in a metamorphosis that had overtaken religion in America during the preacher's lifetime.

Jonathan Edwards, Beecher's Protestant surrogate for a patron saint, had never doubted that the spirit of God "bloweth where it listeth." Moreover, he had divided Scripture for colonists who agreed with him. The Holy Ghost came upon some men unawares, saving them eternally, and, inscrutably, passed others by. Edwards detailed this mystery in a moving, sometimes frightening, description: *A Faithful Narrative of the Surprising Work of God.* By mid-nineteenth century, however, republicans behaved as if they had domesticated God's Spirit, at times even avowing by their speech what their actions proclaimed—that the Spirit had no choice but to accept them if they walked a particular path, which, as it happened, was accessible to all men. Charles Grandison Finney actually prepared a manual on how to have a revival, insuring results outside the church exactly "in proportion to the union of prayer and effort within."[26] The matter was no longer the prerogative of Providence. Whereas before men waited on God's pleasure, they were able now to command—even control—the Infinite. Why is it that "you have not a revival," Finney roared, and pointing his finger at the culprits, he thundered the answer that those convicted by his preaching already knew: "because you don't want one. Because you are not . . . putting forth efforts for it."[27]

Now perfectly well committed to human ability, Beecher rejected not only Finney's startling new measures, such as female prayer in the sanctuary, but also the vulgar extension of Taylor's theology. Nathaniel Taylor spoke of sinful man having "power to the contrary." His audiences listened and returned to their closets to reflect and meditate. Finney howled against the "logical perversions which have filled the world with *cannot-ism*,"[28] and heart-happy pietists listened and approved, often as not with shaking and shrieks.

New England villagers of colonial times had for the most part lived alike—they ate the same lean fare, wore similar dress, and spoke a common, forthright, salty language. Intention converged with happenstance in their condition. Notwithstanding the inescapable conformity of a frontier existence, there is room to believe that in the puritan theocracy members of the established church who, in striving to make their election sure, deliberately chose for themselves the authenticating life of sobriety and righteousness, also insisted that until the dreadful day of doom, the least the probably-reprobate could do was to move toward perdition quietly, obediently respectful of the admonitions of the covenanted. Though obviously pharasaic, the Puritans thus marked were no more—nor any less—hypocritical than other men. It was simply their fate to exhibit the prideful human heart by solemn and confident acceptance of the obligation to enforce proper environment for the Lord's own saints, whoever they might be. Thus it fell out in colonial New England that the saved and the lost might very well appear indistinguishable to the outward eye. One could no more tell from visible forms who was a Christian than he could identify a witch by her walk.[29] Membership within the Christian community was a matter of having inwardly owned the covenant. The Great Awakeners, however, who often deserted convention and encouraged the soul's fateful encounter with Satan (not only in the sanctuary, but in tavern, market place, crossroad, and field), also in large measure displaced the dark uncertainty of the inmost heart with the reassurance arising from the undeniable evidence of having publicly turned from the ways of sin. The development was not illogical among those who believed it possible for man to assist himself toward heaven, and to remember how he had done so. By conforming to a ritual experience, many were, thus, made confident of redemption, and enabled to point with the specificity of the lines upon a map or the hands of a clock face to that time and place at which their names had been inscribed within the book of life.

The conclusion that men do not gather figs of thistles is not forbidden by Beecher's union of revival and reform, for that relation leads ineluctably to a notion of conversion, externally realized, outwardly proven. Beecher quarreled, though, with the crass and insistent form of Finney's prophecy. Whether in the pulpit or out of it, Charles Grandison Finney, the attorney turned evangelist, made use of ridicule, even raillery. By his actions as well as by pronouncements, he mocked "stiff" ministers, the "too fastidious" churchfolk, and the "sanctimonious starch" of both.[30] Lyman, however ebullient, did not outrage propriety, and he feared, advisedly, that stylish Unitarians of Boston equated the tasteless enthusiasm of some of Finney's converts with the essence of evangelism, and, until pressed by his church officers to do otherwise, stood aloof from the agitator.[31] "Finney, I know your plan," Beecher warned, "and you know I do; you mean to come into Connecticut and carry a streak of fire to Boston. But if you attempt it, as the Lord liveth, I'll meet you at the State line, and call out all the artillerymen, and fight you every inch of the way to Boston, and then I'll fight you there."[32] Matters fell out quite differently, though, when Finney did arrive; as much as in him lay, Beecher accommodated himself to the visitor, although the two revivalists disagreed over what might be the authentic and becoming outward signs of that inward change that is true conversion. Once Beecher interrupted Finney in public assembly, to interpret what the invading firebrand was saying. The exchange that followed appears as an irenic episode in Finney's *Autobiography:* "I tried . . . not to appear to contradict Dr. Beecher, but yet thoroughly to correct the impression that he had made."[33] Elsewhere, and likely with more accuracy, Finney in pointed reference to a "Doctor of Divinity" whose position in the exact circumstance was "Miserable!" implied that the encounter had been a contentious one.[34]

Although Beecher both expressed and affected the drift toward externalization of religion, his vision was much less narrow than Finney's, and not for all the world would he have consciously debased or restricted the gospel. If enough were made of the patterned, regulated conversion, then that outward experience might come to be regarded as of itself enough to satisfy the demands of commitment. Finney early in his career began to move in the direction of that culpable stance from which he could "hold forth for a whole winter at the Broadway Tabernacle without a word he uttered reaching the nearby Five Points, center of New York's poverty and vice."[35] Beecher never lost sight of the pathos and ugliness of society when it was examined by the gospel's naked light. However much he might misjudge the Christian's obligation regarding so monstrous an evil as slavery, Beecher still dreamed of a millennium free of all "violence and fraud."[36] God's final restoration would be in no way "partial in its influence, like the sun shining through clouds on favored spots, but co-extensive with the ruin." Lyman envisioned a redemption that was not restricted to the ground of the soul, but revitalizing to the whole wasteland of society, bringing liberty to those so crushed by the tyranny of land monopoly that the "sickness of a week and often of a single day makes them paupers"; affording release to those fed into the maw of industry, and doomed to "wear out their days in ignorance and hopeless poverty"; and insuring dignity to those shunted into "camp and navy, where honor and wealth await the few, and ignorance and an early grave the many."[37] Never doubting that "the blessings of God upon exertions of men" would "introduce and perpetuate" man's happiness, Beecher looked for the remedy for the human condition in a "new direction to the physical, moral and intellectual energies of men,"[38] and a "change . . . in the prevailing forms of government."[39] The masses, more comfortable with provincial application of the gospel than in contemplation of reconstructed communi-

ty, gave practical heed to Finney. Lyman sought a combination of revival and reformation, by which the whole world
would be changed. Finney urged dramatic personal conversion. Finney's star shone brighter. Lyman's began to fade.

When he was past seventy, Lyman came again to North
Guilford, his early home whence "two generations" had
"gone off the stage" since last he lived there. He stepped
once more onto the "white oak floor" of the house of his
childhood and saw "the very place where Annis Benton,"
who cared for him in his infancy, "used to sit at her wheel
and spin." Beecher climbed to the garret, then groped his
way to the "cellar, dark & damp." Standing within the walls
that had sheltered him for the first eighteen years of life, he
took comfort in the memory of his chores—how he had
brought cider and turnips from below stairs, or nightly
helped draw out the trundle bed. But outside, "every tree
was gone, like the generations of men," and it was only with
the "eye of imagination" that he saw the farm as it had been,
for "the fences were all removed." The "few persons" whom
he sought out did not know him, nor would he have known
them. "Everywhere the surface was the same, but the generations [had] . . . changed." Not a little sobered, he "passed
the meeting house & burying ground & returned" to New
Haven, where changes no less drastic wounded his heart less,
because he had been there more often and had sustained the
blows one by one. It was good to be again in the familiar
setting of Yale, where everybody, as Lyman put it, had
always been "amazed to see how young and handsome I look
and how sprightly I walk."[40] Lyman at this period might
easily have wondered if he were not temporarily rejuvenated.
Old friends did not recognize him in the man who, tricked
out in pressed jacket and brushed boots, had become almost
a dandy. His letters strongly suggest that the elegance was
indicative of a subtler alteration than a measure of recaptured
youth and happiness evoked in response to Lydia's warmth.
"What may not be expected when your eye shall watch over
me . . . & your sweet smile reward me?" he asked of his
wife.[41] But if his heart was keen, his mind was growing dull.
Life was ebbing, and Lyman knew it. He drew the thin sheets

of the calendar about himself, realistic and fervent in his resolve to postpone, as he was able, any truce with time.[42]

Now and again Beecher wondered if the ability to cast a spell over an audience were still his. Once, after speaking in New York, he was overcome with a melancholy sentiment "he did not often feel," that his "sermon was a failure." The apprehension was relieved, not dispelled, by the press report that "although the fire of his youth was not there, there was vigor enough" and "words . . . weighty with wisdom."[43] The captivating sermon, however, had become the unexpected dividend, not the predictable return of Beecher's pulpit appearances. Recalling the declining years, a faithful constituent told of how a Missions Board, in arranging a meeting, passed over Beecher, normally the speaker, and "without consultation or apology" substituted another. When the intruder began his address with appropriate regret that "infirmities of age" and "fatigue of travel" had unfitted the "celebrated Dr. Beecher" for the platform, Lyman, only momentarily stunned, "sprang to his feet and cried out . . . 'There is some mistake . . . I was never better in my life.' " Before the interloper could compose himself Beecher leapt into the breach and, "off at full speed . . . electrified the audience" in a speech that was "spontaneous . . . simply grand . . . magnificent" and "full of fire, impulse, and Beecherism."[44] The achievement was a tour de force, though, and was surely recognized as such by those who knew and loved the old doctor. Edward, requesting of his father a short autobiographical sketch for a forthcoming volume, left sad evidence of the old man's deterioration in a maladroit suggestion to Lyman that Lydia "could ask [him] . . . the questions and write down" the answers for him.[45]

Lyman, approaching the end, began to see a generation's failure to build a new Jerusalem in the American wilderness reflected in his own frustration. There were limits to his gloom, but the bright intervals declined in number and duration. Increasingly he sought to trace order and design in the pieces of his life.[46] The deterioration, which became tragic after his return to the East, was visible before he left Cincinnati.

"As his powers began to decline," wrote Lane's faithful
Professor Allen, there was sadness at Walnut Hills, "a depres-
sion which spread itself as a gray, wintry cloud over the
sky."[47] Lyman renewed his effort to organize sheaves of
papers and reams of sermon manuscripts that for years he
had carefully dated and kept, and dutifully dragged from one
residence to another. Sometimes he had sold extra homilies
for as little as twenty-five cents,[48] but always he had saved
enough for the green boxes. He became obsessed with the
task, swapping sheets from box to box and from pile to pile:
"my lectures all in this box . . . my revival sermons in this;
and then—" with the attempt to "find some dimly-remem-
bered fragment" the conclusion was invariably a heap "confused and scattered" and the characteristic pledge toward a
"distant tomorrow . . . to rebegin and never finish."[49] An
undated record, in his hand, may well be a part of the
chronicle of his final departure from Cincinnati for the East.
He had come back to his home "to pack" his sermons after
having "spent an hour in selecting" and arranging them "on
the floor in some 20 piles." "I found them," wailed the
disconsolate Lyman, "scattered all over the floor . . . I stood
& exclaimed Oh—three times long & loud . . . then got on my
knees and after two hours I got them in heaps again . . . tied
each bundle tight . . . & put them into my valise. . . . "[50] So
long as he retained even a tenuous hold upon reality, those
papers exercised "a deadly & bewildering power" over him.
Surely it was possible to see in his effects a pattern that
would point to the meaning of his life, and, by extension, of
all life. "He feels," wrote Charles, "as if he could not die in
peace & leave his life's works to lie waste. Hence he returns
again & again to the hopeless task . . . spends hours on hours
in vain searching, and fruitless & painful shufflings & fum-
blings in manuscripts that *will* not come into order nor be
anything but dead . . . documents."[51] Saying good-bye to his
beloved Tom, on perhaps that son's last visit, the old man
almost wept, as he pled, "Oh, Tom, I wish you could live
with me and help me arrange my papers."[52] The sermons fell
in no easy order, nor offered quick solution to the mounting

tension that arose from Beecher's faith that life was good and
his observation that it was not.

The details of his life were slipping from his memory, and
those that remained in his consciousness were no more susceptible to systematic arrangement than were his sermons.
His children had begged him for years to write his autobiography, but, alas, he could not. Too senescent to recall his
own story, he gave the task to Charles, or, rather, Charles
took it, and advertised for anecdotes, and the letters his
father had posted by the score. To his brother Henry Ward,
Charles wrote, mildly incredulous that the progress of the
book revealed a vitality the musty manuscripts did not; for as
he worked Charles discovered a quality to his father's life
"intensely exciting, the memory of which is almost per-
ished."[53] While Charles gathered the papers, Harriet and
Catherine plied their father with questions, seeking information to fill in the gaps. Spasmodically he reminisced.[54] They
wrote it all down.

When Lyman Beecher's *Autobiography* was thus finished
by other hands than his, Charles came down from Newark
and read the work aloud. "It is glorious, beautiful," Harriet
wrote to Catherine.[55] More so surely for them than for their
father, for in large measure it was their story. Moreover, by
this time Lyman could not have absorbed much of what
Charles had accomplished. Concentration was now difficult
in the extreme. Beecher's outward history had long since
disintegrated into that succession of commonplace humiliation
and defeat familiar to any whose wasting frame outlasts the
mind. In the lucid periods—fewer and shorter—that he enjoyed, it was abundantly clear that his inward eye was fixed
upon the infinite future. Now and again he looked back. To a
young lad, several generations and many years removed from
the circumstance of creeping death, he said, "I was a little
boy once. Did you know it?" On another occasion, after
listening to a reading from one of his own sermons, he
remarked softly, "I have heard it before."[56] Mostly, though,
he waited, like one whose visit is finished—like a traveler
whose bags are packed and whose account is settled and who

is ready, even eager, to depart the temporary shelter and begin the journey home.

While he waited, those who loved him watched as well, suffering keenly over nature's insults to the aging prophet. Devotion was in greater supply than dignity, yet their faithful ministry to the fiercely independent old man brought needed grace to a distressing situation and added to the evidence that in his children Beecher's soul went marching on. The meaning and justification of his existence was visible in them.

Notes to Chapter XIV

1. [Lyman Beecher], Philadelphia, May 18, 1838, to Lydia, Beecher Collection, Stowe-Day Foundation. The signature has been cut from the letter.

2. Samuel J. Baird, *History of the New School*, p. 547.

3. *Ibid.*, p. 553.

4. *Autobiography*, II, 524.

5. *History of the Foundation and Endowment of Lane*, p. 8.

6. John Vant Stephens, *The Story of the Founding of Lane: Address Delivered at the Centennial of Lane Theological Seminary, June 25, 1929* (Cincinnati, 1929), p. 17.

7. *Ibid.*

8. ALS, Salmon P. Chase, Cincinnati, May 12, 1845, to Samuel B. Findlay, Lane Collection of the Cincinnati Historical Society.

9. *Autobiography*, II, 528.

10. *Ibid.*, p. 352.

11. Esther Harriet Thompson, "Life in Old Litchfield."

12. ALS, Lyman Beecher, Marietta, July 24, 1839, to Lydia, Beecher Collection, Stowe-Day Foundation.

13. Henry Philip Tappan, *A Review of Edwards's "Inquiry into the Freedom of the Will"* (New York, 1839), *passim*.

14. ALS, Mary Perkins, [Hartford], November 19, 1848, to Harriet, Beecher Collection, Stowe-Day Foundation.

15. Edward D. Morris, "The Theologians of Lane," in *Thirty Years in Lane* (n.p., n.d.), p. 140.

16. Lyman Beecher, "A Reformation of Morals Practicable and Indispensable," in *Sermons Delivered on Various Occasions*, p. 73.

17. Lyman Beecher, *Views of Theology*, p. 122.

18. *Autobiography*, I, 460.

19. *Ibid.*, II, 74.

20. Perry Miller, *The Life of the Mind in America: From the Revolution to the Civil War* (New York, 1965), identifies "the domi-

nant theme in America from 1800 to 1860" as the "invincible persistence of the revival technique," and acknowledges Beecher's part in the phenomenon, pp. 7-9.

21. Almon M. Warner, "History of the Walnut Hills Congregational Church of Cincinnati," in *Papers of the Church History Society of Ohio*, XII (Oberlin, 1901), 34-35.

22. Henry Howe, *Historical Collections*, II, 290.

23. Robert Gray Gunderson, *The Log-Cabin Campaign* (Lexington, 1957), p. 67.

24. ALS, Lydia Beecher, New York, May, 1845, to her son Joseph, Beecher Collection, Stowe-Day Foundation.

25. *Autobiography*, II, 250.

26. Charles Grandison Finney, *Lectures on Revivals of Religion*, ed. William G. McLoughlin (Cambridge, 1960), p. 325.

27. *Ibid.*, p. 36.

28. *Ibid.*, p. 379.

29. It was just this circumstance which complicated the Salem witchcraft episode in which rectitude was not accepted as proof of righteousness.

30. Charles Grandison Finney, *Lectures on Revivals*, p. 220.

31. *Autobiography*, II, 108.

32. *Ibid.*, p. 101.

33. Charles Grandison Finney, *Charles G. Finney: An Autobiography* (London, 1892), p. 266.

34. Charles Grandison Finney, *Lectures on Revivals*, p. 170.

35. Perry Miller, *Life of the Mind*, p. 20.

36. Lyman Beecher, *Six Sermons on the Nature, Occasions, Signs, Evils, and Remedy of Intemperance*, p. 79.

37. Lyman Beecher, *A Sermon Addressed to the Legislature of Connecticut*, p. 7.

38. *Ibid.*

39. *Ibid.*

40. ALS, Lyman Beecher, Brooklyn, August 28, 1848, to Lydia, Beecher Collection, Stowe-Day Foundation.

41. ALS, Lyman Beecher, [New Haven], August 26, 1847, to Lydia, Beecher Collection, Stowe-Day Foundation.

42. Lyman Beecher, "God in the Storm," p. 261.

43. ALS, Lyman Beecher, New York, February 7, 1849, to Lydia, Beecher Collection, Stowe-Day Foundation.

44. James C. White, *Personal Reminiscences*, p. 38.

45. ALS, Edward Beecher, Boston, February 4, 1847, to Lyman Beecher, Beecher-Stowe Collection, Schlesinger Library, Radcliffe College.

46. [Lyman Beecher], a memorandum in MS, Walnut Hills, June 19, 1850 [to Henry Ward Beecher], Beecher Collection, Yale University.

47. Edward D. Morris, *Thirty Years in Lane*, p. 188.

48. ALS, Lyman Beecher, Litchfield, December 3, 1823, to Cather-

ine, Beecher-Stowe Collection, Schlesinger Library, Radcliffe College.

49. *Autobiography*, II, 516-517.

50. ALS, Lyman Beecher, n.p., n.d., to Lydia, Beecher Collection, Stowe-Day Foundation.

51. ALS, Charles Beecher, Boston, May 21, 1856, to Henry Ward Beecher, Beecher Collection, Yale University.

52. *Autobiography*, II, 517.

53. ALS, Charles Beecher, Galesburg, Ohio, March 22, 1857, to Henry Ward Beecher, Beecher Collection, Yale University.

54. Forrest Wilson, *Crusader in Crinoline*, p. 403.

55. *Ibid.*, p. 436.

56. [Lucy Jackson White], MS description of Beecher's last days, Beecher Collection, Stowe-Day Foundation. Mrs. White was the daughter of Beecher's third wife, Lydia Jackson, by a former husband.

Chapter XV

Soul Marching On:
Heirs of Beecher's Spirit – Before and After 1863

... *The Lord hath said of* New-England, *Surely they are my People*, ... Upon this Basis have all the *Saviourly Undertakings* of the Lord been founded ... and upon this bottom do we unto this day abide. The solemn work of this day is ... not to lay a new Foundation, but to continue and strengthen ... that which hath been laid. ... If we ... deceive the Lords Expectations, ... then All were lost indeed; Ruine upon Ruine. ... The name and Interest of God, and Covenant-relation to him, it hath been written upon us in Capital Letters from the beginning ... as to *Sons* and *Children* that are Covenant-born unto God, Are not we the *first* in such a Relation? ... O what Parents and Predecessors may we the most of us look back unto, through whose Loins the Lord hath stretched forth the line of his Covenant, ... It hath been a special Exasperation unto Adversaries and Ill-willers, that despised New-England hath publickly avouched and challenged a special Interest in God. *As for our Advantages* ... time and strength would fail to reckon up what we have enjoyed ... the Eye and Hand of God, watching and working every way for our good; ... Encouragements, and a wall of fire round about us. ... God sifted a whole Nation that he might send choice Grain over into this Wilderness .... therefore let us in the fear of God learn this great truth today, *That the great God hath taken up great Expectations of us,* ...

New-Englands True Interest
William Stoughton, 1631-1701

Beecher Family 1855 (Yale University Library, Manuscripts and Archives)

Thomas   William   Edward   Charles   Henry Ward
Isabella   Catherine   Lyman   Mary   Harriet

Piecing together the mosaic of their father's life, the Beecher children understandably projected the image of a splendid old saint, weary in God's work, but not of it. They tell of how their father, in tidy sequence, and with no "regrets of mortified ambition," relinquished his duties at Cincinnati; and they note the "appropriate resolutions" adopted by the Board of Trustees.[1] Not for a minute was Lyman deceived by the fair words, which were full of "due honor but . . . not . . . support."[2] Yet it is true that in May 1851 he walked away from Lane without bitterness and without looking back. He wrote to Henry Ward that he had "fought a good fight," and, though confident that his achievement was "a matter of history," still hoped to "rescue from oblivion" that record of his labors which was locked in "sermons & lectures & miscellaneous addresses."[3]

Immediately, therefore, in the summer of 1851, he had turned toward Brunswick, Maine, where his daughter Harriet Beecher Stowe—recently arrived[4]—had, in typical family fashion, established that defensible balance between responsible activity and a keen enjoyment of the sea air and the rugged coast, obliquely expressed in "Earthly Care a Heavenly Discipline."[5] Instinctively seeking the same personal ecology, Lyman, according to the *Autobiography,* was for several months occupied in "preparing his writings for the press," while a guest in his daughter's home; but by the time the season had changed, he was comfortably pursuing "literary labors" in his own hired house in Boston.[6]

Lydia Jackson Beecher has left a partial record of the same transition and of the time that followed, at once less tranquil and far more mundane. It is highly colored by anxiety over money matters, and there are, moreover, echoes—not all of them faint—of the clash of strong wills in fierce disagreement over the allocation of obligation and privilege in caring for the aging doctor, and over acknowledgment of the one upon whom the mantle of the abdicating patriarch should properly fall.[7]

Beecher's third wife was eminently "efficient and practical,"[8] becoming attributes for the companion of Lyman's middle and twilight years, and doubtless indispensable characteristics for one who had been, as she had, successful entrepreneuse of a ministerial rookery.[9] Her life (no more relentlessly stalked by death than Lyman's[10]) had, nevertheless, made her peculiarly sensible to the costliness of illness and dying;[11] but even had this not been so, her Cincinnati experience would surely have alerted her to the practical hazard of providing for Lyman. It was not just that he could never be trusted to use the red handkerchief ordinarily and to keep the white one as a "special one for public."[12] Rather it was that, with his obliterating genius for living in the present, he simply did not bother to save for another day. "The Lord always has taken care of me," he boasted, "and I am sure he always will." So strongly did he hold to this faith that he could bed down in untroubled sleep beside a wife who lay awake and weeping over financial problems the whole night through.[13]

"When we closed up at Lane," wrote Lydia, "we sold all our goods & chattels for $300, to be paid in monthly" installments, an arrangement, incidentally, which failed of fulfillment and left them, as she said, without "means of support except the promise" of their friends.[14] In the actual drama, there were roles neither for a distinguished man of letters, retiring to the leisure of editorial activity, nor for a penniless woman, frightened by the prospect of an indigent old age and the humiliation of subsisting upon the largess of in-laws. But the fact is inescapable that Lyman had accumulated no estate. Free-handed as he was open-hearted, he had shared with others as gladly as he had importuned their aid. Nor had he looked narrowly to accounts.

When, for example, a certain Josiah Bissell, attempting to establish a line of "Sabbath-keeping stages through Central New York," appealed to Lyman, the doctor was so entranced with the notion of a mail and passenger coach that did not desecrate the Lord's day by Sunday runs, that he raced

upstairs to his wife's bedroom, determined to find a contribu-
tion. There, in a bureau drawer, he discovered seventy-five
dollars that had been collected by the ladies of his Boston
church for the purpose of buying a carpet for the bare floor
of the Green Street parsonage. Without asking, Lyman took
the money, which was rolled together, and, never bothering
to count it, delivered the whole sum into the hands of the
grateful Bissell.[15] Innocent improvidence alone, though, did
not account for Lyman's insolvency. There were those who
were indebted to him.

At his retirement, Lyman Beecher, who had "secured"
primary income for Lane, and, in effect, through personal
effort, "erected the buildings, founded the library, and endowed two professorships"[16] was due almost four thousand
dollars in unpaid salary.[17] The trustees had never risen above
the financial difficulty that had begun with the Tappan
brothers' disaffection over abolition. Directly after Arthur
sustained serious loss in the panic of 1837, he "calmly and
resolutely set about making needful arrangements" that "the
blow fall as lightly as possible on others,"[18] but, unfortunately, he gave no support thereafter to the Seminary. Beecher had received prompt word from New York that a draft of
his on Mr. Tappan had "been dishonored on account of his
suspension of payments."[19] Nevertheless, the redoubtable
Lyman continued to serve faithfully. The fact, therefore, that
at seventy-six he was occasionally preaching as often as seven
times weekly may indicate straitened circumstances, as well
as enduring vitality.[20] The ex-president's claim upon Lane
was not settled until seven years after his departure.[21] Meanwhile Boston friends, in "sentiments of highest esteem,"
presented him with a modest life annuity.[22] Lyman, who
always entrusted "financial arrangements to the hands of his
several wives," turned all monies over to Lydia,[23] but that
was not the end of economic hardship. When Lyman's amazing sturdiness persisted, some who had "wished many years
of health" for him, grumbled at the ongoing expense for one
so far advanced on borrowed time as he.[24]

If Beecher's last days were sad, they were not so in his eyes
because of leanness of fare. Meagerness—even penury—Lyman

could sustain. He was subjected, however, to a less support-able burden in the familial controversy that often swirled about him in his declining years. Even more grievous was defection from the tradition in the lives of his offspring, a development that troubled him no less than their tardy acceptance of the creed. In their various ways the Beecher children did forsake the conventional standards and trappings of their father's faith. It is easy, therefore, to say that their abandoned symbols point accusingly to a more far-reaching failure than theirs, and that there is indication of Lyman's inability in the end to influence his generation any more lastingly than he could shape the affirmations of his house-hold. But it is a matter not so much of charity as of reflection to see that, in point of fact, Lyman succeeded grandly, precisely because in his children, who moved upon the basic assumptions of their father, his soul, quite as much as theirs, found true and lively expression.

After Lyman was past middle age, centrifugal forces began to threaten the structure of the Beecher community whose members, because they were bound together by intangibles of the spirit, had long withstood that erosion which customari-ly follows separation or inequality of estate among relatives. At a grand family reunion, celebrated in Ohio shortly after Lyman's heresy trial, two of his children saw each other for the first time, and some had met only once before.[25] They gathered, however, in rapport that arose, not out of physical proximity, but from a mystique that focused upon the gold-en days when all the living Beechers had been crowded together into the inadequate confines of the Litchfield manse. For years the enclave successfully expanded and em-braced any born, or inducted, into the clan. So for the gathering of 1835, Catherine, constitutionally unable to resist supervising others, had composed a "Song of Remembrance" (of indifferent prosody, but commendable warmth) designed for the lusty, unison voice of the whole assembly. Truth to tell, it was far more reminiscent of the composer's past than of anybody else's. The verse recalled "naughty tricks / and snickering jokes" to which James, for example (who did not see light of day until twelve years after Lyman quitted

Connecticut), could not possibly have been a party. Catherine's poem also made references to such Bantam Hill eccentrics as "Deacon Trowbridge" and "crazy Dine," whose names Hattie and Henry Ward recognized, if they did so at all, only by acquaintance with oral tradition and tribal lore, for these two had still been toddlers when the family removed to Boston. Yet, oddly, there was a cogency in Catherine's composition, because the joy of the things she remembered lay in their transparency to an essence that informed all their lives and cemented the Beechers together. When they sang of the "old church / uncushioned, cold and bare," but still warm and cheerful,[26] they hymned an existence that, in all its vagaries, yet revealed a common faith. Their music was a parable of how singleness of spirit leavens the lumpy life, and it was a spirit unmistakably learned from their father. His happy, nostalgic children also gave jubilant witness, as with joined hands they surrounded Lyman in a circle of love, and together with him gladly sang "Old Hundred."[27] The obvious community of that gathering did not outlast Lyman. Paradoxically, the loss of it attests to Beecher's enduring influence upon his children.

By the time of Lyman's appointed death, their concord was strained, if not destroyed. Impervious to many solvents that divide the ordinary families of men, the Beechers split upon the shoals of theological opinion (always a passion with them), and upon the sharp reef of individual will, because they were neither biddable to unsolicited advice nor tolerant of what they considered aberrant action or attitude in each other. The consequence of Lyman's career is illuminated in their personal histories. Each of Lyman's children reproduced in his own way, not the pattern of the father's life, but an example of his faith and a demonstration of how the spirit of the man enlivened and sometimes dignified that which—otherwise—might have been only bizarre or ridiculous.

James, the youngest of them all, merits special attention, because he was a peculiar trial to his father, and thus a compelling illustration of the influence of Beecher's character. But James' extension of his father's spirit did not by any means appear as conformity to the shape of Lyman's life. In his son James, Lyman, always concerned for his children's conversion, encountered much more than resistance to the Holy Ghost—a reluctance Lyman understood in the contrite who were well advised to exercise caution lest they heed a demonic voice.

James insolently defied the establishment. Until he was suspended from Dartmouth[28] "he associated with wild young men . . . played cards & rode about"[29] excelling only in low "wit . . . and wickedness," while brazenly enjoying sanctuary because he was Lyman Beecher's son.[30] Sufficiently tamed to be readmitted and graduated, James immediately unsettled his father by demanding benediction and stipend for a year's jaunt to the Orient—a proposal to which the shaken Lyman, seventy-three at the time, said: "I cannot give my consent without doing violence to my judgment & conscience & heart." He added that if James did go to the East, it would bring down upon his troubled parent "great grief & . . . sorrow which most probably" would "so affect [his] . . . health as to shorten [his] life."[31] James went. Five years later he returned, chastened and converted, to enroll in Andover Seminary, fulfilling the promise his brother Tom had detected in spite of James' "proclivity toward vulgarity" even "bestiality," because James was truly his "father's son by nature both in mind & body,"[32] and in common acknowledgment with him of the imperative demands of God's Spirit.

Only briefly, though, did James tarry at home. Soon he was off again to the Orient, but this time as a missionary of the Seamen's Bethel in Hong Kong, a ministry he interrupted to enlist for service in the American Civil War. Almost immediately thereafter, James challenged the popular notion that blacks could not be transformed into disciplined soldiers and quite properly became distinguished as colonel of the "First North Carolina Colored Volunteers."[33] Having thus vanquished Satan, escaped Chinese sea-pirates, and proved his point, the mature James nevertheless continued to suffer from wounds of family combat, complaining to Harriet in 1862 that while he had been in China "nobody wrote to" or "seemed to care for" him.[34] The sentiment was quite akin to that of the young James, who, never less than liberated, had always rejected the "amazing condescension" and free counsel of his family, and had once sworn, "The next beloved elder sister or kind brother I visit it shall not be my fault."[35]

The unfettered, self-determining James finds scant place in his father's official *Autobiography*, not a single word of rejoicing for the return of this prodigal to the fold, although an entire chapter— "The Lost Found"[36] —relates how Charles, once a seminarian and long a heretic, forsook the musician's life in New Orleans and reaffirmed the faith of his father. Yet the ambivalent James, quite as much as the recusant Charles, was exponent of Lyman's own confession. Moreover, by obliging his brothers and sisters to respond to his problem, James furnished the occasion of further revelation of Lyman's impact upon the family.

Throughout the feverish episodes of the youngest Beecher's life the other members of the family, siblings as well as parents, held strong opinions about the situation and voiced them publicly. Nobody was neutral, and, as often happens when folk act in conscience, there were set a "man at variance against his father, and a daughter against her mother,"[37] and worse, in the multiplying tension and strife. It is their principle, though, and not their prejudice that instructs. The conflict and partisan alliances among members of the Beecher family, whatever else they show in their baffling and complex variety, illuminate the core of Lyman's character; for they exhibit, often in stark profile, individuals whose minds and wills had been sharply honed in granulating encounter with their father, children whose hearts had inherited and emulated Lyman's courage by which they, too, therefore, risked solitary—even unpopular—commitment, and dared face any adversary—including family or infinity, if necessary—to maintain their real or imagined integrity. As for James, his tortured pilgrimage led him finally down the lonely path to suicide.[38] Though assuredly melodramatic, the conclusion of his fervid story stands as a reminder of one who, if he acted at the end in wild, unbalanced, pitiable decision, was even then not without courage of conviction and a willingness to chance danger and accept penalty.

Individuality in the Beechers was religious in orientation, but protean in form. It was often manifest as humanitarianism, markedly so in Catherine.

No one could have denied that Catherine Beecher was dominant. Some considered her domineering. "Isn't it time Robert went to bed?" she once inquired of her hostess, a Mrs. Porter; and then, looking in the direction of the woman's young son, added positively, "All children should go to bed at eight." Master Porter promptly retreated. Later during the same evening the family whose hospitality she was enjoying (and that by her own invitation, if she were in her customary situation) elected to sing hymns. Miss Beecher interrupted when the chorus of one ran, "I am nothing, Lord, Oh nothing—thou art all, all." "I am *not* nothing," she declared.[39] The vignette is typical. Her concern could be obnoxious, but it was born of unshakable conviction that her fellow creatures were stamped—as she was—with dignity and worth, and that it was her duty to assist all to understand themselves similarly. Her actions were her own, but her spirit was like her father's. We must bring the "whole nation" to the "light of intellectual and moral daylight," Lyman had said, adding confidently, "This can be done."[40] Not from the time when Catherine first vowed by doing good to overcome her grief for the drowned Alexander Fisher, until the last month of her life, when she was still busy with a plan "to consult heads of . . . institutions, and superintendents of . . . schools"[41] did she relax her effort to recast human nature into its proper dimension. Just so did Lyman practice his religion.

Soberly conceding that there was no "extensive sphere of usefulness for a single woman" outside the "school-room,"[42] Catherine wrote to her father that she was determined to save the world through education—giving herself particularly to promoting "endowed institutions"[43] that would insure liberal instruction for women. Though no more willing than Miss Sally Pierce to restrict the training of females to china painting and chamber music, Catherine sensibly concluded that there was no reason why homemaking should not be taught as scientifically as Euclid, nor any insuperable barrier to

acquainting the female mind with ladylike arts and intellectual disciplines in the same curriculum. Though a crusader for
women's just place in society, Catherine did not question
that heaven had assigned woman a secondary role in the
universe; but she contended that man had ignored and denied
the true potential of her sex. As for rights, Catherine—no
suffragette—still felt that her sisters were due equal rights
among themselves. Like her father, she deplored the fallen
creation. Yet by her realistic attempt to redeem misguided
society she accepted it, though never imagining that the
shape of Eden could be improved upon as a paradigm for
happiness or humanity.[44] Consequently Catherine juxta-
posed tedium of existence and the infinite mercy in the same
way that Lyman had delighted in bifocal lenses, equally
adaptable to the study of philosophy or the shooting of
pigeons.[45] Thus Catherine's *Domestic Receipt Book* explains
how to make and use yeast in the baking of bread,[46] and
wisely cautions against experimenting with new dishes when
entertaining guests.[47] If an unmarried and, frankly, now
unwanted Catherine had wistfully informed mothers and
housekeepers through the pages of this volume that their lot
was preferable to that of "imperial queens," it was a religiously committed Beecher who assured them that their
heavenly Father "sympathize[d] ... with all [their] ...
cares."[48]

In a long career, undaunted by limited finance and chronic
ill health, Catherine published more than two dozen
books,[49] innumerable circulars, addresses, and articles, all
the while migrating like a gypsy from East to West and back
again, establishing schools from Hartford to Dubuque.[50]
Between times she espoused causes and pontificated on national phenomena from Indian removal (which she deplored[51]) to calisthenics (which she heartily endorsed, because, typically, in one group of young ladies whom she
examined she found that for the sake of "curvature of the
spine" and other "deformities among them, not one quarter
[had] ... the proper figure"[52]). No cause was too obscure
to escape her notice or too unpopular to outflank her assistance. Perhaps no one else except another Beecher would

have championed the cause of Delia Bacon—in which affair Catherine, more than in any other situation, exhibited that distinctive perspective of morality which justified in a measure the division of nineteenth-century Americans into three categories: "saints, sinners, and Beechers."[53]

Delia Bacon was of privileged ancestry. She was sister to Leonard Bacon, Nathaniel Taylor's successor as minister of the First Congregational Church in New Haven, and thus, by definition, a true Connecticut celebrity. Remembered in American letters for her mad notion that Shakespeare's plays were written by another than he, Miss Bacon was not yet in the grip of her monomania when for a time during 1845 she had kept company with one Alexander McWhorter, a minister and also a member of the Yale faculty. Whatever ardor there had been between these two cooled under circumstances that were variously reported. Miss Bacon's umbrageous friends labeled McWhorter a cad; his associates described Delia as a forward young woman who had pursued a male. The Rev. Dr. Bacon, appearing before his denominational consocation, charged the alleged suitor with "slander, falsehood, and conduct dishonorable." Wisely, that ecclesiastical body deemed action "unnecessary."[54] "Convinced that no private influence would be exerted to redress this high-handed injustice," Catherine Beecher thereupon characteristically rallied, as she termed it, to "an outrage upon the female character and sensibilities, which, considering its objects, its nature, and its authors, is without parallel in the history of civilization."[55]

When the other Beechers awakened to what Catherine was planning, they were stunned. Mary wrote frantically to sister Hattie, beseeching help in stopping the "meteor," and telling how Kate was *secretly* preparing" to publish "the whole story," not even sparing papa's sacred old friend, Dr. Taylor, who was at that time esteemed professor of divinity at Yale.[56] Where Beecher was pitted against Beecher, and Catherine opposed to family friend, the residual stuff of the heritage was exposed. One believed in God, himself, and neighbor, and one discharged obligation to each by loyalty to all. But if there were conflicting claims, the priority was

unambiguously that of God, and of his truth.[57] It was as
nothing and less than nothing to Catherine that she had often
been self-invited guest of the Taylors for weeks on end. [58]
Her announced intention was to "attack Yale college & clear
the ministry of such men as Dr. Taylor," doubly guilty in her
eyes because McWhorter lived under his roof. Even the most
embarrassing detail, said Mary, "if she thinks it *best,* she will
certainly put it in."[59] Lyman disapproved, but was helpless.
The completed work, *Truth Stranger than Fiction,* which
incidentally the wretched Delia implored her benefactress not
to publish, was ill received. It aroused Leonard Bacon, and
was too much even for the professional aplomb of Dr. Taylor.[60] Catherine—a true Beecher—was not subdued, and presently began work on yet another of her attacks upon the
theology of Jonathan Edwards, an endeavor in which she was
skillful enough to give sharpened meaning to the wounded
astonishment of a Teutonic theologian who even in his native
Germany had heard of this creature abroad, and wailed:
" . . . a woman that can write an able refutation of Edwards
on 'The Will?' God forgive Christopher Columbus for discovering America!"[61]

Anecdotes of the Beechers (and their name is *legion*),
though intrinsically fascinating, are far more than that. A
substructure of character underlying the distracting activity
of the amazing family informs their eccentric personality,
and transforms trivia into significance. Beecher folk were, in
some respects, not unlike the Scottish Highlands that nourished certain of their forebears, and sheltered those who
crystallized the symbols Lyman's children cast aside. As the
heather, though bending wildly with the wind, is so bound to
the rock beneath as to be well-nigh immovable, so the Beechers, nodding, even straining, in the direction of cross-currents,
were fixed by intransigent commitment that transcended
human reference or temporal condition. In James and in
Catherine, erratic forays, articulated prejudice, and missionary zeal arose from acknowledgment of obligation of such
long-continued and deep-rooted scruple as to pass their power to avoid or put away. Lyman had at some pains delineated
the matter: true faith "supported by sanctions of eternal life

and eternal death" plainly "required love to God with all the heart, and impartial love for men."[62] Beecher children, therefore, did not confuse the essence of religion with its propositional forms. Years after Lyman's death, Henry Ward could laughingly express confidence that his father had surely "repented of [his] . . . orthodoxy long ago in heaven,"[63] because the son understood, as "everybody else knew," that although Lyman thought himself "great by his theology," he was, in fact, "great by his religion."[64] At another time and in another place, Henry Ward, with disarming candor, explained the nature of his father's influence: "When I was a boy, I learned some hymns, and committed to memory an indefinite number of texts, and waded a certain distance into the catechism, never getting through it; and I forgot them again very quickly. But I do not think all of them put together exercised any material influence upon me one way or the other—they did not remain in my mind to be understood when I was older; but a great many things which my father did, but which neither he nor anybody else spoke of, have had a strong influence on my whole life. . . . I had an ideal of what a man should be and should do, and it stood me in stead better than any amount of catechetical instruction could have done."[65]

Faith for the Beecher children was a decisive act, and man was both able and responsible in the matter. Scorning the notion that children's teeth are set on edge because their fathers have eaten sour grapes, Lyman had held men "accountable . . . for their voluntary exercises and deeds."[66] So was it with his offspring. Moreover, Beecher was contemptuous of those who did not grasp the nettle because their nerves were made of shoddy, and he denounced them as unworthy by reason of their *unwillingness to encounter opposition and obloquy, and loss of confidence.*"[67] In appearing to take metaphorical arms against their father, therefore, righteously militant Beechers were rather acting upon precepts learned from him, and, at least in their own opinion, volunteering to serve with the ranks of the angels. They did not withhold allegiance because Armageddon had not come; and until summoned by heaven to engage in that final struggle, they were quite capable of making apocalypse of accident. Evidence of their kinship with Lyman lay not in identical actions, but in common sensitivity to the moral dimensions of life. Like their father they accepted the obligation attendant to being born in the image of God.

Thus, Henry Ward, most celebrated pulpiteer of all of Lyman's preacher sons, presented in his Brooklyn sanctuary a picture of Jehovah so watered down that Lyman could by no means endorse it, and even complained that one of the celebrity's sermons had "annoyed him exceedingly." Henry "had no business to tell sinners of the Love of God without telling them of the wrath of God." Still, the old revivalist admitted honestly that he could "not tell how much" the desire to help "men that would not listen to" any other kind of "preaching had to do with Henry's" public theology.[68] Exactly here Henry behaved as a son of Lyman, who, never forgetting the ultimate goal of saving men by whatever desperate or devious means were necessary, always had "regard [for] time and circumstance in respect to" proclaiming difficult truth and also to "the preparation of the Church to receive it."[69] It was Lyman himself who had warned Charles Beecher to be cautious with church folk so as to "provide no mark for the enemy to fire at."[70]

Harriet remembered her father preaching so powerfully against slavery as to draw "tears down the hardest faces of the old farmers in his congregation."[71] His prayers, she wrote to Frederick Douglas, "indelibly impressed my heart and made me what I am from my very soul, the enemy of all slavery,"[72] yet her attack upon the peculiar institution, by which she demonstrated the Beecher mettle, was from a position much closer to the stance of Theodore Weld than to that of her father.

Tom Beecher first entered the Christian community in Litchfield, Connecticut, where churches did not have stoves until after 1812, and only then over the outraged protests of traditionalists; but in nineteenth-century America he built a house of worship in Elmira, New York, accommodated with "gymnasium, library, theatre, and a 'romp room' for the children in the daytime which served as a dancing room for

the young people in the evening."[73]   Thus he proved himself
heir to the spirit, not of the troubled man who had sadly
helped to close the Cornwall Mission School (as he believed,
for the common good), but of that fiery parson who had
vowed to a conventional parish that he would make fishing
respectable there.

Even the dream of Lyman's suffragette daughter Isabella[74] was, though perverted, another expression of individuality. Favored with a revelation from heaven, Isabella predicted a *"maternal government"* of the world, with herself
called to the presidency of a commonwealth whose benign
influence would spread "slowly but surely over the whole
earth." Hers was the faith that affirms the unlimited potential of humanity, and assumes responsibility with regard not
to risk, but to need.[75]

The behavior of the Beechers, however dissident, is not
accurately styled rebellious. Assuredly they appeared to be at
war with Calvinism, and there is no denying that they rejected both the spoken admonition and external paradigm of
their father. As the matter stood, though, whether considered
in Harriet's defection to the Episcopal church, Charles'
vertigo of compromise in periodic flirtation with heresy, or
Catherine's busy-ness with projects and publications, the essence of the breed was an irrepressible spirit, which drove
their bodies on missions of charity as relentlessly as it denied
them peace in any sanctuary save the reduction of all insight
and industry to theology. Their father had left them a treasure that was both scourge and blessing.

Moreover, what Lyman bequeathed to his children he gave
to his generation in such measure as they would receive it.
Lyman Beecher's goals seemed—like desirable fruit on the
topmost bough—ever to elude his grasp. He did not unite
men of Christendom into a vast army, moving against wickedness; he did not reform society, or even teach it temperance;
he never convinced his peers that his word was synonymous
with Edwards'. But he did not fail in the prophetic obligation. During his lifetime religion in the young nation began to
exhibit a new dimension. Although it would be extravagant
exclusively to credit Beecher with the genesis or tax him with

any blameworthy character of the nature emerging in American religion, to ignore his influence in the estimate of what happened is both incognizant and ungrateful. Men encountered Beecher as an influence—whether paternal or mystic— for the sake of his person, not for what he said, although they long remembered and quoted his words, usually attempting, unsuccessfully, to communicate the exact way in which he said this or that.

Lyman's sermons were effective because *he* preached them. The yellowed manuscripts of old exhortations refused to come to life, and seemed moribund, if not dead, because the strong voice of their creator prophet had begun to quaver and his accusing finger to tremble. The life of his sermons was in him. Lyman never confused prophecy with printer's ink and instinctively resisted readying his sermons for publication. It took more time, he said, "to fit one . . . for the press . . . than to prepare five for the pulpit."[76] Little wonder. When he was in the natural milieu of the pulpit he could emanate a numinous power.

"One very hot day in summer, and in the afternoon," a parishioner related, "I was in church and Dr. Beecher was going on in a sensible but rather prosy, half sermon, when all at once he seemed to recollect that we had just heard of the death of Lord Byron. He was an admirer of Byron's poetry, as all who admire genius must be." He raised his spectacles, and began with an account of Byron, "his genius, wonderful gifts, and then went on to his want of virtue, and his want of true religion, and finally described a lost soul, and the spirit of Byron going off, wandering in the blackness of darkness forever! It struck me as with an electric shock, and left an imperishable memory."[77] For all Beecher's words—no doubt, splendid words—the green memory here is of a man of great heart grieving for another. Just so did Lyman Beecher enforce his faith with others, "not because he was a profound theologian or an acute metaphysician, or a man of wide literary culture; . . . but because he was a man always most thoroughly in earnest . . . living every moment under the impression that he had a great work to do for God and which must be done at once, not a minute to be lost."[78] That work was to publish the message of which he himself was a summary—that man, by God's design and pleasure, is created free and able, and that man's happiness lies in the realization of the potential of this good estate. Beecher's person, his devotion, these things remained, burning in the souls they warmed; and in them his soul went marching on. But his weary old body finally crumbled, and he died on Saturday afternoon, January 10, 1863.

Notes to Chapter XV

1. *Autobiography*, II, 541.
2. [Lyman Beecher], Walnut Hills, June 19, 1850, to Henry Ward Beecher, Beecher Collection, Yale University.
3. *Ibid.*
4. Calvin E. Stowe in 1850 accepted a call to the chair of natural and revealed religion at Bowdoin. Two years later he went as professor of sacred literature to the Theological Seminary at Andover.
5. Annie Fields, *Life and Letters of Harriet Beecher Stowe*, p. 121.
6. *Autobiography*, II, 543.
7. The situation, of course, has more reference to Lyman's family than to him. See, e.g., ALS, Tom Beecher, Hartford, November 6, 1848, to Henry Ward Beecher; ALS, Lyman Beecher, Boston, October 17, 1855, to Henry Ward Beecher; ALS, Harriet Beecher Stowe, n.d., n.p. [though obviously in the mid-1850's] to Henry Ward Beecher; ALS, Harriet Beecher Stowe, n.p., n.d. [mid-1850's], to Henry Ward Beecher, all of which are in the Beecher Collection, Yale University.
8. James C. White, *Personal Reminiscences*, p. 26.
9. ALS, Lyman Beecher, Boston, September 24, 1836, to Thomas Brainerd, Beecher Collection, Yale University.
10. Lydia Jackson Beecher, "Family Record," MS, Beecher Collection, Stowe-Day Foundation.
11. Round robin letter from the Beecher children, separately signed and dated, beginning with James Beecher, Brooklyn, December 28, 1847, to Lyman Beecher, Beecher Collection, Stowe-Day Foundation.
12. James C. White, *Personal Reminiscences*, p. 40.
13. *Autobiography*, II, 227.
14. [Lydia Jackson Beecher], Boston, 1852, to Lyman, Beecher Collection, Stowe-Day Foundation.
15. *Autobiography*, II, 227-228. Also see James C. White, *Personal Reminiscences*, pp. 21-23, for the sequel to the incident.
16. *Autobiography*, II, 421.
17. D. H. Allen, "Circular, to the Friends of Dr. Lyman Beecher, and of Lane Seminary," Beecher Collection, Stowe-Day Foundation.

18. Lewis Tappan, *Arthur Tappan*, p. 281.

19. *Autobiography*, II, 420.

20. Typescript of an ALS, Harriet Beecher Stowe, February 1, 1851, to Henry Ward Beecher, Beecher Collection, Yale University Library.

21. *Autobiography*, II, 549-550.

22. ALS, John Tappan *et al.*, Boston, January 1, 1853, to Lyman Beecher, Beecher Collection, Stowe-Day Foundation.

23. Typescript of an ALS, Harriet Beecher Stowe, n.p., n.d., to James William Kimball, Beecher Collection, Yale University.

24. Typescript of an ALS, Harriet Beecher Stowe, n.p., March 4, 1858, to Lydia, Beecher Collection, Yale University.

25. *Autobiography*, II, 362.

26. MS, "A Song of Remembrance," poem to be sung, written by Catherine Beecher, Beecher Collection, Stowe-Day Foundation.

27. *Autobiography*, II, 363.

28. Lyman Beecher Stowe, *Saints, Sinners, and Beechers*, p. 384.

29. ALS, Nathan Lord, president of Dartmouth, June 6, 1845, to Lyman, Beecher-Stowe Collection, Schlesinger Library, Radcliffe College.

30. [Tom Beecher], Hartford, November 6, 1848, to Henry Ward Beecher, Beecher Collection, Yale University.

31. MS notation, Lyman Beecher to James, *verso* of ALS, James Beecher, Farmington, October 10, 1848, to Lyman, Beecher Collection, Stowe-Day Foundation.

32. [Tom Beecher], Hartford, November 6, 1848, to Henry Ward Beecher, Beecher Collection, Stowe-Day Foundation.

33. Lyman Beecher Stowe, *Saints, Sinners, and Beechers*, p. 385; Dudley Taylor Cornish, *The Sable Arm: Negro Troops in the Union Army, 1861-1865* (New York, London, and Toronto, 1956), pp. 226, 268. Cornish observes that James Beecher, in addition to discharging military responsibility to his troops, "went further to help those men prepare for the lives they would lead as free men after the war was over." See also Joseph T. Wilson, *The Black Phalanx* (New York, 1968), p. 469; *Official Army Register of the Volunteer Force of the United States Army for the Years 1861, '62, '63, '64, '65* (Washington, D.C., 1867), Pt. VIII, 206.

34. ALS, James Beecher, Washington, January 27, 1862, to Harriet Beecher Stowe, Beecher Collection, Stowe-Day Foundation.

35. ALS, James Beecher, Hartford, August 15, 1845, to Lydia, Beecher Collection, Stowe-Day Foundation.

36. *Autobiography*, II, 461-481.

37. *Gospel According to St. Matthew*, X:34.

38. Mark M. Boatner, *The Civil War Dictionary* (New York, 1959), p. 56.

39. Lyman Beecher Stowe, *Saints, Sinners, and Beechers*, p. 134.

40. Lyman Beecher, *A Plea for the West*, p. 48.

41. Mae Elizabeth Harveson, *Catherine Esther Beecher*, p. 238.

42. *Autobiography*, I, 507.

43. Catherine E. Beecher, *Educational Reminiscences*, pp. 154-155.

44. Catherine E. Beecher, *Letters on the Difficulties of Religion* (Hartford, 1836), pp. 82, 170, 324.

45. *Autobiography*, II, 516.

46. Mae Elizabeth Harveson, *Catherine Esther Beecher*, p. 276.

47. Catherine E. Beecher, *Miss Beecher's Domestic Receipt-Book*, p. 280.

48. *Ibid.*

49. Mae Elizabeth Harveson, *Catherine Esther Beecher*, p. 149.

50. *Ibid.*, pp. 145-147.

51. Emily Noyes Vanderpoel, *Chronicles*, p. 244, reproduces Catherine Beecher's "The Indian's Lament," a poem she wrote upon "hearing that measures were taken to remove the remaining Indians in our country across the Mississippi."

52. ALS, Catherine Beecher, Columbus, February, 1855, to Lydia and Lyman, Beecher Collection, Stowe-Day Foundation.

53. Lyman Beecher Stowe, *Saints, Sinners, and Beechers*, p. [7], quotes Leonard Bacon as saying in the second half of the nineteenth century that America was "inhabited by saints, sinners and Beechers." The phrase, of course, is suggestive of Sydney Smith's observation that "the French say, there are three sexes,—men, women, and clergymen," a mot similar to Lady Montagu's proverb affirming that "this world consists of men, women, and Herveys."

54. James Hadley, *Diary (1843-1853) of James Hadley, Tutor and Professor of Greek in Yale College, 1845-1872*, Laura Hadley Moseley, ed. (New Haven, 1951), p. 313.

55. Mae Elizabeth Harveson, *Catherine Esther Beecher*, p. 190.

56. ALS, Mary Beecher Perkins, [Hartford], March 10, [year missing], to Harriet Beecher Stowe, Beecher Collection, Stowe-Day Foundation.

57. Lyman Beecher, *A Sermon on the Death of Mrs. Sands*, p. 9.

58. Rebecca Taylor Hatch, *Personal Reminiscences*, p. 34.

59. ALS, Mary Beecher Perkins, [Hartford], March 10, [year missing], to Harriet Beecher Stowe, Beecher Collection, Stowe-Day Foundation.

60. ALS, Nathaniel Taylor, Yale College, October 12, 1850, to Lyman, Beecher Collection, Stowe-Day Foundation. Cf. Catherine E. Beecher, *Truth Stranger than Fiction* (Boston, 1850).

61. Charles Edward Stowe, *Life of Harriet Beecher Stowe*, p. 26.

62. Lyman Beecher, *The Faith Once Delivered to the Saints*, p. 4.

63. Lyman Abbott and S. B. Halliday, *Henry Ward Beecher*, p. 606.

64. Charles Edward Stowe, *Life of Harriet Beecher Stowe*, p. 501.

65. William C. Beecher and Samuel Scoville, *Henry Ward Beecher*, p. 69.

66. Lyman Beecher, *The Faith Once Delivered to the Saints*, p. 11.

67. *Ibid.*, p. 23.

68. MS, n.p., n.d., dictation by Lyman Beecher to his daughter-in-law, Beecher Collection, Stowe-Day Foundation.

69. *Autobiography*, II, 472.

70. *Ibid.*, p. 476.

71. Charles Edward Stowe, *Life of Harriet Beecher Stowe*, p. 152.

72. *Ibid.*

73. Lyman Beecher Stowe, *Saints, Sinners, and Beechers*, p. 372.

74. *Ibid.*, pp. 344-353. Married to John Hooker, Isabella was prominent in the suffragist movement, although she believed in liberation of her sex that went far beyond the matter of insuring them of the vote. See also John Hooker, *Some Reminiscences of a Long Life: With a Few Articles on Moral and Social Subjects of Present Interest* (Hartford, 1899), *passim.*

75. MS Diary of Isabella Hooker, Beecher Collection, Connecticut Historical Society, p. 41. See also Kenneth Andrews, *Nook Farm* (Cambridge, 1950), Ch. 2, for the story of Isabella's remarkable diary discovered in the waste of an old bar.

76. *Autobiography*, I, 546.

77. E. D. Mansfield, *Personal Memories*, p. 140.

78. Calvin E. Stowe, "Sketches and Recollections," pp. 221-222.

Epilogue

Brooklyn's Plymouth Church was still hung with Christmas evergreens when Lyman Beecher's funeral entourage entered the sanctuary, bearing his body in a coffin of handsome rosewood, heavily mounted with silver (a conceit the fallen warrior would never have chosen, or even noticed). Things meant little enough to Lyman, and he left few behind. An 1855 will entrusted to Lydia his entire and modest estate, save for the books that were still in the keeping of Professor Allen at Lane. Those were for James. A codicil designated Charles as guardian and executor of sundry manuscripts, letters, and copyrights—a practical necessity, obviously and wisely arranged by the son himself,[1] but a doubtful bequest of which to reconstruct the shape of the man's stature.

Other men than Lyman have failed in the attempt to discover the man in the baffling welter of his papers: the very deciphering is a torment. One of his daughters volunteered three negative rules for reading her father's writing. "If there is a letter crossed, it isn't a *t*. If . . . dotted, it isn't an *i*. . . . If there is a capital . . . it isn't the beginning of a word."[2] Yet, there are clues; for in the morass of abbreviations and pictographs of his manuscripts, certain clear, readable words recur endlessly and leave no doubt regarding the subject of the pages, or the loves of his heart. They are strong words, nouns and verbs that point beyond themselves to men and action, and to God. What Lyman asked and what he understood of life is referable to sin and grace and the human will. Sin is black; but grace abounds, and the will is free. "When the old man lays off his helmet for the last time & wipes from his brow the sweat & dust of the battle," wrote an admirer, "there will be moist eyes through the nation." Then he added, "His will be bright."[3] The judgment was clairvoyant. Less than a fortnight before his death Lyman had an experience he so strongly believed to be a sight of heaven that his very countenance became "luminous." "Oh, such scenes as I have been permitted to behold," he sang,[4] but he rejected any offer of another to rejoice with him. "You cannot enter into my experience," he said. Not his selfishness, but the inability of others to see and respond as he did, made it so. It was ever thus. East Hampton had heard what he said, and not understood what he meant. Litchfield listened with her ears, but not with her heart. Boston repeated the anecdotes and forgot the anguish. And the West censured him because he yearned for the whole wide world.

Of course there had always been some who knew him for no ordinary mortal. Many were arrested by him, but they did not see what he saw, even when they followed where he led. It was altogether fitting that his friend, Dr. Bacon of New Haven, should have delivered the impressive oration. The choir chanted "Blessed are the dead, who die in the Lord." Nearly all the clergymen of the city were represented, and many from other places.

After the benediction, "the body was . . . taken out-of-doors . . . and shadows began to fall before the throng of people, who desired once more to look at the noble dust, departed."[5]

Notes to the Epilogue

1. "Last Will and Testament" of Lyman Beecher, Surrogate's Court, Kings County, Brooklyn, New York.
2. Calvin E. Stowe, "Sketches and Recollections," p. 234.
3. ALS, Lyman Beecher, New York, February 7, 1849, to Lydia, Beecher Collection, Stowe-Day Foundation. Beecher, in this letter, reported to his wife what a reporter had written of him in the press.
4. *Autobiography*, II, 557.
5. Photostat of a press clipping reporting Beecher's funeral, without indication of source, Beecher Collection, Stowe-Day Foundation.

Appendix

Lyman Beecher's Children

CATHERINE ESTHER BEECHER, 1800-1878, a pioneer in higher education for women, eldest of Roxana and Lyman Beecher's children, was born in East Hampton, Long Island. After her mother's death, 1816, she shared with her aunt the care of the household until her father remarried. Self-taught in Latin, mathematics, and philosophy, she was briefly on the faculty of a private girls' school in New London, Connecticut. The sudden death of her betrothed, Alexander Metcalf Fisher, in 1823, was the occasion for reordering her plans and reexamining her religious faith. She determined to devote her life to good works. In 1824 she established a school at Hartford for young ladies that became a model of excellence and innovation in women's education. After moving to Ohio, when her father became president of Lane Seminary, she founded western schools for women. Though committed to broad education for women, she was a determined and out-spoken anti-suffragist. Author of eighteen major works whose subjects range from introduction of scientific methods into domestic economy to attack upon Calvinism, she was to her life's end a tireless worker and indefatigable reformer in spite of perennial problems of poor health and finance.

WILLIAM HENRY BEECHER, 1802-1889, son of Roxana, born at East Hampton, Long Island, studied theology first with his father, Lyman, and then at Andover Seminary. Apprenticed to a cabinetmaker without success, he tried his hand at merchandising before turning to the ministry as a career. His first church was at Newport, Rhode Island, and thereafter he served a succession of parishes, among which were Batavia, New York; Toledo and Euclid, Ohio; and

Reading and Brookfield, Massachusetts. He was not adroit in handling relations with his congregations and usually left his parishes under strained circumstances, and was almost always harassed by dyspepsia and lack of money. At Brookfield he also served as postmaster. After his wife's death he made his home with his daughters, Roxana and Mary, in Chicago, where he died.

EDWARD BEECHER, 1803-1895, son of Roxana, born at East Hampton, Long Island, was educated first at Yale and later at Andover Seminary. After a year as tutor at Yale, he accepted the pastorate of the Park Street Church in Boston, and four years later, 1830, was invited to become the first president of Illinois College in Jacksonville, a position he held for fourteen years. Called back to Boston in 1844, he was for better than a decade the minister of the Salem Street Church. In 1855 he returned to the West, serving as pastor at Galesburg, Illinois, until 1871, when he removed to Brooklyn. At the age of eighty-one he grew restive in retirement and went back to a schedule of weekly preaching, which he maintained for five years at the Parkville Congregational Church of Brooklyn. An ardent abolitionist, and friend of Elijah P. Lovejoy, by whose side he stood guarding Lovejoy's press from rioters the night before the editor was shot, Beecher was one of the organizers of the Illinois Anti-Slavery Society. Among his many publications was *The Conflict of the Ages* (1853), which accounted for man's depravity through a fall that had occurred in a pre-existent state.

MARY FOOTE BEECHER PERKINS, 1805-1900, daughter of Roxana, born at East Hampton, Long Island, was the only one of Lyman's children who, having reached maturity, did not participate in public life as educator, reformer, or preacher. She wrote no books. After graduating from Miss Pierce's school in Litchfield, Connecticut, she moved to Hartford, where she lived for the rest of her long life. While she was teaching at her sister Catherine's Female Seminary she met Thomas C. Perkins, a Hartford attorney, whom she shortly married. Thereafter she lived a happy, though private, life.

GEORGE BEECHER, 1809-1843, son of Roxana, born at East Hampton, Long Island, was prepared for Yale by his parents. At New Haven he studied divinity with Nathaniel Taylor and subsequently was ordained by the Presbytery of Cincinnati, over the objection of conservative churchmen there. He held successive pastorates in Batavia and Rochester, New York, and, finally, Chillicothe, Ohio. Considered one of the most gifted of the family, George, when he was thirty-four years old, was discovered in his beloved garden, dead by a gunshot wound that was pronounced accidental.

HARRIET ELIZABETH BEECHER STOWE, 1811-1896, daughter of Roxana, was born at Litchfield, Connecticut, and, though the most famous of all Lyman's children, did not achieve celebrity until the publication of *Uncle Tom's Cabin* (1852), when she was already middle-aged. She had moved to Ohio with her father when he accepted the presidency of the theological seminary at Cincinnati, and there, in 1836, she married Calvin Ellis Stowe, professor of Biblical literature on her father's faculty. In 1850 her husband accepted a professorship in Bowdoin College in Brunswick, Maine. It was in New England that Mrs. Stowe's anti-slavery sentiment became intense, and there that she produced the novel that sold three hundred thousand copies within a year of publication. For almost thirty years thereafter she wrote an average of one book a year. Though successful as a writer, she was never prosperous, for she was not astute at business, and her husband was even less so. She was quite popular in America and England, but a controversial figure—in America because of her stand regarding slavery, and in England because of the spirited attack on Lord Byron included in "The True Story of Lady Byron's Life," which appeared in the *Atlantic Monthly* in 1869. During the last decade of her life she lived in a sort of dream world, and her last years were completely tranquil.

HENRY WARD BEECHER, 1813-1887, child of Roxana, born in Litchfield, Connecticut, was the most well known of Lyman's sons. Educated at Amherst and at Lane Seminary, he began his ministry at an obscure Presbyterian church in Lawrenceburg, Indiana, but moved shortly to another church of the same denomination in Indianapolis. In 1847 he accepted a call to become pastor of the newly organized Plymouth Church in Brooklyn, New York. Always successful as an effective orator, he was sometimes controversial but throughout his life enormously popular. Internationally famous, as preacher and author, he attacked slavery, sold slaves for ransom money to purchase their freedom from his pulpit, campaigned for Lincoln, espoused generous terms for readmission of Southern states to the union, and endorsed evolution as evidence of man's progress. In sensational trials (1874-1875) following accusation of adultery, he was acquitted by civil and ecclesiastical courts, but, though deserted by some, retained support of his church and continued a popular preacher. His death marked the end of a forty-year pastorate of the Plymouth Church.

CHARLES BEECHER, 1815-1900, son of Roxana, born in Litchfield, Connecticut, was the last of Lyman's children by his first wife. Educated at the Boston Latin School, Lawrence Academy of Groton, Massachusetts, Bowdoin College, and Lane Seminary, he lost his faith as a young man and spent a season in New Orleans as a music teacher and a clerk. Reclaimed for the ministry by his brother, Henry Ward, he was in 1844 ordained as pastor of the Second Presbyterian Church of Fort Wayne, from which he was later dismissed for his liberal views. Subsequently he was minister of Congregational churches in Newark, New Jersey, and Georgetown, Massachusetts. The Essex North Conference convicted him of heresy in 1863 because of his belief in the pre-existence of souls, but several years afterward the conference rescinded the verdict. He edited the influential *Plymouth Collection of Hymns and Tunes* (1855) and also published his anti-slavery sentiment. In 1870 he moved to Newport, Florida, to preach to poor blacks. Seven years later he returned to the East, and between the years 1885 and 1893 he served a church in Wysox, Pennsylvania. His last years were spent at the home of his daughter in Georgetown, Massachusetts.

ISABELLA BEECHER HOOKER, 1822-1907, daughter of Harriet Porter, was born in Litchfield, Connecticut, and was still a child when her father removed to Cincinnati. She came to Hartford in 1841 to study in the Female Seminary her sister, Catherine, had founded, and lived in the home of another sister, Mary Perkins, while she was at school. In Mrs. Perkins' home she met John Hooker, who was a clerk in the office of her brother-in-law. Isabella and John soon married, and together they studied Blackstone. When the young bride discovered the legal discriminations against women she began a life-long struggle for female liberation. She was one of the founders of the New England Suffrage Association; she wrote and published on the subject of freedom for women (*Woman-hood: Its Sanctities and Fidelities,* Boston, 1874); and she lectured frequently on her enthusiasm to the extent of completing a formal speaking tour of the West in 1870. She was successful in having introduced in the Connecticut legislature, annually for seven years until it was finally passed, a bill that gave married women the same property rights as their husbands. In 1871 she addressed the Committee on the Judiciary of the United States Senate. After passing seventy years of age, she took a less active part in public affairs than formerly, but she continued her interest and activity in women's liberation to her life's end. Also she shared with her half-brother and sister, Charles and Harriet, a keen interest in spiritualism.

THOMAS KINNICUT BEECHER, 1824-1900, son of Harriet Porter, was born in Litchfield, Connecticut. His early and manifest aptitude for science almost convinced his father that his career lay elsewhere than the professional ministry. Nevertheless, after graduating from Illinois College, Thomas studied divinity with his father, and served as a minister of the Congregational church at Williamsburg, New York, before moving, in 1854, to Elmira, New York, where he became minister of the Independent Congregational Church. With the exception of a brief period as chaplain of the 141st New York Volunteers during the Civil War, Thomas remained in Elmira until his death. He was a great favorite of all classes and religions. Unconventional in the extreme, he was expelled by the Ministerial Union for holding religious services in an opera house. Undaunted, he continued an individualistic and highly effective ministry. Under his leadership, and according to his plans, the congregation built a church that included a gymnasium, a library, a theater, and a dancing room. There was also a pool table in the basement. Although he published no books, he contributed regularly to the Elmira *Advertiser*. He found some outlet for his scientific interest through keeping the town clock in repair.

JAMES CHAPLIN BEECHER, 1828-1886, son of Harriet Porter, and last child of Lyman, was born in Boston. Less obviously inclined to intellectual life than Lyman's other children, James, after graduating from Dartmouth, spent a period at sea and in the Far East. He returned from the Orient to study divinity at Andover, and, ordained as a missionary in 1856, went again to China, where, until 1861, he served as chaplain of Seamen's Bethel in Hong Kong. After accepting a lieutenant-colonelcy of the 141st New York Volunteers, of which his brother, Thomas, was chaplain, he was promoted to colonel in 1863, and given command of the First North Carolina Colored Volunteers. Later he was mustered out with the rank of brigadier general by brevet. Reentering the ministry, he served several churches at Oswego and Poughkeepsie in New York, and, subsequently, the Bethel Mission in Henry Ward Beecher's church at Brooklyn. James, never in good health after being wounded during the Civil War, died by his own hand at Elmira, New York, where he had gone to take the water cure.

Index

Abolition. *See* Slavery controversy
American Anti-Slavery Society, 192
American Colonization Society, 187
Antislavery movement. *See* Slavery
    controversy.
Atwell, Dinah, 118

Bacon, Delia, 276-277
Bacon, Leonard, 136, 220, 276-277,
    288
Baldwin, Ben, 102
Barnes, Albert, 207, 231
Beecher, Catherine, 21-22, 23, 24,
    26n, 79, 103, 109, 170-171, 195,
    210, 261, 280, 289 (biog.)
  character, 16-17, 274-277
  death of fiancé, 104-107
  poems and hymns, 94, 102, 270-
    271
  speeches, 169
Beecher, Charles, 41, 118, 175, 189,
    194, 260, 261, 273, 280, 287,
    292-293 (biog.)
Beecher, David, 31, 33, 89, 159-160
Beecher, Edward, 22, 106, 119, 137,
    234, 253, 259, 290 (biog.)
Beecher, Esther, 22-24, 88, 89, 103,
    229
Beecher, Frederick, 118, 229
Beecher, George, 24, 89, 103, 119,
    291 (biog.)
Beecher, Harriet. *See* Stowe, Harriet
    Beecher
Beecher, Harriet (infant), 88
Beecher, Harriet Porter, 23-25, 31,
    76, 87, 104, 118, 137, 222, 227-
    230, 239
Beecher, Henry Ward, 21, 28n, 102,
    118, 125, 210, 216, 217, 229,
    267, 271, 278-279, 292 (biog.)
Beecher, Isabella. *See* Hooker, Isa-
    bella Beecher

Beecher, James, 24, 120, 270, 271-
    273, 277, 287, 294 (biog.)
Beecher, Joseph, 31
Beecher, Lydia Jackson, 230, 239-
    240, 251-252, 259, 267-269, 287
Beecher, Lyman
  Autobiography, 261, 273
  Boston pastorate, 120-121
  Calvinism, 89-90, 101-104, 160,
    217-222, 247, 251-253
  children, 21-25, 32, 43n, 59, 87-89,
    102-103, 118-120, 175, 252-253,
    266 (port.), 270-281, 289-294.
    See also names of individual
    children (cf. family tree, 12)
  Cincinnati pastorate, 239, 253
  conversion, 41-42
  death and funeral, 282, 287-288
  East Hampton pastorate, 50-62
  emphasis on physical exercise, 175
  family tree, 12
  financial problems, 59-60, 77, 117-
    119, 268-269
  foster parents, 31-33
  health, 31-32, 56, 64n
  heresy charges, 209-222
  honorary degree, 137
  influence of James Gould, 75; of
    Nathaniel Taylor, 133-142; of
    Timothy Dwight, 37-43, 50
  Kemper suit, 249-251
  Lane presidency, 179, 189-202,
    236-239, 249-250, 267
  lineage, 31
  Litchfield pastorate, 61, 72, 76, 87,
    94, 117-120
  missionary interests, 151-156
  move to Ohio, 15-20, 24-25, 179,
    189
  opposition to Catholicism, 156-
    157; to duelling, 57-58; to liquor,

92-95, 240; to Unitarianism, 136-139
parents, 31, 42
patriotism, 70, 90-92
personal papers, 260-261, 267, 281, 287
personality and behavior, 20-21, 51, 56, 87, 102, 104, 139-142, 149-151, 157-158, 175, 199, 216-217, 238, 241-242, 258-262
physical appearance, 14 (port.), 15, 68 (port.), 148 (port.), 240, 248 (port.), 258-259
political activities, 253-254
preaching style, 17-18, 125, 259, 281-282
revivalism, 18, 50, 53, 78-79, 124-125, 254-258
stand on church music, 158; on disestablishment, 78-80; on slavery, 197-199, 279
Views in Theology, 235, 244n
voyage to England, 240-242
wives, 22-25, 53-56, 87, 102-104, 118, 222, 227-230, 239-240, 267-269, 287. *See also* names of wives (cf. family tree, 12)
Yale experiences, 34-43
Beecher, Mary. *See* Perkins, Mary Beecher
Beecher, Nathaniel, 31
Beecher, Roxana Foote, 22, 31, 53-56, 59, 60, 61, 63n, 76, 87, 88, 102-104, 118, 120, 239
Beecher, Thomas, 24, 119, 217, 260, 279-280, 293-294 (biog.)
Beecher, William, 21, 119, 289-290 (biog.)
Beecher home (Cincinnati), 179, 226 (illus.)
Beecher home (Litchfield), 86 (illus.), 87, 117-118
Benton, Catherine, 31, 32
Benton, Lot, 31, 32, 55
Bissell, Josiah, 268
Bolivar, Simon, 91
Boston, 17, 121-122, 149-150
Boudinot, Elias, 154-156
Bradley, James, 190
Buel, William, 95
Buell, Samuel, 50-52, 55

Bunce, Isaiah, 153-155
Burr, Aaron, 57
Burr, Betsy, 89
Burritt, Elihu, 240
Byron, 22-23, 281

Calhoun, John C., 161
Calvinism, 85, 89-90, 126, 131, 133-142, 159-160, 213-215, 217-222, 235, 250-252
Catholics, opposition to, 156-157
Catlin, Grove, 92
Champion, Judah, 69
Channing, William E., 115, 151
Chase, Salmon P., 250
Chittenden, Betsy, 54
Chittenden, Mary. *See* Hubbard, Mary Chittenden
Christian Alliance, 242
Church ownership dispute, 123-124
Church-state relations, 67, 75-80, 123-124
Cincinnati, 168 (illus.), 169-171, 192, 195, 237
Clay, Henry, 57
Clinton Academy, 59-60
Colonization movement, 178-179, 187, 193-194, 197-198
Cornelius, Elias, 138

Daggett, Herman, 154-156
Damnation, 104-110
Davis, Tudor, 50
Decatur, Stephen, 91
Dedham (Mass.) church, 124
Discrimination against minority groups, 147, 151-157
Disestablishment of the church, 67, 75-80, 83n
Douglas, Frederick, 279
Duelling, 57-58
Dwight, Sereno E., 136
Dwight, Timothy, 29, 37-43, 50, 57, 93, 121, 135, 152, 156, 196

East Hampton, N. Y., 49
East Hampton Presbyterian Church, 48 (illus.), 55-62
Education of ministers. *See* Theological education
Edwards, Jonathan, 19, 42, 78, 87,

110, 134, 138, 218, 251-252, 254, 277, 280
Emmons, Nathanael, 77, 105

Finney, Charles Grandison, 181-182, 201, 254-258
Fisher, Alexander Metcalfe, 100 (port.), 105-107, 274
Fitch, Eleazer, 207
Foote, Eli, 53
Foote, Harriet, 54, 101
Foote, Roxana. See Beecher, Roxana Foote
Foote, Samuel, 88
Foreign Missionary School (Cornwall, Conn.), 151-156
Fox, Emily, 153
Freedom of the will, 217-222, 247, 250-258

George III, King of England, 69
God's sovereignty, 107-109, 217-222, 247, 251-252
Gold, Harriet, 154
Gold, Theodore, 152
Gould, Henry Guy, 69
Gould, James, 74-75
Grandison, Charles, 54
Green, Ashbel, 207

Hall, James, 197
Hamilton, Alexander, 57
Hand, Esther, 52
Hanover Church (Boston), 124-126, 132 (illus.), 141
Harrison, Julia, 191
Harrison, William Henry, 253-254
Harvard College, 123, 167
Harvey, Joseph, 154
Hastings, George, 180
Hooker, Isabella Beecher, 24, 118, 280, 293 (biog.)
Hooker, John, 285n
Hopkins, Samuel, 108-110
Hubbard, Mary Chittenden, 70, 102
Hubbard, Russell, 152
Huntington, Abel, 52
Huntington, Dan, 72

Infidel Club, 52, 59

Jackson, Andrew, 57, 174, 209
Jackson, Lydia. See Beecher, Lydia Jackson
James, Thomas, 51
Jefferson, Thomas, 37, 60, 74

Kemper, David, 249-250
Kemper, Elnathan, 174, 249
Kemper, James, 173-174, 177, 209, 249

Lane, Ebenezer, 173
Lane, William A., 173
Lane Theological Seminary, 167, 170-183, 188 (illus.), 189-202, 208 (faculty port.), 236-239, 249-250, 269
Liberal-orthodox Presbyterian controversy, 209-222, 225, 230-236, 249-250
Litchfield, Conn., 69-72, 120
Litchfield Congregational meeting house, 72, 95
Litchfield Female Academy, 73-74, 104
Livingston, John Henry, 167
Lyman, Huntingdon, 200

Mahan, Asa, 192, 198, 199, 201
Man, doctrine of. See Freedom of the will
Mann, Horace, 111n
Manual labor institutional programs, 174-176, 184n
Mason, Lowell, 158
McWhorter, Alexander, 276-277
Ministerial training. See Theological education
Missionary work, 151-156
More, Hannah, 76
Morgan, John, 199, 201
Morse, Jedediah, 123

Napoleon, 91
Nettleton, Asahel, 235
"New Haven Theology," 134, 207, 225
New School Presbyterians, 212, 213-215, 225, 230-235, 249-250
Northrup, Sarah, 153

Oberlin Collegiate Institute, 190, 201, 205n
Obookiah, Henry, 151-152
Old School Presbyterians, 211, 213-215, 225, 230-236, 249-250
Oneida Institute, 174, 178, 181

Paine, Thomas, 36
Park Street Church (Boston), 124-125, 133, 136-137
Parker, Theodore, 159-160
Patriotism, related to religion, 13, 70, 90-92
Payson, Dr., 125
Peabody, Ephraim, 170
Perkins, Mary Beecher, 22, 118, 252, 276, 290-291 (biog.)
Perkins, Tom, 118
Pierce, Sarah, 72-74, 274
Plan of Union (Congregationalists and Presbyterians), 55, 167, 207, 213, 225, 231, 233
Porter, Ebenezer, 159
Porter, Harriet. See Beecher, Harriet Porter
Prentice, Charles, 154
Presbyterian Old School-New School Controversy, 212, 213-215, 225, 230-236, 249-250
Puritanism. See Calvinism

Rachel (bondservant), 89, 103
Reeve, Tapping, 74-77
Reeve, Mrs. Tapping, 76-77
Revivalism, 18, 29, 78-79, 254-258
Revolutionary War, 69-70
Ridge, John, 153

Second Presbyterian Church (Cincinnati), 239, 253
Sectionalism, 160-161
Seminary training. See Theological education
Sherman, Roger, 33
Shipherd, John Jay, 201
Slavery controversy, 147, 171-172, 182, 187, 189-200, 234
Smith, Samuel, 13

Society for Promoting Manual Labor in Literary Institutions, 177
Sparks, Jared, 115
Stiles, Ezra, 36-37
Stone, Timothy, 154
Stoughton, William, 265
Stowe, Calvin E., 125, 134, 191, 200, 217, 223n, 238-239
Stowe, Eliza, 223n, 229
Stowe, Harriet Beecher, 24, 101, 109, 118, 120, 133, 175, 210, 252, 261, 267, 271, 273, 276, 279, 280, 291 (biog.)
Stuart, Charles, 197

Tabernacle Church (Salem, Mass.), 138
Tallmadge, Benjamin, 103
Tappan, Arthur, 178-179, 182, 201, 269
Tappan, Lewis, 178, 182, 194, 195
Taylor, Father, 158
Taylor, Nathaniel, 18, 116 (port.), 131, 133-142, 149, 215, 218-219, 231, 232, 233, 255, 276-277
Temperance, 92-95, 240
Theological education, 167, 172-177, 180-181, 184n, 189-202, 236-239
Thome, James A., 200
Tocqueville, Alexis de, 160-161
Tracy, Uriah, 71
Trollope, Frances, 169
Tyler, Bennet, 133-134, 223n, 235

Unitarian controversy, 17-18, 115, 122-126, 133-142

Vail, F. Y., 177-178
Voltaire, 35, 39

War of 1812, 90
Ward, Andrew, 53-54
Ware, Henry, 115, 123
Weatherby, James, 214
Weems, Mason L., 92
Weld, Angelina Grimké, 234

Weld, Theodore, 177-182, 191-194, 197-199, 202, 234, 279
Whitefield, George, 78
Wilson, Joshua, 203, 209-222, 230, 232, 233
Woolworth, Aaron, 52

Wright, Frances, 169-170

Yale College, 30 (illus.), 34-43, 243n

Zillah (bondservant), 89